REVERB, TX

HARLIN ANDERSON

REVERB, TX

Copyright © 2017 by Harlin Anderson

All rights reserved. No portion of this book may be reproduced or transmitted by any means whatsoever without the express written permission of the publisher.

Printed in the United States of America

First Edition, 2017

ISBN 978-0-9985554-0-9
GMGB01

Cover design by Darin Bradley
Interior layout and design by Aaron Leis

Goliad Media is a production house based in Denton, TX, showcasing art, literature, music, and mixed media. We dream of empty places.

goliadmedia.net

DEDICATION

This one goes out to my Jewish Vikings soon to be raising hell on the Northside. Hasta luego, Kap and Giddy.

CONTENTS

Introduction
1

Part One: Mandy
7

Part Two: The First Texas Coastal Expedition
45

Part Three: The Jackson Clan
91

Part Four: High Desert Waltz
121

Part Five: The Second Great Texas Goastal Expedition
205

Acknowledgements
243

INTRODUCTION

DISPATCH

I'd forgotten I ever wanted to be a writer by the time I walked into that dingy practice room at Rubber Gloves Rehearsal Studios in Denton, Texas. Seven years writing the back of DVD boxes in a cartoon factory will have that effect. Darin Bradley and Chris Welch had been meeting at Gloves for months, maybe longer. They were secret meetings to discuss a clandestine undertaking. I arrived unprepared, carrying only three cool tallboys in a plastic grocery sack. Mismatched leftovers from a night spent listening to records with friends in my garage. I had no clue what was in store for me. In fact, I was clueless that anything at all lie in wait.

We drank beers and smoked cigarettes for a while. I was finishing up my second tallboy when we finally got down to business.

"There's a reason we asked you here tonight," said Darin. "Chris and I have been working on a project. We're starting a company."

"We're gonna put out records," said Welch. "Sorta like a label, but we'll do more than just music. We'll do books and art, too."

"What's it called?"

"Goliad Media."

"That sounds fucking badass. Anything y'all need my help with, just name it."

My mind jumped immediately to shows. Promoting. Organizing. I'd done a little bit of that here and there over the last dozen years. It was fun, and I didn't suck at it.

"Seriously, y'all. Whatever I can do. I'll help with shows, smoke BBQ for the bands. Anything."

Darin and Welch glanced sideways at each other and didn't say shit for a second. The pause scared me. Hurt me. Maybe they had better people lined up to help.

"We want you to be a part of it," said Darin. "But not that way."

"Oh."

"We want you to be Goliad's first author, said Welch. "We want to publish your book."

"But I don't have a book."

"You don't have a book, yet," said Darin.

"Shit, y'all. I don't think I brought enough beers."

Two hours later I was doing shots with Darin at Mable Peabody's Beauty Parlor and Chainsaw Repair, a friendly gay bar with blacked-out windows and coolers that don't always cool what you're drinking to the temperature you want it cooled to. I don't remember what we were shooting, probably Jager or something with Red Bull, but I can mostly recall trying to wrap my head around the time frame of finishing a book that didn't even exist.

"It's a little quicker turnaround than is typical for writing a book on assignment, but we're trying to put out three releases in our first year. Music, literature, and art."

"Well, I've got a few ideas I used to kick around. Should we set up a meeting and see which one you like best?"

"Oh, we'll meet, but I already know what project I want you to work on. It's not a novel. More of a collection of essays."

Clearly this dude was drunk.

"A collection of essays?"

"Not your typical essays. A new essay. Basically, we want you to go different places in Texas and find interesting stories. Write those down. Put seven or eight of them together, and there's your collection."

To be fair, Darin was most assuredly more eloquent in his description of the project, but Darin is also much smarter than me, so there is no possible way in hell I could ever attempt to recreate his description.

"So, I go places. Find cool shit. And write about it?"

"More or less."

"And how long to I have to get this done?"

"Don't worry about that right now. Just enjoy the moment. I promise you'll be fine. I think you've already got some strong material for the collection."

"Like what?"

"Remember that trip you took to see Mandy Patinkin?"

"Yeah."

"Well, that would be a great place to start."

PART ONE

MANDY

ONCE UPON A PICNIC TABLE

The lights were working fine the night before. It was a Thursday, and the regular crowd convened on the patio at Dan's Silverleaf for what promised to be one hell of a Texas storm. Big, dark, ominous clouds rolled across the horizon and settled into a looming perch directly above the Denton town square.

We sat at picnic tables, downing grown-up beverages, pausing only to brandish smart phones for photo opportunities. The sun slouched behind the cloudscape and turned the sky an electric shade of sherbet.

Dan's has long been the go-to destination for cold beers and storm watching. It used to be one of the only bars in town with a covered patio, where you could smell, hear, and feel the downpour without getting soaked to the bone. About thirty minutes before any big weather blew through, an internal countdown would commence, screaming at us that time was running out to make it to Dan's before the sky opened up and dumped buckets on anyone not yet under the safety of cover.

The initiated among us knew to heed the countdown. And we knew we'd see all our friends come storm time. It was a given. Storm shows up. We go to Dan's. Drink beer and repeat throughout the spring. The regulars. Proprietors of the picnic table community. I was glad to share the light with them that night. It was sure to be a harbinger of good things to come as we prepared to embark upon an adventure that would include tacos, life-threatening acts of nature, commemorative water fountains, the invention of squirt bombs, and the greatest tenor voice the Milky Way galaxy has ever known.

Friday would be a holiday of my own creation. The Cartoon Factory where I worked wouldn't even be a memory. Instead, I would pilot my minivan to Lufkin, Texas, where I would finally see Mandy Patinkin sing in real life. No more YouTube. No more CDs. No more records. I was headed out to Lufkin to watch Mandy sing.

DENTON

Leah is my wife. She's a doctor, but not the kind that cuts you open to fix you up. The soul and the mind are her domain. And she knows all the rights places to put commas and dashes and shit, too. We met in college. I invited her to a Super Bowl party, but she never showed. Then I made her a mix CD, but that didn't work either. A couple of semesters later, we had a class together, and I guess I finally wore her down because here we are.

Not too long ago, we bought a house in Denton. A '70s ranch-style home next to a park. The streets are wide, and there are lots of trees, and it's quiet. I found an old bar on Craigslist and put it in the garage. Now I call it the Barage. We like to have friends come over and sit out there and listen to records and sip beer and tequila and sometimes sangria. We got a smoker and three dogs, and we've fought hard and made sacrifices to have all that and still live in Denton. Not everybody gets to stay in their college town forever. Maybe that's a good thing. Who knows?

I came to Denton for the first time in the mid-'90s to compete in a regional U.I.L editorial writing competition that was being held at the University of North Texas. It was my junior year of high school. After I turned in my story, I wandered to the edge of campus where there was this massive, fuck-off crowd packing what I now know to be Hickory and Fry streets. All the people were out that day for this thing we used to have called Fry Street Fair, a kick-ass music festival that ran for almost thirty years. It's been dead nearly ten now.

I can still feel the rush of standing so close to such a beautiful chaos. Music invaded all the empty spaces. Flooded ears attached to young bodies and sparked an outbreak of movement. Hippie chicks twirling and smiling and skipping. Metal dudes rocking with their heads and throwing up horns. I didn't dare step off the curb and into the crowd for fear that I would never find my way back out. But I must have gotten close enough. Because I'm still here despite all the forces that push and pull on a person—and the changes a small town with a cool music scene goes through when it stops being small and people start talking about it.

I'VE GOT A MANDY PROBLEM

"You're going where to see who?"

That's what the guy at the kennel asked when I dropped my dogs off on the morning of our departure. It wasn't an uncommon response when I told people about my little adventure. Most folks would probably know Mandy if they saw him, but they might not know his actual name. Inigo Montoya is a different story altogether.

Everyone's heard the tragic tale of how the six-fingered man killed his father and marked him for life with the point of a sword. They know all about the quest for revenge that consumed his existence and the words he practiced over and over again, dreaming of the day he would come face-to-face with his father's murderer.

"Hello. My name is Inigo Montoya. You killed my father. Prepare to die."

It's a testament to Mandy's incredible talent that he was able to so fully assume the identity of the character that people often remember the role more than the man himself. Not to mention the challenge inherent to a Jewish man of Russian and Polish decent transforming into a swashbuckling Spaniard with a talent for swordplay. But he made the transformation look easy, in the process becoming a pop culture fixture.

The Mandy story neither begins, nor ends, with *The Princess Bride*. He won an Emmy for his role as Dr. Jeffrey Geiger in the riveting, prime-time hospital drama, *Chicago Hope*. I've always maintained that Mandy's departure after the second season is one of the main reasons *ER* stole the spotlight and *Chicago Hope* eventually got canceled. Don't get me wrong. I loved *ER*, but no performance on either show could hold a candle to the magic of Mandy Patinkin playing the preeminent heart surgeon in the entire world. Plus, the role allowed Mandy the occasional opportunity to sing, which is exactly what I'm supposed to eventually get around to talking about.

Were I to trace the roots of my Mandy adoration, it wouldn't lead back to *The Princess Bride* or *Chicago Hope* or even *Homeland*. No, my Mandemonium comes from my mom. Music and books are two of the most important things in the world to me, and my mom has a hand in both. The love of reading came from countless childhood trips to the library, and I became a music junkie after she gave me a copy of Paul Simon's greatest hits on cassette.

Mom made sure there was always music around while my brother and I were growing up. The radio in her tank-like, diesel station wagon was constantly set to the oldies station, and I learned every lyric as she sang along with all the memories from her youth. There were, to be sure, some bumps along the road. I still consider her Celine Dion phase a dark period, but for the most part, she knew good music when she heard it. Mandy was a big part of that tradition. Mom always had a fondness for show tunes, and Mandy scratched that itch.

My brother Sinclair and I used to hate her Mandy tape. We had a soft spot for his version of "Puttin' on the Ritz," but the rest of the songs seemed to us an indecipherable tangle of crazy old-person music about cardboard coffee cups and sad bastards who needed to borrow a dime. We cringed whenever she played it. Which was a lot.

I remember when that tape finally died. We were on a family vacation and the cassette melted down mid-play somewhere around Denver. Mom was crushed, but she should have expected it. She'd played and rewound, played and rewound, over and over again in a hot car all the way from Texas. The poor tape just couldn't hold up. Many years later, when I first started collecting records, I tracked down a copy of that very same Mandy album on vinyl and bought it immediately. The plan was to give it to her for Mother's Day or a birthday or some special occasion. I stuck to that plan until the record arrived at my house. The minute I put it on, the plan was shot. It took only a few bars of Mandy to forever change the course of my destiny. And by forever change the course of my destiny, I mean turn me into a big enough Patinkin fanatic that I would drive all the way to Lufkin to see him in concert.

So let's recap. Mom loved Mandy, so I loved Mandy, which led to a road trip to see him sing, even though no one knows who the hell I'm talking about unless I say Inigo fucking Montoya. I had no idea who would be interested in driving to Lufkin, which isn't exactly a tourist hotspot, to see Mandy Patinkin, who they might not even realize is world-class singer. It was gonna take a special kind of road warrior to hop that train.

The thing about road trips is that they can be a lot more fun with a proper caravan of adventurers. The loner road trip works when you have shit rattling around in your head that you need to work out. The couple's road trip is great for romantic stuff, although my wife will call bullshit since we still haven't gone on a honeymoon. (It's only been like nine years, so I'm not sure what the big deal is.) But the *event* road trip—a jaunt to see a concert or a festival of some sort—is always better with a group of people.

LOCAL BAGGAGE

Folks who know me well know that I'm a reluctant traveler at best, which is ironic since I'm supposed to be writing a whole damn book of stories about visiting interesting places. I get the travel panic real bad. Airlines always lose my luggage, and I don't much like sleeping anywhere but my own bed.

Once in my early twenties, I flew solo into the Seattle-Tacoma airport. My brother was working as a park ranger in the Elwha River Valley, and the plan was for me to fly up and drive his car home because he had to work until the day before classes started. The flight was fine—I slept most of the way—but I started feeling lonely the minute I stepped off the plane. There was nothing familiar. No tones of home. I was 1,600 miles away and still thinking about what was going on in Denton.

The only other person on the hotel shuttle was a soldier about the same age as me. I didn't pay the dude much attention until it was time to check in, and the friendly clerck at the front desk asked him where he was from.

"Texas, ma'am."

"I been to Dallas once. You from Dallas?"

"No, ma'am. I'm from Lewisville. It's just north of Dallas."

My ears pricked up. This dude lived like fifteen minutes from me.

"Excuse me, buddy. I couldn't help but overhear. You're from Lewisville?"

"That's right."

"Dude, I live in Denton."

"Small world, man. Hey, you hungry? I was gonna drop my bags off and see if I could find someplace to get a steak and a beer. I ship out in the morning, so it's my last night stateside."

"Sounds good to me. It's not like I know anyone around here, so it'd be great to have some company from back home."

Things were looking up. I'd found a security blanket. Never mind the fact that I'd only been gone about five hours and shouldn't have needed one.

We met back up in the lobby about thirty minutes later and grabbed a cab to some restaurant the clerk recommended. We ordered ribeyes and tall frosty mugs of beer and talked about how the steaks were better in Texas. I should have asked him about where he was going or what his job was, but all we did was look for things we had in common. Had we eaten at the same places? Been to the same bars? Did we know any of the same people? Ever end up at the same parties? When we'd forged a superficial connection, we ordered another round of beers and made plans to hit a casino.

I was in over my head from the get go. Flashing lights and bells and celebratory sirens and cocktail waitresses everywhere I looked. My soldier friend bought us beers and then grabbed a seat at the blackjack table. I was on a budget, so I found something with a cute dealer and a small buy-in. Ten minutes later, I was up seventy-five bucks. Another ten, I was down to my last five. I was embarrassed about losing all my money and wanted to leave, but my buddy was on a hot streak. He tossed me twenty-five bucks in chips just stick around. To not leave him behind.

I cashed in fifteen bucks, folded it up, and shoved it deep into my wallet. With the remaining ten, I bought a beer and headed back to that game with the cute dealer. I tried to play more conservatively this time around. Make it last longer. I milked the roller coaster for about thirty minutes before I almost busted again. Afraid to risk any more money, I ordered another beer and sat by the table trying to figure out how to flirt with girls in unfamiliar territory.

I didn't exactly go down in flames, but it wasn't pretty. I wish I'd known enough to know that flirting with girls on the clock in a casino is a waste of time. Dealers just want to win, and they don't get paid to lose their hearts. My friend didn't do much better. His luck had taken a turn for the worse since I'd last seen him. He was down a hundred bucks.

"Damn. That's a lot to lose."

"Fuck it. I get paid again next week. And besides, I won't be someplace like this for a long time. Let's get another beer."

It ended up being two more beers and then a cab back to the hotel. I was fairly numb in the moment, but I knew I was gonna be full of woe and worry in the morning. I was supposed to have some cash set aside for the trip home, and now most of it was gone. This would have never happened to me in Denton. I wished I was home about as hard as I've ever wished for anything. It was time for bed, but there was still the matter of goodbyes.

"Well, dude," I said. "Good luck. I hope you make it back safe."

"Man, I need you to do me a favor."

What the fuck could this guy want from me? I hardly even knew him.

"I got a little brother who is about to start school. He'll probably end up in Denton. I need you to watch out for him. Be there if he needs advice or help moving or some shit. Show him around town."

The beer kicked back in, and I started feeling real noble.

"For sure. Me and my friends would be happy to show him the cool spots in Denton. Anything he needs. I'll treat him like my own brother."

The soldier went red in the eyes, but I don't think it was my willingness to show his brother where to get drunk and meet girls that did it to him.

"Thanks, man. I owe you one."

"Nah. You don't owe me anything. Just be safe."

The soldier gave me his brother's phone number and told me where he went to school. He said that the next time he got to talk to his family, he'd tell his brother to expect my call and to listen to me because I was a good dude who'd watch out for him. I carried that phone number around in my wallet for a year until I finally threw it away along with an expired CPR certification and an old Subway sandwich punch card.

ENTER THE VERDES

"Juan Verde, you down for a road trip?"

"What you got in mind?"

"Lufkin."

"Lufkin?"

"Me and Leah and my brother and his lady are gonna go see Mandy Patinkin."

"The Princess Bride guy?"

"That's the one."

"What's he gonna do? The Inigo Montoya thing?"

"Nah, man. He's gonna sing."

"He's a singer?"

"Dude. He's a big-time Broadway star. Motherfucker's won a Tony. His version of 'Somewhere over the Rainbow' is the most beautiful thing I've ever heard."

"You want to drive all the way out to Lufkin to see the dude from *The Princess Bride* sing a bunch of show tunes?"

"I'm telling you, man. This shit's not to be missed."

"Fuck it. Camie loves that dude, and I love road trips. We're in."

And so I assembled my loyal band of traveling companions. Sure, I was a little worried that Juan Verde might convince his wife, Camille, that a trip to Lufkin was a worthy use of vacation days by promising some *Princess Bride*-related festivities, which there almost certainly would not be. Sinclair and his lady, Dawn, on the other hand, were going into this with their eyes wide open. They were not expecting a vengeance-obsessed Spanish swordslinger or any Rob Reiner antics. As far as the Verdes were concerned, I could only hope that the intoxication of a proper Texas road trip would make up for the absence of Inigo Montoya.

MANDY DAY

I woke up half hung over and anxious on the morning of our departure. Staring off into that staggering lightning cloud kept me at the bar too long, and I was definitely feeling those last couple of Jägermeisters. I was nervous about road tripping with the Verdes because aside from complimentary refrigerated air, I sometimes fail to see the beauty in traveling. Don't get me wrong, you could scour this whole damn planet and not find two better people than Juan and Camille, but hanging out at a bar or a backyard BBQ is an entirely different scenario than squeezing into a minivan for hours and then sharing a small cabin for a couple of nights. Especially when one of the people in that minivan is a negative, no-traveling bastard like myself.

It was clear that the success of the Patinkin Expedition rested on shoulders other than my own, and the Verdes were a damn good start. Natural born travelers. Juan restores classic Honda

750 motorcycles. He takes them down to Austin on the backroads or out to bike shows where he can win trophies. And Camie's an artist. She loves maps and bright colors and creates these whimsical paintings of foxes riding bikes or cats in that *Dia de Los Muertos* style. Visit their home, and you'll see pictures of excursions to everywhere imaginable. Their fridge is a brochure for a dream vacation. I hoped riding the highway with folks like the Verdes would give me a feeling of invincibility. Like even bad shit, if it were to happen, would be happening for a good reason.

Our friends were waiting on the front Porch when we pulled up. They had backpacks and coolers and whiskey and a three-liter of Squirt. Camille hopped in the back with Leah, and Juan climbed into the co-pilot's seat. Their general aura of positivity put me at ease. Things were gonna be all right. We'd hit the Mexican grocer on the way out of town to stock up on *fajitas marinadas y tablitas mas sabrosas* then make tracks for Crockett, Texas. There was plenty of time to get to the cabin, rendezvous with my brother, and scoot through the Davy Crockett National Forest and into Lufkin before Mandy took the stage. Nothing could stop us, now.

Except the Dread 35 Corridor.

THE BACKBONE OF AMERICA

Back in the late '80s when Sinclair and I were young, my family moved from Minnesota to the great state of Texas. Technically, we'd been living in South Dakota, but we all root for the Minnesota Vikings, so it's more or less the same thing. Dad was already in Texas, which left Mom with the unenviable task of packing two kids into a station wagon and driving from one end of the country to the other. I gotta give it to her, though. She never so much as looked at a map or stopped to ask directions. Dad wasn't exactly thrilled.

"Why in the world would you make that long of a drive with no map?"

"You told me to stay on I-35 until we got to Texas. Who needs a map for that? It's one highway, the whole time."

With the exception of the year I spent studying journalism at the University of Missouri, I've lived my entire life in the shadow of Interstate 35. My family, to this day, is still connected by that nightmare of a highway. Mom's in Waxahachie, Texas, Sinclair is in Austin, and Dad is in San Antonio. Even though it's the fastest route to my family, I avoid I-35 just as much as I possibly can. I've seen enough accidents and bad drivers racing up and down America's spine to know that it's only a matter of time before you get caught in the shit. The more hours you log on I-35, the more likely you are to die there.

Sure enough. My traveling companions and I got stuck on that damn highway in front of the Medieval Times in downtown Dallas for about an hour and a half. No one was moving so much as an inch, and the rain that never quite arrived the night before was steadily creeping closer. Our comfortable traveling time cushion was wearing thin. By the time we escaped the city and landed at that strange little BBQ joint in Ennis where they had a whole squadron of model airplanes hanging from the ceiling and severely fucked up Juan Verde's order because they wouldn't let him place it at the counter, the storm was right on our asses.

THUNDER AND LIGHTNING

The shit hit the fan the minute Sinclair and Dawn showed up. And I mean really hit the fan. Hit the fan so bad that they wouldn't even get out of the car. Juan Verde and Camie and Leah and I were nursing beers under a covered patio, but we were still getting soaked from the thigh down. The thunder that had been missing from Dan's the night before was rolling now. Window panes shook with each sonic explosion, and branches all around us broke loose from their trees. Sinclair and Dawn didn't budge from his Nissan Cube. They were waiting for a lull in the storm before making a break for the cabin. I couldn't blame them, but we were starting to get pressed for time. Mandy was way the hell on the other damn side of the Davy Crockett National Forest, and he would wait for no man.

Sensing the futility of continuing to wait out the storm, Sinclair and his lady bolted from his Cube as we held the door to the porch open for them. There wasn't much ground to cover, but they got drenched all the same. Just as the door slammed behind them, the mother of all lightning bolts gave birth to a boom that rattled the roof.

"Jesus," said Sinclair. "I'm glad the show is tomorrow."

"Bro."

"Yeah?"

"The show is in an hour and a half."

"It's tonight? I thought it was tomorrow."

"No such luck."

"Well, how far away is Lufkin? Do we have some time to wait this shit out?"

"We need to leave in about fifteen minutes. Twenty at the most."

Sinclair said nothing for a moment before walking over to his bag and solemnly pulling out a bottle of whiskey.

"Shit," he said. "I really thought the show was tomorrow."

He took a glass from the cupboard and poured himself the kind of drink you deserve after driving through that nightmare. I was about to do it myself. It made me think about the beer I was drinking, and how another one would be a seriously bad idea. The storm showed no signs of abating, and forests can be very, very dark places. Any hint of the moon had vanished behind the storm clouds. Lightning alone lit the sky. The drive would be treacherous. It would be so easy to forget about the concert. To sit on the dock and drink spirits and watch the storm. I mustered the courage to say as much, but Juan Verde was steadfast.

"Hell, no! We came all this way just to see Mandy. The damn tickets are already paid for. We can't let a little spring rain stop us."

Juan Verde was a few more beers into the bag than me, but that didn't mean he was wrong. For more than one reason. It wasn't just us I had to worry about. Somewhere out there in the darkness, my mom and her friends were making their own way to the show. Storm be damned, we were headed in to the forest, and Mandy willing, we'd come out alive on the other side.

MAD DASH FOR MANDY

Chaos reigned in the rush to depart. Three couples bounced about the modest cabin, grappling for mirror space, prepping drinks for the road, and frantically searching for Wi-Fi passwords that would unlock the precious directions through the woods to Mandy's house. As I changed into the clothes I could only hope were appropriate for a night at the theater in Lufkin, Texas, I began to feel very tired. Tired from the night before. Tired from the drive down. And tired of being mostly sober this far into the happy hour. My traveling companions downed last-second whiskies as I readied my trusty minivan for the journey ahead. It was fucking go time.

The cats and dogs downpour intensified as we darted, one by one, from the safety of the cabin. It reminded me of some old war movie where the heroes are taking fire from all sides, and their only hope for escape is to make it to the chopper alive. But there's no way to cover someone when the enemy is Mother Nature. None of us would emerge unscathed. Our best-case scenario would be to avoid lightning bolts and branches long enough to arrive at the van somewhere between soaked and fucking drenched.

No one died that night between the cabin and my minivan, but the journey through the forest hadn't even begun. As the two side doors slid shut, I cranked the wipers and hit power on the radio. Sinclair and Dawn took the back bench, Leah and Camie reclaimed their spots in the middle, Juan Verde and I manned the front, and Denton rapper AV the Great took over the stereo. The rain came so hard and heavy it drowned out the lyrics. All we could hear above Nature's din was the rattle of soccer-mom van speakers never meant to blast bass.

Cautiously, I began to pull out of the small circle drive in front of the cabin. Visibility was negative-to-zilch. Wind and rain everywhere. I was driving by intuition. This was not going to end well. A Thunderous CRACK split the night and an entire tree limb crashed to the ground in front of us, blocking our path to Mandy. We sat in there in stunned silence as the dark skies poured forth, threatening to wash out the simple gravel road that connected us to civilization.

There is a line in *The Princess Bride* that has always stood out to me. Wesley and Buttercup have just emerged from the Fire Swamp, only to find themselves face-to-face with Prince Humperdinck and his henchmen. Buttercup, hoping to spare Wesley's life, barters herself for her true love's safe return to his ship. Humperdinck agrees, though he has no intention of letting his rival go on living. Wesley knows as much, and when the Six-Fingered Man attempts to play out the charade, Cary Elwes straight shuts him down with a classic bit of movie badassery.

"*We are men of action. Lies do not become us.*"

In the case of Juan Verde and the tree limb in the road, my friend proved beyond the shadow of a doubt that he was a straight up man of motherfucking action.

While the rest of us sat there in a mixture of shock and awe, Juan Verde sprung from the passenger seat, darted into the road, and dragged the limb clear of our path. In a flash, he'd returned to the van, soaked but heroic, ready to resume our journey. We were already running late, and the weather certainly wouldn't do us any favors.

It was heinously dark. The rain was relentless. I began to feel an incessant tightening in my neck. Stress. I couldn't shake the thought of arriving at the theater too late to see Mandy. Forced to wait in shame in the lobby until intermission—or worse yet, be refused entrance altogether. That truly would have been the Humperdinck at the end of our Fire Swamp. I wanted to drive faster, but I could barely see the road.

I wish I could say that the tree limb Juan Verde vanquished was the only arboreal obstacle we faced that night, but it would be a lie. All the way through the Crockett National Forest, there were branches and limbs in the road. Sometimes, nature's debris would be in our lane, forcing us into oncoming traffic. Other times, we'd never even see the downed tree. There would be only the sudden shock of headlights bearing down on us before darting back where they belonged at the last second after avoiding the limbs in their own lane. It was a white-knuckled drive through the storm on a road I'd never been down before. No recognizable landmarks. No elation at reaching the halfway point. No possible way of knowing when we were "almost there." We were flying blind in a shitstorm, spurned onward by the siren song of Mandy and chased like hell by thunderbolts from the gods.

The comfort and safety of the Dan's Silverleaf patio seemed a million miles away. I wanted to be there so badly. To forget about driving through forests and storms and let my worries slip away in the bliss of a Friday buzz. My adventurer's spirit had begun to wane.

Every time I travel. Airlines lose my luggage. I miss flights. Storms. Traffic jams. And now lighting. A fuckton of lightning. I'm never leaving Denton again.

I felt the grumpiness like a wet blanket. I feared I would become short-tempered and surly and ruin everyone's night. I have seen what these moods of mine do to my wife, and I didn't want to subject my companions to it. I needed something to break—the storm, the tension, anything—before I melted down.

As if on cue, the mix CD I'd prepared reached its final tracks, where I'd strategically placed Mandy's version of "Somewhere over the Rainbow." The rain surrounding us was so loud that no one really noticed. I believe Sinclair was the first to catch on. Sitting there in the last row, he must have been transported back to childhood days in the way *way* back of a station wagon. Maybe he even remembered that fateful drive into Denver when Mom's Mandy tape melted. Gradually, from Sinclair to Dawn, to Camie and Leah, the Mandy buzz spread until it reached Juan Verde.

Juan's voice jumped an octave, like an excited kid: "Is this Mandy?!"

"This is what we're going to see?"

It was dark as fuck, but I could *feel* the grin on his face.

"Start this shit over and turn it up!"

And just like that the spell was broken. I don't mean it was broken in that the rain vanished and the moon lit our way. But the knot in my neck eased, and we blasted Mandy so loud that it drowned out the storm. It occurred to me that I'd spent so much time worrying what everyone would think of the show—of Mandy—that I'd forgotten to be excited. But my friends' reaction to this hidden track had changed all that. I'd sold them short—they trusted that I wouldn't drive them to the far reaches of East Texas for a show they'd hate. They trusted that I'd get them through the storm and the trees alive. They were artists and thinkers and *bon vivants*, and they were bullish about finding magic in the unexpected.

My taste for adventure was renewed, but I was still nervous about making it to Mandy before the curtain went up. The violent weather and the darkness made it impossible to make up time. I began watching the mileage markers.

Thirty-five miles to Mandy. Then twenty. Then fifteen. We weren't going to make it on time. My head started spinning. How much would we miss? How long would he play? Do shows in Lufkin work the same was as they do in Denton, where everything starts at least an hour late? Finally, we reached the edge of the forest and the outskirts of Lufkin only to be greeted by . . . nothing. No wind. No rain. No thunder. No lights. Lufkin had gone dark.

OUT IN THE TALL TREES

My friends and I weren't the first traveling party to ever cross the Crockett National Forest in the rain. Some years back, Dan Mojica, proprietor of Dan's Silverleaf, and his buddy, Harold, were headed through that very forest on their way to the World Championship Fiddler's Festival of Crockett, Texas. They weren't dealing with a downpour, but there was a heavy mist that turned the red clay into a thick sludge. Dan and Harold had been partying all the way out to East Texas. By the time they reached the part of the forest where it was nothing but logging roads and campgrounds, they were out of beer.

"We pulled off somewhere for gas and a couple twelve packs," Mojica told me. "But we were in the middle of a dry county. Shit out of luck. So I asked if there was anyplace close by we could pick up some beer. That's where the story really starts."

A friendly local took pity on them and clued Dan into this little bar located even further into the woods. Armed with a suspect directions—a right at the third logging road, go about a mile, and then a left at the second logging road—they hopped back into Harold's 1972 Ford pickup and were on their way. Everything was wet, and the roads were getting slick, but Harold wasn't about to go slow. Not even with his Rottweiler Jake tied up on about twenty foot of rope in the bed of the truck. Dan, on the other hand, could feel them slipping in the shit, and he was justifiably concerned.

"Harold, brother. You might wanna slow down."

"Whatever."

The truck kept fishtailing all over the road, and Dan was getting more and more worried, and Jake the rotty was looking around like even his dog brain could process just how fucked he was if Harold rolled that shit.

"Seriously, man. I think you might need to slow it down a little, Harold."

"Fuck that, Dan. I got it under control."

Right about then, the fishtailing got serious, and Harold spun the truck into this big-ass bar ditch. Jake bailed the fuck out at the first sign of trouble. For a while he was up and running, then he was getting drug, then running again, then drug, and eventually Dan lost sight of him.

"I thought that poor bastard was dead as hell," said Mojica.

But Jake did not die. In fact, he emerged unscathed. A little freaked out and muddy as shit, but fit as a fucking fiddle. Harold's truck was not so lucky.

"We were sunk up to the rims in mud," Dan said. "Both tires had slipped right off the back wheels. We were completely screwed, but I couldn't shake how gorgeous it was with the mist hanging over everything and the pine trees shooting up into the clouds. It was a beautiful spot to be stranded in."

For lack of a better plan, Dan and Harold decided to spark a joint and try and figure out what to do next. It wasn't ten minutes before they saw an El Camino coming from the opposite direction. When it got close, they could see that there were two big chainsaws and a couple of twelve packs of Old Milwaukee in the back.

"We could tell right off that that these guys were coming from the same place we'd been headed," said Dan. "And whatever they were up to was probably not cool in the eyes of the law. They didn't look like legitimate loggers."

The dudes in the El Camino stopped to investigate the out-of-towners stuck in the mud at the bottom of the ditch.

"What the hell happened to y'all?'

"We sorta spun off the road."

"Say, Boss!" yelled the local in the mist to the local behind the wheel. "Ain't we got that chain still?"

The two men unearthed a swing set chain from somewhere deep in the bed of the El Camino and proceeded to double wrap that fucker around a sturdy spot on Harold's truck. The one called Boss got back behind the wheel and went to work freeing the Ford from its clay prison. There was a fair amount of mud slung and some serious squealing from the belts, but ten minutes later, the truck was back on the road. This left just one problem: Harold had only one spare and two of his wheels were straight-up fucked.

"Y'all know anywhere we can pick up a spare?" asked Dan.

"Say, Boss! Ain't we got us another Ford tire still?"

And sure enough they did. Forty-five minutes after Harold had spun them into the ditch, Dan and his friend and Jake the rotty were back on the road to the beer store. Boss and his sidekick made them a gift of that extra tire and disappeared down the road and into the mist never to be seen again.

"We finally got to the place that was supposed to be a bar," said Dan. "But it was more like a house that was actually a bootlegger's shack. The second we walked in the door, everyone started starring at us, so we bought four twelve packs and got the hell out of there. I still think it was a miracle. And I like to believe that Boss and his buddy are both still alive telling the same story wherever they're drinking beer for the night."

"Damn. You make it sound like a whole different world, Dan."

"East Texas, brother. Some of those motherfuckers look straight-up amphibious."

THE SHOW MUST GO ON

Lufkin was still waiting for the lights to come back on. It made for an eerie drive through the city. The streets were empty except for utilities trucks scrambled by dispatchers that no doubt had their hands full. The only illumination came from generator-fed emergency lights in a handful of buildings. Occasional sirens echoed in the darkness. The haunting silence lingering after the storm's wrath filled me with hope. Maybe the show was delayed by an act of Mandy-loving God.

We reached the Angelina Arts Alliance about forty minutes late. There was a bus from a senior citizens center parked out front, and people were milling about the entrance. My heart sank. They'd already canceled the show. What other explanation could there be? I pulled into one of the few open parking spots not occupied by a fallen branch and braced myself for the grim news. The air was cool as we walked toward the darkened theater. Maybe we could at least get our tickets as souvenirs.

Everything was in shambles. A kindly lady promised that she remembered putting our tickets in an envelope marked with Leah's name, but they were impossible to find inside the very, very dark ticket office nestled inside a slightly less dark theater left powerless in the black of night. I was too afraid to ask the question of the hour, so Leah went looking for answers. She returned too quickly.

"What is it?" I asked. "Is it canceled?"

"No," she said. "Mandy is going to sing."

I wish to hell this was the part of the story where I tell you all about my powers of total recall and recant every detail of the spectacular show in the darkness in Lufkin. But this is not that part of the story. I started life with a pretty good memory that's been dulled by drink and smoke and cluttered with way too many trivial facts about the original *Beverly Hills 90210*. When it comes to Mandy and the darkness, all I have are chicken scratch notes on hotel stationary and the spiritual tinnitus from a musical display I never thought I'd witness in conditions I couldn't have imagined. I get lost in a flood of emotional reverb and everything comes out like a rambling bastard coked up on gratuitous profanity.

Yeah, man. I went all the fucking way to Lufkin to see Mandy fucking Patinkin. It was fucking incredible. This big-ass storm knocked out all the power, and we had to drive through the goddamned forest while trees were falling all over the place. Juan Verde had to jump out of the car and drag this big fucking limb out of the road or we never would have made it alive. Then we get to the damn venue, and man, the fucking power was out. We were all bummed on account of the show probably being canceled, but dude, Mandy wasn't having that shit. He came out like a damn champ and killed that shit in the darkness. No lights. No AC. No mic. Fucking nothing, man. Just a piano player, Mandy's voice, and a couple of fucking flashlights. The bastard didn't even play Somewhere over the Rainbow, but it was still cool. Sometimes he held the flashlight right under his face motherfucking Leprechaun-style. It was the shit. Fucking for reals.

Although that's an accurate description of my Mandy recollections, it really isn't the greatest approach. Or at least that's what I expect my editor would say. I wish there was some way to make you understand how overwhelming it is to try and put into words a night so incredibly surreal. From the moment we took our seats, it was clear we were to be treated to a show the likes of which no one had ever experienced. Hundreds of thousands of people have seen Mandy on the big screen or Broadway or even his shows with the great Patty LuPone. But I've got to believe those of us in the audience that night in Lufkin are the only people on Earth who've seen Mandy Patinkin perform an entire concert in the dark. And I have it on fairly high authority that Mandy himself would agree.

"I want to thank you all for sticking around," said Mandy. "There's no power, but the show must go on. This is going to be a night none of us will ever forget."

I remember those words often. The idea that Mandy and I could someday be simultaneously regaling someone with the story of that show gives me chills. It's like old timers telling war stories or gray-haired hippies talking about dropping acid at Woodstock.

I remember that night in Lufkin. Never seen such a storm. Knocked out power all across town, but it couldn't stop Mandy. His version of "It's Only a Paper Moon" was the most wonderful thing I've ever heard.

But the night wasn't all picture-perfect fairy-tale fodder. It got pretty damn stuffy without any air conditioning and all, and the crowd, mostly older white folks, found it particularly difficult to clap in rhythm during the parts that required audience participation. Mandy, a consummate showman, took everything in stride, even when some crazy old bitty asked if he ever planned on returning to *Criminal Minds*. Seriously? Everyone knows he hated that fucking show. He detested the violence and vileness and putting abducted women in boxes and cages and shit. Mandy graced her with "Next question" and moved on.

In a way, it almost didn't feel like a concert at all. It was the act of a dedicated host trying to save an intricately planned party derailed by circumstances beyond his control. The intimacy of the affair was not lost on Mandy.

"Something about tonight makes me want to tell stories. It reminds me of being in my studio. There would be some people sitting on my couch, and I'd make them listen to me."

Trust me when I say that everyone in the audience immediately embarked upon some version of the same fantasy. A very simple, innocent fantasy that entailed sitting on the couch at Mandy's place listening to him tell stories or ordering Chinese food or delightfully informing telemarketers that he was not at all interested in upgrading his cable package. I, for one, would have gladly hung on every word as he read me a death sentence.

The story I tell most from that night is very short, but I believe it's the Mandiest moment of the entire evening. Near the end of the show, in a second disastrous twist of fate, the power was restored and the lights and the AC came back on.

Mandy stopped mid-song. "Off!" he shouted. "Turn them off! Off or I walk!"

Almost as quickly as it had been illuminated, the theater went dark again.

"Let's pretend that never happened."

Mandy never played "Somewhere Over the Rainbow," but he did just about everything else. He told jokes, supervised the arrangement of camping lanterns on the stage around him, subsequently demanded that said lanterns be immediately removed, and even tossed a bottle of water into the audience, which he quickly repossessed for a reason I tragically cannot remember. This was not an artist collecting a check and going through the motions. Mandy seemed to fully recognize how special this night was—that we were allies, bound and determined to hold onto the magic for as long as we could.

When the final note had been sung, and we launched into a standing ovation, I caught sight of my mom down near the front row. The whole "no power in the box office" thing had turned the assignment of seats into a land rush scenario. Mom must have gotten there early because she was close enough to the stage to see

Mandy up close and personal. Sinclair and I made our way down to her row to see how she'd weathered the storm, but she was already talking before we could even ask.

"Harlin! Sinclair! I met Mandy!"

"What?"

"It was so cool! He came out to talk to the audience after the power went out. He was such a nice man. He kept thanking us for being here and telling us we should stick around because it was going to be such a fun night."

"Seriously," I said. "You actually spoke to Mandy Patinkin?"

"I did. He was so gracious and so funny. It was really, really cool."

My mom has a strange talent for just sort of bumping into famous people. She's met Pele a couple of times, got to know the lead singer of Golden Earing pretty well, and once spent a day hanging out on the set of a video shoot with Warrant. She's also the only reason I got to briefly meet one of my other heroes, Elvis Costello, but that's another story for another day—probably even another book.

Anyway, Sinclair and I weren't entirely surprised that Mom had met Mandy. I just wished I'd been there to share the moment with her. Mandy probably would have gotten a real kick out of little old mom and her two bearded sons making a pilgrimage to Lufkin to see him sing. We would have surely become best friends and enjoyed many wonderful summer vacations, Thanksgivings, and Passover feasts together.

I didn't say much on the trip back through the forest to our cabin. Sometimes I get real quiet and reflective after experiencing something I want to hold onto so badly. I'll keep playing the scene over and over in my mind, hoping that it will get burned into my grey matter even though I know the details will slowly fade until all I'm left with is a faint aftershock of the original feeling of the thing. It's important to hold on to all those moments for stories that will be written down—or swapped over camp fires or during patio hangs when the weather is nice. And so I try my damnedest even though I know that everything is fleeting and my memories of momentous events, when shared, will be an insult to the magic of a moment that flickered for an instant once upon a time.

THE SQUIRT BOMB

Juan Verde and Leah started it. There's no doubt about that. They're secret shot buddies who've been known to sneak off for Irish Car Bombs on nights out at the Silverleaf. Leah is a sucker for sweet shit like flavored vodka and Red Bull. Sometimes she'll walk straight up to Kate Covington Best, the sweetest, kindest bartender in the history of Dan's Silverleaf and the first lady of Slobberbone, and order a flavor instead of an actual drink. We get away with shit like that because we're regulars and mostly loveable.

But out there in the woods next to the lake, we didn't have many flavors or mixers at our disposal. It was pretty much just the Beam and that three-liter bottle of Squirt. So we improvised.

The Sultans of Shots started tinkering with ratios and different temperatures and glasses while the rest of us sorta watched but mostly just drank whatever we were already sipping. There was a lot of laughter and probably some taste testing, and in the end, The Squirt Bomb was born. Credit for the concoction falls squarely on the shoulders of Leah and Verde. As for the name, well that was more of a group effort. Had we an audio recording of the night, I'm sure we could identify the heroic trailblazer that first combined the words "squirt" and "bomb," but since it was a handle born of inebriation, that piece of history is lost to us forever. In its place, I have no shortage of warm memories of tipsy giggling and jubilant exclamations as we downed a second round and realized just how damn tasty the comingling of Squirt soda and Jim Beam bourbon could actually be.

In the post Squirt Bomb era, music took center stage. Glasses clinked and cans were crushed as we took turns plugging iPods into Sinclair's portable job site radio. Camie leveled my brother with this badass song, "Kudzu," by Daniel Markham, a Denton musician by way of Lubbock who makes the best friends when he's high. Sinclair nodded his solemn approval then countered by laying down some Temples. Juan Verde and I had never heard of them, but we were hooked before the chorus. Talk turned to how they were playing the Austin Psych Fest that year and just like that a plan for another road trip was hatched.

Life, as it is known to do, would take some turns, and none of us Denton folks ended up making it down to Austin to see Temples or any other band, but in the moment the possibilities were infinite and we never thought we'd ever miss another show we wanted to see no matter where it was going down. That's the power of a Squirt Bomb.

REGRET

I never even unbuckled my seatbelt at the Davy Crockett water fountain, which is connected to the Davy Crockett Spring, which gets its name from the fact that Davy Crockett camped there on his way to the Alamo. Sinclair and Dawn were the first out of the van for a drink from the fountain and a photo opportunity. Leah and Los Verdes were right behind them. But not me. I'd have something to drink soon enough. No need to get out of the car for an old, stone water fountain. That's what I told myself, but I didn't believe it.

I remember looking sadly in the rearview mirror as we pulled away. Was this my story? A grumpy fuck too lazy to walk twenty feet for a sip of water from a landmark honoring one of my childhood heroes? I'd been down this road before. Stubborn refusal or fear of testing the waters leaving me on the sidelines while friends and family dove right in. This was shaping up to be another Mexico, but I guess that was okay. I'd spent years getting good at regret.

JUMP MOTHERFUCKER

The summer before my sophomore year of high school my dad took me and my brother to Cancun. One of the few friends he'd been able to hold onto after the divorce had a time share down there. We stayed for two glorious weeks of scuba diving, exploring the beach, and endless hours at the pool trying like hell to figure out how to flirt with girls. On the last day, we drove three hours to this insane jungle oasis. The kind of place where you couldn't even bring in sunscreen because they didn't want anything to pollute the water. Tourists don't pay top dollar for murky water. They want that shit to look like the brochure.

There were dozens of these mysterious boxes hung from trees and various poles along the road to the oasis. My Spanish wasn't anywhere near good enough to decipher the signs on the boxes, but I could tell you didn't want to be standing anywhere near one of those fuckers. My Dad's buddy with the time share was married to a lady from Mexico, so his kids were all fluent. I asked my friend Chris about them.

"They're for the bees, man."

"The build houses for the bees on the side of the road? Shouldn't they be on honey farms or something?"

"No, bro. The bad bees. Those shits they told us about in science class."

"The Africanized bees?"

"The what?"

"Killer bees?"

"Yeah, man! The fucking killer bees. I heard those assholes are gonna be in Texas in like six months."

"What happens to the bees when the go in the box?"

"They don't come out. Mexico bout to save the motherfucking day, cabron!"

He busted into some kind of half-nationalistic victory dance right there in the back of the jeep. He pulled himself up by the roll bar and screamed into the wind. I was holding on to his belt in case he slipped when I started thinking how stupid it was to brave a trip down a killer bee-infested road and then pay for the privilege of baking in the heat for hours without sunscreen. The bees seemed like a quicker, less expensive way to go.

The line to get into the jungle oasis took about forty minutes, but even I had to admit that the place was a straight-up paradise. Pristine water lapped at sand like pulverized crystal. There were exotic birds, and I like to remember there being monkeys in the trees. We set up our day camp in a manicured spot that came with a waitress. Chris and his sister's boyfriend ordered beers even though they weren't old enough because the waitress didn't give a fuck.

We swam in the ocean for a while and floated in a sort of natural lazy river. It wasn't as big as the lazy river at the Wet 'n Wild water park next to Arlington Stadium, but it was natural and probably didn't have as much pee in it. I would have been happy to lounge there all day, but Sinclair had found something more exciting. He herded my reluctant ass through a path in the jungle to a bridge over a cave that opened up into a deep lagoon. The water was dark and calm. Hypnotic. I started to ask my brother what was so important about a stone bridge, but it was too late. There was barely time to gasp between his triumphant leap and the instant his body crashed into the pool below. Sinclair resurfaced in an instant and yelled at me to join him. A twitch somewhere in my legs was all in on the action, but my mind shut that shit down before I even got close to the edge.

I began to calculate. Jump angles and velocity and the likelihood of catastrophic injury should I chicken out halfway through and take a header into a giant lava rock. I spent an hour on top of that bridge. I watched all my friends—and people older and younger than me—plunge giddily into the waiting water. No one got hurt. But still, I couldn't turn off that part of my brain fixated on danger or public embarrassment.

Eventually, someone got clever and used girls against me. It might have been my dad or my brother. Who knows? Maybe it was even the girl herself. An act of kindness. All I can say for sure is that I eventually jumped, and I'm fairly certain I was goaded into it by a girl. Some of that "don't you want to look brave in front of all the pretty girls" bullshit. I'd seen enough people jump to know logically that I probably wouldn't get hurt. But getting over that hump was a bitch. Good thing nothing gets a guy over the hump like a girl.

The first jump passed in a flash. An "oh shit" followed by a "whoosh," and then it was all over but the splash. I was laughing before I broke the surface, and I scrambled up the rocky path back to the bridge for another go. Over and over and over again I flung myself from the bridge into the waiting arms of the cool water. Like a mother, she never dropped me. Breaking my fall with an exhilarating rush each and every time until the sun started to sink and I began to curse myself for every jump I wasted paralyzed on a bridge in the jungles of Mexico. I didn't notice the killer bee boxes on the way home. I was too busy with my regret.

GRIZZLY DRINKING

We'd been milling about on the empty streets playing the "is it open yet" game for almost an hour when the bartender finally unlocked the doors to Bear Hall. The space opened up like a cavern once you got through the entrance. The interior was a mash-up of exposed brick and wood. So much wood. Like some giant wizard waved a magic wand over a forest and turned it into a Texas roadhouse. There was a massive stage in the back corner of the bar and a couple of doors that opened onto a little patio. A majestic, L-shaped bar dominated the room. The friendly Lufkinite bartender greeted us promptly, and we wasted little time pulling up stools and making ourselves at home.

"Where y'all in from?"

"Denton," said Juan Verde. "Came out for the weekend."

"What brings y'all all the way out here?"

"We rented a cabin on the lake. Came out to see the Mandy Patinkin concert over in Lufkin."

"She put on a good show?"

"Not bad."

He set us up with a round of something cheap that was on special the night before. They were cold, and that's all that mattered. We started to explore the joint. Some lubricated spelunking in a rustic wooden wonderland scratched all my itches. I wandered into a side room with a couple of pool tables and a juke box and a long wooden table. The place was literally everything I'd ever wanted in a bar. I was already falling in love, and I didn't even know all its secrets.

Juan Verde and I finished our beers and headed back for another round. The bartender was talking in a real animated way to a lady who hadn't been there when we came in. He saw us out of the corner of his eye.

"Y'all ready for another one?"

"Yessir," I said. "Wouldn't mind a shot of something, either."

"We can make that happen."

I ordered a couple shots of tequila and we settled in for a chat with our new friend.

"We wandered around town for a bit today. Nice place. Quiet. But nice."

"It ain't always quiet. We had some excitement just a bit ago."
"Yeah?"
"No doubt. You see that lady I was talking to?"
"Yup."
"Well, she owns the hotel across the street, and this girl that cleans the rooms over there quit today. Swore she saw a ghost. Dropped everything and walked right out. Said she's never going back."
"No shit? A ghost?"
"That's what she said. I've spent plenty of time over there, and I've never seen anything strange like that, but the girl was pretty freaked out. The look on her face gave me the damn creeps."
"You think she really saw a ghost?"
"I don't know, man. But she sure thinks she saw a ghost, and that's got me thinking twice. That's why we opened late today. I had to help across the street before I could get things set up here."

I was thinking about calling an audible for some late night ghost hunting when Leah rushed over. She was fired up about something.

"You guys have to come see what we found."
"What is it?"
"Just come with me."

Leah led Juan and I to a little door in a neon-filled corner near the bathrooms. She pushed it open and the late afternoon sunlight smacked me in the face. I squinted and slid my sunglasses back down as we passed through the door and emerged into a beautiful courtyard filled with tables fashioned out of giant wooden spools. There was a single-wide trailer right in the middle and some signage promising taco sales. By the time my eyes settled on a familiar shade of blue paint—Silverleaf blue—I had already decided that Bear Hall must be where the Valkyries take warriors when they fall on the field of battle.

We settled into a couple of tables underneath a metal awning. This was exactly what we'd been looking for. Easy and comfortable. It might could have even given Dan's a run for its money had it been in Denton. And run by Dan. The Silverleaf isn't the go-to gathering spot because it's got the nicest amenities or the best drinks. Locals gravitate toward the little juke joint in the Industrial Street Arts District for the vibe, and that comes from Dan. You can serve all the Moscow Mules in fancy brass mugs in all the world, but that doesn't change the fact that a bar with Dan in it is always better than a bar without him. He was all Bear Hall needed.

We were drinking and staring longingly at that taco trailer when a weathered old interloper shuffled into the courtyard and over to our table. I would have been fine acknowledging him politely before closing ranks, but I was traveling with far more welcoming folks. Camie invited him to join us, and a conversation blossomed. I still had half an eye and most of my mind on those tacos, but what was left of my attention caught that the newcomer was a veteran of the music game. Gigging, booking, promoting, and just plain watching. He'd done all of it once and most of it twice. He was a nice enough fellow, but he weren't no taco.

We took turns trekking to the bar for more beers and shots. Before I knew it, I was nice and loose and chatting up our wayfaring music buddy about throwing one king hell show right there at Bear Hall. He'd wrangle up some of his musician buddies, and I'd bring a crew from Denton, and we'd pack that damn bar and the hotel across the street, ghosts be damned. I was just about to invite him back to the cabin for dinner when that magical taco trailer opened for business.

We don't mess around when it comes to tacos in the great state of Texas. Well, mostly. There are those that try to fancy up a street taco and sell it for six bucks, but unless you got an urban spoon up your ass, you know where to get the good stuff. Start by looking for a hole in the wall. If the menu is in English, you're in the wrong place. Try again. If you see sour cream anywhere in the joint, get the hell out. Tacos ain't supposed to be fancy. They just need to be simple and greasy and delicious. Bonus points for taco spots with a big *molcajete* filled with homemade salsa and a gurgling reservoir of fresh made *horchata*. Always—and I mean always—do your due diligence on the *barbacoa*. Some of these culinary crooks will try to pass off stewed beef as sweet cheek meat. Don't be fooled. True *barbacoa* looks a little gnarly, but it'll go down easy and kick a hangover right in the ass.

Leah beat us all to the counter. She'd done it up right, too. One of damn near everything and every salsa they had. We tore into those tacos, went back for seconds, and then tore into those. You can never get your fill of quality Mexican food. At least not in Texas.

My belly was full, and my head was light as I returned to the bar for one last round. Juan Verde was buying a Bear Hall T-shirt.

"I can't not get a shirt from the coolest bar in East Texas. It's got a damn bear right on it. No way you can pass that up."

I turned to the bartender and ordered a couple whiskeys. He started pouring, and I looked at Juan Verde, and my wheels started spinning.

"Say, man," I said. "Y'all got any Squirt soda back there?"

Dude just stared at me.

FOUNTAINHEAD REVISITED

We piled into the van with every intention of heading straight back to the cabin. The fridge and the cooler were fully stocked, and Sinclair had finally found some fishing lures. No need to press our luck in a strange town with a beers on our breath. But as we cruised past the Davy Crockett water fountain for the second time that day, something inside me snapped.

I flashed through a highlight reel of myself, sitting on the sidelines, watching the scene unfold. There were the countless car trips I spent with my nose in a book, driving my poor dad halfway to batshit as he pleaded with me to pay attention to the beauty—mountains and trees and wildlife—all around me. There were parties and weddings and discos in foreign lands connected by the common thread of a wannabe writer hanging back by the bar, too mortified to step foot on the dancefloor and foolishly clinging to false hope that watching life was just as good as living it. There was the drawer in my college desk that became the final resting place of every phone number of every girl I never could muster the nuts to call. The fireman's pole I was too afraid to slide down as a kid. The journalism degree at Mizzou that I abandoned because the easy scene of old friends was too much to resist. The trip in Europe I cut short for no reason other than to go home early. And my dad again.

Urging me at every turn. Begging me to go out and experience the world before life became a nine-to-five juggling act of bills and responsibilities.

That stubborn reluctance and inescapable timidity I'd carried with me my entire life became an untenable burden there in the streets of Crockett, Texas. I'd reached the mythological crossroads. Travel the wrong course, and I'd spend the rest of my life writing the back of DVD boxes for FUNimation, the leading distributor of Japanese anime in North America. The thought of it made my chest tighten. I was already getting aged out, and there is only so much you can say about magical titty warrior princesses clad in costumes that shred on demand. But there was another road. A drink of water from a forgotten monument was as far down that road as I could see, but the mystery of what might come next was exactly what I hoped for every morning and every evening as I sat in my van listening to sports talk radio and raging at the clogged lanes on my daily commute.

I yanked the wheel of the van into a u-turn. The boisterous rabble from the back ceased instantly as necks craned to identify the reason for the deviation in course. We skidded into the parking lot, and I slung the gearshift from "D" to "P."

"What are we doing?" asked Leah. "I thought we were going back to the cabin?"

"When I was a kid—and Sinclair can back me up on this—I used to wear a coonskin cap everywhere I went. It wasn't real coonskin. Just some imitation shit I picked up at Disney Land. But it was my favorite thing in the world."

"He did," said Sinclair.

"I must have watched about a hundred hours of the Davy Crockett show starring Fess Parker. Did y'all know he played both Davy Crockett and Daniel Boone? The man was a true gift to humanity."

"I did not know that," said Camie.

I pointed at the fountain. "I'm getting some of that water, and I'm getting water at every other fucking commemorative water fountain I see for the rest of my life."

There was nothing remarkable about the Davy Crockett water. It was not especially cool, and the stream was weak . . .

HARLIN ANDERSON

A GOOD TEXAS MAN, PART I

Knapik ain't from Texas, but he's trying his Cleveland ass off to live up to the high standards. He just don't want anyone to know it.

Aside from being a long-suffering Browns fan and looking a little like a garden gnome after a two-day bender, Knapik is good people. He's handy with tools and quick to volunteer whenever someone needs help. He loves music, and there's a good chance the local festival ain't got folks to work the door the last two years without his efforts. Sometimes he runs his mouth like a grumpy asshole, but deep inside the man there's a heart like a half-nuked marshmallow.

Once upon a time, Knapik fell into a little bit of unexpected good fortune that could have made life easier for him and his lady. Instead, he went right out and adopted the Skittles Kids.

I call them the Skittles Kids, well, because they called me Skittles first. Juan Verde put little Joshy up to it one year at the Golden Jesus Chili Cook Off on account of I put peanut butter cups in my chili. The name stuck. Now every time I see his brood, all three of them come tearing ass at me screaming, "Skittles!" They're pretty damn adorable, so it's hard to get annoyed.

The Knapiks rescued the Skittles Kids from an absolutely god-awful, undeniably horrible, fucking-tragedy of a situation. They were scattered across foster care, but Andy and Heidi fought hard to get them all reunited. He told me the specifics of the story in the waning moments of this year's 35 Denton Music Festival while we leaned against a fence on the patio at Oak Street Draft House. We were almost too tired to drink and some of the details drifted up into the night and disappeared forever. But the long of the short of it is that the Skittles Kids didn't have a frozen shit's chance in hell until they became Knapiks.

It ain't easy to go from no kids to three kids all at once, but Knapik puts everything he's got into it. He takes them to concerts, on vacations to New Orleans, teaches them about collecting records, and answers about a thousand "why?" questions every damn day. Sometimes, it looks like it's wearing on him. Like he might be too old and too tired to pull it all off. But then one of them calls him Dad or does one of those amazing things only kids can do, and just like that, Knapik catches his second wind.

One of my favorite things when I visit Leah at work is to walk out of her building and see Joshy and his Daddy up ahead of us, holding hands and shuffling past that big fountain in front of the library as they head home to swim in the pool he built for his kids so they can learn there's nothing in the world like being brave enough to jump off something solid into whatever water waits below. You ain't even got to squint your eyes or anything to believe that they are flesh and blood. I guess someday Denton will have a whole herd of Knapiks running around town. God help us all because that Joshy is gonna be a hulk.

ALL GOOD THINGS

The next day, we watched Sinclair and Leah fish while we listened to Beck's *Morning Phase*. I was grumpy, and nobody caught shit, but the two things had nothing to do with each other. I had begun to ache in anticipation of the absence of Sinclair, and I was dreading the final curtain on our weekend escape. That's another thing I'm real good at. Lamenting the end of something that isn't even over yet.

We repacked our bags and loaded up our cars and cleaned up the cabin. Trash bags full of empty beer cans sat next to trash cans that had already been filled with empties. I put on sunglasses to hide the storm in my eyes and hugged Sinclair goodbye. A feeling like I barely knew my brother ripped through me. It was my fault.

I didn't visit him once while he was teaching English in Russia. We swapped emails, but the pictures and stories were so sad. I didn't want to go there. I couldn't be bothered. Not even when the little Russian Blue kitten he loved got sick and died because that's what happens to things you love in cold, hard places.

Part two of the same story played out in Washington D.C. Sinclair went away to grad school and fell in love with Dawn. The only thing I really knew about her is that she was working on a Ph.D. in civil engineering with a specialty in concrete. She loves Vince Guaraldi, her parents own the local donut shop in Taylor, Texas, and she was quickly becoming the most important person in my brother's life.

But I missed all of it. The friends he made. His battles with bed bugs. Bocce Ball and drinks on Sundays. The time he spent earning his security clearance as an employee of some spooky government contractor. I should have visited more. That's what a good brother would have done. I did manage to make the trip out for his graduation, but I can't say with any degree of honesty that I actually saw him walk across the stage. And that's about all the sins I can stand to confess for now. It was time to try and move forward.

"We're close now, brother." I said. "We need to do this more often."

"Why do you think we moved back?"

"I'm just glad you did."

We said our goodbyes and dropped off the key and got in our cars and drove away. Somewhere down the road, we stopped at a mega gas station and bought BBQ sandwiches and caramelized corn puffs. Leah and Camie played games on their phones while Juan Verde and I ran the gamut of my wallet of burned CDs and the tall trees rewound themselves into cities and suburbs and then all of the sudden we were back in Denton pulling up to Casa Verde.

"What y'all gonna do for the rest of the day?"

"Probably go to Dan's. They're spinning records on the patio this afternoon. You?"

"Probably go to Dan's."

Our East Texas Mandy Patinkin adventure was over, but there was still some weekend left. A handful of hours we could spend hanging out with friends, distracting each other from the vicious reality of Monday morning when we would cease to be explorers and instead waste forty hours of perfectly good sunshine with our collective asses planted in office chairs. It's not fair that we live in state as big and beautiful and full of wonder as Texas—yet we squander so much of our lives under fluorescent lights. This is the reason we drink.

THE ONCE AND FUTURE PATIO

The founding members of Denton DJ collective The Nice-Up Crew had their gear set up on the little stage at the end of the Silverleaf patio closest to Hickory Street. They had to be careful walking around because the boards were old and warped and one boisterous step could send vibrations coursing through the wood like an electrical current until they reached the needle of the turntable and skipped it across the grooved vinyl. That stage is gone now. Torn out and replaced with a new bar and a walk-in cooler. There's a new stage now at the other end of the patio. It's bigger and better and it doesn't make needles skip.

That's not the only change. The old bar that used to run the length of the patio is gone, too. Chunks of it are scattered across Denton. Dan turned some into stepping stones between the little decks in his back yard, and I've got two sections sitting on my patio. Someday I'll find the perfect spot for them. Until that day, they'll just be heavy slabs of concrete with a storied past.

The biggest change from those days—the most gapping void—is the loss of the picnic tables. The alpha and omega of this story. The happy spaces I shared with friends the night before leaving for Lufkin and immediately upon my return have disappeared. Banished to make room for tables that take up less space and accommodate more people because our town won't stop growing. The powers that be won't allow it to stop. Real estate brokers and visitor's bureau lackeys lured the masses to the 940 with the promise of small-town charm and a thriving music scene and then did all they could to destroy both. Our beloved picnic tables are just another item on the list of casualties.

But not all change is bad. Juan Verde and Camie have added a little Green Bean to their family since that magical night in Lufkin. You'll see her tottering around at shows or rolling her toy car across the smooth, sturdy boards on that new Silverleaf patio stage. She'll never know the picnic tables or where the old bar used to be, and that's just fine. Because she'll grow up and take over for us when we're old and tired and don't want to fight "progress" anymore. She is a child of the old Denton, but she'll have a role to play in shaping its future. Or maybe she'll simply grow up and take her parents' sense of adventure and a little of the spirit of Denton to a new place where she can be part of community not unlike what existed in 76201 not so long ago.

Children and cities are not so different. They start small and grow big. The people who love them want only the very best for them. They shepherd and guide them for as long as possible, but eventually we must all let go so they can become whatever they will become.

Part Two
The First Texas Coastal Expedition

GAS STATION CURRY

I travel polite. Please. Thank you. Yes, sir. No, ma'am. All of those words that make mothers and fathers real proud. Out on the patio at this gas-station-turned-Indian-restaurant-and-wine-store, I'm too bashful to interrupt anyone's conversation. But I need a lighter. The people seem friendly enough—except they're not my people. These are Austin people. Sinclair's people.

I camp out next to a bar that's not being used for anything and wait for someone to start smoking. A girl with tattoos and pin-up hair sitting with a corporate bro is the first to get the craving. I sneak over and real gently ask if I could borrow her lighter for a second. She hands it to me and kinda half-ass bullshit smiles. The bro is annoyed. I can't tell if it's because I'm standing there or because she's smoking. It stinks of a doomed first date.

Austin is due south of Denton by about three and a half hours. The curry station is right off Interstate 35, so you can almost feel the cars flying by. Little streaks of light there for a second and then gone. I watch them while I smoke. Sinclair and I were supposed to travel that road tomorrow on our way to Mile 60 of the Padre Island National Seashore, but the red tide fucked up our plans. Now we'll be taking a different road to a different beach to steer clear of the evil in the water. We leave in the morning. There are people inside sitting at a table with Sinclair and Dawn that I have not seen in years. Only booze can obliterate that awkward silence. Maybe I'll buy a bottle of wine on my way back to the table.

MORNING OF THE VERY BAD PHONE CALL

My bag was packed and waiting by the door, so I'd be ready when Sinclair got home. We were leaving for the coast at noon. Some members of our traveling party had dropped out on account of the red tide, a disturbing phenomenon often caused by an algal bloom of toxic dinoflagellates. You can't swim when that shit's in the water. It can kill fish, or even manatees, and it's hell on people with asthma or other respiratory problems. There is no exact science to the factors or conditions that spawn red tide, but when the surf changes color, you stay away from the water. Somehow, Sinclair still managed to piece together a caravan of adventurers willing to make the trek all the way to the coast in search of a place with clear waters. All we needed was a little luck with traffic on our way out of Austin, then it would be full speed ahead until we hit the sand.

All that hope and glory bullshit flew the fuck out the door the minute Sinclair opened it. He had this look on his face like something had gone horribly, terribly wrong.

"Brother," he said. "I think this trip is cursed."

"What happened?"

"There was actually murder, believe it or not."

"What the fuck? Who got murdered?"

"My buddy's cousin. Someone shot him on his doorstep at like three in the morning."

"What the fuck for?"

"No clue, man. Someone rang the bell, and when he answered it, they shot him."

"Holy fuck."

"They were close, too. My buddy is in a bad way."

"I'm sorry, brother."

"No. I'm sorry. You came all the way down for this, and it's falling apart faster than I can try and put it back together.

"You ain't gotta be sorry, Sinclair. If the universe wants to throw red tide and random shootings at us all in one weekend, there's not a damn thing we can do about it."

"Everyone has pretty much dropped out at this point."

"I figured as much."

"I mean, we could still try to go it on our own, but it's probably not a good idea. My buddy and his friend were gonna be driving our anchor truck. Big fucker with a winch in case anyone got stuck. You need at least two vehicles to make it through the sand."

"What about Bruns?"

"Dropped out when he heard about the murder. Said it was one too many bad omens."

"Kinda hard to disagree"

"Like I said. We could head down on our own, but —"

My phone rang when it shouldn't have been ringing. It was my wife.

"Hold that thought. I gotta to take this."

A neural car alarm blared in my head, triggering an icy burn of misfiring nerves at the base of my neck before sliding down the length of my spine and settling into a sick pool of dread deep in the small of my back. She hardly ever calls, and she definitely shouldn't be calling right now. She should be at her appointment. A text, maybe. But not a phone call. This could only be bad.

"Hello?"

Nothing. Just a pause like a telemarketer.

"Leah?"

More silence. Then a sound like a little kid desperately trying to catch a runny nose followed by sob choked into submission.

"It didn't have a heartbeat."

THE VERY BAD PHONE CALL, PART II

The sun was bright in my eyes, but I smoked two cigarettes just to keep from going back inside. What was I gonna say to Sinclair? Less than forty-eight hours ago, everything was mostly fine and we were headed to the beach with no baggage but some coolers, sunscreen, and camping chairs. Now everything was ruined. Someone was dead. Things in the ocean were drowning in clouds of red algae that would tolerate no life. I've had my fair share of shit go wrong while traveling, but I'd never seen anything get so fucked up with such a vicious quickness. I took a very deep breath and then opened Sinclair's front door.

"Everything all right?" he asked me.

"I just got a very bad phone call."

"What does that mean exactly?"

"That thing we were happy about. The thing we celebrated with beers at the Carousel Club?"

"Yeah."

"We can't be happy about that anymore."

Sinclair threw his cell phone at the top of the coffee table and didn't say anything for a minute.

"I'm really sorry to hear that, Harlin."

He looked me in the eyes so hard that I almost couldn't take it.

"I'm as sorry to hear that as anything I've ever been sorry to hear in my life."

"I know."

"How's your lady?"

"She's sad, brother. Really fucking sad."

"What can I do? What do you need?"

"I'm hungry, Sinclair. I'm hungry and I think I want to drink. Can you take me somewhere we can do those things?"

"Yeah, man. I can do that."

40 SPINS WORTH OF BEER

I was feeling pretty fucked out by the time we left End of an Ear, a favorite vinyl-hunting spot of Sinclair's. Money has a way of slipping through your fingers in a town like Austin, and I was already doing the mental math only two days removed from payday. There's so much shit you can spend money on in that city. Good food and endless things to drink. Live music. Records. More drinks.

I'd been good and limited myself to just a couple records. A cool little garage rock band I'd never heard of and this kick-ass Todd Terje double record that set me back thirty bucks all by itself. My wallet was definitely looking for soft landing spot. Someplace to lay low and recharge. A joint with dim corners that no one bothered to look into. I needed a dive bar and a juke box, and that's exactly what I told Sinclair.

"I know a spot," he said.

Navigating the city was a clusterfuck on account of the Austin City Limits music festival. I'd gone once back in college, and had a great time, but that was years ago. Since then, it had grown from a Friday, Saturday, Sunday party to a big-ass, double-weekend blowout. That's the thing about throwing a good party. Word gets out and then everyone wants to go. Making room for that many people can disrupt an entire zip code, but nobody knows that as well as Austin folks. Our capitol city is a prime destination for every asshole that crosses the Texas border.

Sinclair snaked his way into the back parking lot of a place I recognized straight off.

"Is this Deep Eddy?"

"You been here before?"

"Only once. But this is exactly the place I had in mind when I said I wanted a dive bar."

"It's like I read your mind, right?"

"Almost."

"What do you mean 'almost'?"

"I mean you didn't actually read my mind, Sinclair."

"Maybe not the way they read minds in movies, but you gave me a general direction, an inkling, and I took you to exactly the spot you were thinking of. I read your fucking mind. You know how I did it?"

"I don't know. Magic?"

"Because I fucking know you better than anyone in the world will ever know you. Same as you know me. Parts of us are the same because we come from the same places. Learned from the same people. We could not see each other for ten years, and the minute we were in the same room, I'd know exactly what you were thinking just as sure as you'd be able to read every expression on my face. So don't tell me I didn't read your mind because I fucking did."

"You win, Sinclair. You read my mind."

The dim interior of Deep Eddy's was a salve for my brokenness. No one paid any attention as we walked through the door. There was a threesome of graying barflies camped out at the table by the juke box, and I cursed them silently for taking the spot I wanted. Sinclair laid claim to a table in a dark corner near the front of the shotgun bar. We ordered drinks. Something fancy for brother man. Maybe a Sculpin IPA. I asked a tall bartender who looked a lot like someone's crazy uncle for a Lone Star and a whiskey. I needed something cheap and familiar.

Sinclair and I killed the better part of an hour bouncing back and forth between our table and the bar. Drinks go down faster than you'd think at certain times of day. You get caught up, Mystikal-style, and the gravitational pull of alcohol slings you right around the moon and sends you hurtling toward a row of tap handles. You think nothing of it until later, when the bar-space-time continuum starts doing strange things to your surroundings.

Sinclair was haggling, on my behalf, with Crazy Uncle Bartender over the price of an official Deep Eddy trucker hat when Dawn walked through the door.

"What's he up to now?" she asked.

"You know Sinclair. I mentioned that I wouldn't mind having one of those trucker hats, which is strange since I usually hate trucker hats. I'm very careful about my headwear."

"You don't say."

"Absolutely. See, Sinclair can wear any old hat and pull it off. He's the Loki. I'm the big old bastard Viking brother. I gotta stick to a specific style."

"So if Sinclair is Loki, I guess that makes you Thor?" She tried to keep a straight face, but it was obvious she wanted to laugh like hell.

"We do share quite a few characteristics, and I'm sure there's more than a passing resemblance." I was talking straight out my ass now. "But I'm more of an everyman's Thor. Not so Hollywood. That's why I got to be careful about my hats. Leah bought me a killer fedora for Christmas one year, but I can't wear it because it's got this deep crease down the middle that doesn't leave any room for the top of my head. Sinclair wouldn't have that problem. He'd put that fucking hat on and look just like a young Bruce Springsteen. You know what I'd give to look like a young Boss even for just one day?"

"You've obviously spent more than a little time thinking about all this."

"Hell yes, I have. I don't think you've spent enough time thinking about Bruce Springsteen. It'll change your life."

"Change it how?" she asked.

"I can't answer that for you. Each man and woman has to come to Springsteen by their own road, and that journey of discovery does a number on your soul like little hands mashing up playdough. There's a push and a pull to the experience that leaves you changed."

"How long have you two been drinking?"

"They want twenty-five bucks for those fucking trucker hats," interrupted Sinclair. "Can you believe that? Ten bucks is fair. Maybe fifteen tops. But twenty-five? Not happening. I tried to tell him that it would be good advertising to have an up-and-coming writer wearing their hat all over Denton, but he said he wasn't authorized to give discounts."

"You tried to barter with the bartender?" she asked.

"Can I still be an up-and-coming writer if I'm almost forty?"

"Darlin," said Sinclair, getting real serious in that intense way of his. "People have been bartering with the keepers of the spirits since the days of the very first bartender. It's a helluva lot more natural than handing over paper money stamped with an arbitrary value. And brother, up-and-coming doesn't have a damn thing to do with age. It just means you've got something good inside that you haven't quite figured out how to share with the world. Yet."

Dawn and I just stared starry-eyed at Sinclair for a long minute, both of us loving him in our own ways. He can be a frustrating human to interact with. A riddle personified. But at his core he's generous and caring and pretty fucking amazing. Dawn leaned in and gave him a kiss on the cheek.

"You boys have a good day?"

"Sure did, lady," said Sinclair. "You got any money for that juke box?"

THE VERY BAD PHONE CALL, PART III

Telling people about a Very Bad Phone Call is not fun, and you never, ever want to do it. But you have to tell them or they'll ask about it without knowing, and then they'll be embarrassed. That's the situation I found myself in at Deep Eddy's the night of the Very Bad Phone Call. Dawn didn't know enough of the story to be sad, and it was my responsibility to tell her. Looking back, I would rather have been a coward and asked Sinclair to do it for me while I took a piss or something.

She started to say something that sounded like it might drag me into the darkness I couldn't shake, so I cut her off.

"We can't be happy about that anymore."

"Oh," she said and looked over at Sinclair kind of confused.

"I just found out that we're sad a few hours ago. We should be happy again someday, but not right now."

"I'm sorry."

"I know."

"Are you going home?"

"I asked if she wanted me to. But she's got her mom, and I've got to be in Corpus for a conference on Sunday, and I don't have any fucking idea what I could do even if I was home. What am I supposed to say, Dawn?"

"You don't have to say anything right now, Harlin. I understand."

"Thank you," I buried my eyes at the bottom of my mug of beer and drank until there was nothing left. "I'm empty," I said. Then I got up and walked away.

SPINNING

I slid cash money into the little slot on the juke box and waited for the inner magic of the machine to do its thing. The honky tonk box must have learned math from the same person I did because it paid forty spins on a five dollar bill. I dialed up a pairing of sonic misfits—the Grateful Dead's "Uncle John's Band" and "Hanging on the Telephone" by Blondie—then stopped by the bar on my way back to the table.

"Y'all better settle in," I said, slumping into my chair.

"Why's that?" asked Sinclair.

"Your lady gave us a magical five dollar bill. And when I put that magical five dollar bill into the machine of wonder, it gave us forty spins. The first two have been selected. Dawn is officially on the clock."

Dawn then Sinclair then me then Dawn then me and Sinclair at the same time then Sinclair then Dawn then me, and so forth and so on, ad nauseum. We unleashed the very best that box had to offer. Elvis Costello, The Meters, Van Morrison, Bowie, Graham Parsons, and JJ Cale. After that, there was a break for whiskey and beer and a cigarette on a little patio out back before Sinclair launched us on another go-round highlighted by two Prince tracks, some Flying Burrito Brothers, the Ramones, Junior Brown, and the Mavericks. The bar was beginning to warp around us by the time we reached our last dance, a bleary-eyed ride down Willie Nelson's "Whiskey River." We settled up with Crazy Uncle Bartender and stumbled out into what had been daylight seemingly not so long ago.

"Is that the dark?" asked Dawn "What happened to the light?"

"We burned day into night, baby," said Sinclair. Burned it all out on those forty spins."

We started off in the direction of our cars, dodging groups of musical tourists headed for Zilker Park and the festivities of ACL. Just before the turn off to the parking lot there was a large, crudely drawn sign outside a beer and wine store.

Last Chance for Cheap Booze. Do it.

FUTURE LEADERS OF AMERICA

Me and Will were cruising the empty streets of Terrill, Texas looking for beer. Our friend Dee was dead, and we wanted to drink a couple of cold ones in his memory. I was eighteen, Will was seventeen, and I don't guess it mattered what age Dee would have been because he was never gonna get any older.

Camp RYLA had brought us all together about a couple months back. We'd all three been recipients of the Rotary Youth Leadership Award, which meant we got to spend a week doing team building exercises and listening to motivational speakers and flirting with cute girls in footie cow pajamas. For seven days we lived as close as brothers. Ate together, went to bed and woke up at the same time, and competed against the other cabins in obstacle course races and swimming and shit like that.

The thing I remember most about Dee is how much he loved that song "Brandy" by Looking Glass. His face is all blurry now, and I can't make out the features, but I can still sorta hear him singing:

"Brandy! You're a fine girl. What a goooood wife you would be. But my life, my love, and my laaady is the sea."

He'd get real into it, and me and Will would just be looking at him like "What the fuck are you even singing dude? Don't you know any Beastie Boys or some Smashing Pumpkins or Green Day or something fucking cool?" But he'd just keep on dancing and singing and tell us that someday we'd figure out what cool really was.

A couple weeks after we left Camp RYLA, I got a call from our cabin counselor. He told me that Dee and his family had been in a car accident and that Dee didn't make it. They were headed out on a family vacation. Someone fell asleep at the wheel or maybe Dee was sleeping in the back seat so he wasn't buckled up when some asshole wrecked into them or some other stupid fucking reason to not be alive. Dying so young feels like it should be impossible, but some poor fuckers just can't seem to get old.

We responded to the tragedy the way any conscientious group of young leaders would respond. We met up at someone's house to tell stories about the good times we shared that one week of our lives we were together. We wrote letters to Dee's parents. They were still alive, and I had no fucking idea what to say to them. I'm sorry your son is dead and you lived. I'm sorry you'll have to carry that with you every day of the rest of your fucking life. I'm sorry you are reading this right now and wishing like hell that you could trade places with Dee so he could live a life. Go to college. Get drunk. Get laid. Graduate. Have a career and children. Maybe buy a fucking boat.

I said none of that. Obviously. Instead, I just told them how much Dee loved singing about Brandy. I sandwiched it between a bunch of the prerequisite "He was such a great guy" and "I'm sorry for your loss" bullshit. But the part about "Brandy" was the only real thing I wrote because it was really the only thing I knew about Dee. He was a kid who was a leader, and he was way into Looking Glass and then he was dead. And that's as much of the story as I'll ever fucking know.

Which brings us back around to cruising for booze with Will. We'd promised to stay in touch when we saw each other at Dee's letter writing party, so I made the trek from Waxahachie that Sunday specifically for the purpose of pouring a little out for a fallen homie. Only none of Will's usual hookups were coming through for him. We drove around doing a whole lot of nothing for a real long time. Listening to the radio and making small talk like the virtual strangers we were.

At some point, Will wanted to stop and see his girlfriend. She was having her wisdom teeth removed the next day, and he was dead set on giving her a hug and a kiss before she went into surgery. I couldn't blame him. She was the real deal Texas-style knock-out. Blonde hair, blue eyes, and a country accent. Her family lived in a big house. There was a library off the entry way with more books than I'd ever seen in a person's home. I hung out in there looking at all the titles, so the lovebirds could have some time alone. Besides. She was way too cute for my self-conscious, teenage ass to feel comfortable around anyway. When it was time to go, she gave me a friendly hug.

"It was nice to meet you, Harlin. Y'all don't get in too much trouble tonight."

"Doesn't seem like that'll be much of a problem."

"Take a good look at me, Will," she said. "The next time you see my face, it'll be all swole up like a chipmunk. You probably won't even love me anymore."

"Never happen, babe. I'm gonna love you my whole life."

"You better."

I excused myself at that point. Kissing was probably coming next, and I didn't want to be a creeper sitting there watching my buddy make out. That ain't cool. I lit a smoke and waited by his car. Will had a spring in his step on his way out the front door. He was full of infatuation energy. That cosmic surge that puts a goofy smile on your face after you get done kissing someone you really, really like kissing. I'd only experienced once or twice at that point in my life, but I knew it to be powerful.

"Harlin, I think I got an idea where we can get some beers."

"Fuck yeah, man. Let's do this."

We started driving across town while Will told me about this buddy of his whose folks kept a fridge in the garage. It was usually stocked with some sort of alcohol, and if the garage door was open, we could sneak a few.

"But what if somebody catches us?"

"This dude's like my best friend. His parents wouldn't be surprised to find me in their garage. I'll just tell them I was stopping by to introduce one of my buddies from camp."

"Sounds like a plan."

The garage door was up when we got to the place. Jackpot. We were gonna be able to toast Dee after all. Will and I crept inside without turning on any lights or making any noise. We reached the fridge, and Will eased it open while I watched the door to the house.

"Fuck."

"What's wrong?"

"All they got is wine coolers."

"Works for me, dude."

Will handed me a Seagrams, and we hustled back to his car. Not wanting to get caught wine-handed at the scene of the crime, we stashed the bottles in a backpack, and Will drove us to a dead-end road where we could "enjoy" them in peace.

"Well," said Will. "When I said we should meet up and toast Dee, I never thought it would be with wine coolers."

"Ain't exactly what I had in mind, either. But it's better than nothing."

"You got anything special you want to say?"

"I wish I did, but I can't think of anything. It's shitty that he's dead, but I didn't really know him well enough to say some movie-type shit or anything like that."

"Yeah. Me neither."

"Best to keep it simple then. To Dee."

"To Dee. Hopefully he's someplace better."

We guzzled our wine coolers and chucked the bottles into a field. It's not safe for teenagers to be driving around with empties. Cops probably would have given us extra hell for drinking girly shit. Small-town cops in Texas are like that sometimes. Will drove us back to his place, and we put in a movie and fell asleep before it was halfway over.

A loud knock on Will's door woke us up early. It was his dad.

"Will, can I see you for a minute?"

"Yes, sir."

I looked around Will's room while he was gone. It was military neat. Nothing like my room with its piles of crap everywhere and walls plastered with pictures I'd cut out of magazines. There was hardly any decoration at all. Just some certificates and band awards. In the corner, there was a music stand and a trumpet case. I hadn't even known that Will played an instrument, but judging by the awards, he was pretty hot shit.

When Will got back, I could tell he was heated.

"What's up man?"

"Sonofabitch just punched me in the mouth."

"What?"

"My dad hit me in the mouth."

"What the fuck for?"

"Because he's an asshole. Same reason as always."

"This has happened before?"

"Yeah. He says it's so I don't get the big head. I work my ass off to impress him, but he just hates me more for every good thing I get."

"Shit, man. You want me to say something to someone?"

"Fuck it. I'm gone in a year. I'll get a music scholarship, and I'll never have to come back."

"There's better days ahead, man. This is just the beginning for us. Reach for the future, baby!"

I'd invoked the official slogan of Camp RYLA because I didn't know what else to say when a kid gets punched by his dad for doing nothing but being a good kid. Wine cooler thievery, aside.

"Reach for the future, Harlin. C'mon, I'll walk you out."

Will and I walked through his living room to the front door. We passed right by his dad, but he made no move to introduce me. The sun was bright outside. When we got to my car, we hemmed and hawed our way through a last bit of small talk and then did the whole bro hug thing.

"Don't be a stranger, Harlin."

"Never, buddy. I don't live too far. You let me know if you ever need anything. I got a big room with a couch and a hammock. You're always welcome if you need to get away for a bit."

"Thanks, dude."

"Take care of your girl. She'll be groggy as hell when she gets out of surgery, but she'll be happy to see you."

"Drive safe."

"Shit, man. My ride's a tank. I'm always safe."

I got into my seventeen-foot, six-inch long 1986 Buick LeSabre and began my trek home. I hadn't expected to come face to face with something so sinister, but what the hell could I do about it? Some future leader of the world I was turning out to be. And fuck Camp Ryla. Maybe I could hold my own on a ropes course, but they hadn't done shit to prepare me for what I was gonna find out in the world.

I never saw Will again after that morning. Never so much as called. Sometimes I think of him and Dee, but mostly I don't. The past is just the past, and there's no point in dredging it all up again. Unless you got to write a book or some shit like that.

VERY BAD PHONE CALL, PART IV

Sinclair and I had been drinking for most of the day, and now we were shouting at each other in his front yard. We were heated, but it wasn't a "fuck you" blow up. Just one of those things were two dudes get drunk and shout their hurt at each other.

I don't even know how we got to that point. One minute, we were inside listening to records and sipping drinks, and the next, we were outside smoking cigarettes and Sinclair was telling me that the whole reason he wanted to be a firefighter was to make up for the fact that he wasn't Edward Snowden. It took a few go-rounds before his words started to cut through the haze of drink. When they finally did, I flashed back to that day on the Denton square when the news first broke revealing the identity of the man who'd blown the whistle on the NSA.

"Holy shit," Sinclair had said, turning up the radio and ignoring whatever story I was rambling at him. "I know that fucking guy."

"You know the most talked-about man in America? Fuck, maybe the world?"

"I worked with him. We weren't friends or anything, but I used to see him in the building. We met once."

"Did you know about all that shit?"

"I know about a lot of shit, but I can never talk about it. I'd have to go on the run. Never see anyone I know ever again."

"I'd never let that happen, Sinclair. If you ever had to ditch your identity and start over, I'd go with you. I couldn't let you be alone."

It was easy to talk big because someone else's brother or son was already on the run in a foreign land. It was a kick finding out Sinclair knew the kind of secrets they put in movies, so I made promises I figured I'd never have to keep. But out there in his front yard on 51st street in Austin, I was starting to discover just how much guilt Sinclair was carrying over not being man enough to make an enemy of one of the biggest, most powerful and most ruthless governments in all the world.

"You don't understand, Harlin. People might have died because of me."

"C'mon, Sinclair. I doubt that's true."

"Maybe they didn't die directly because of things I did, but you can bet your ass bad shit happened to people because of things I didn't do."

"You were caught between a rock and a pitchfork, motherfucker. How in the hell can you expect yourself to even remotely know what to do in a situation like that? Governments make people disappear. What if Mom or Dad never got to see you again? Think of that."

We were getting loud enough that spittle was flying. Nose to nose. Sinclair took a breath and tried to dial it down a notch.

"I have. Trust me, I have. But I have a code. It's an honorable code, and I broke it by not saying what I knew. I had the opportunity to do good—but I was afraid."

"So what now? Is that why you're trying to be a fireman?"

"Yeah. Firemen are good. They risk everything to help people. Maybe if I can become a fireman, I can make amends for what I didn't do."

"You gotta find a way to let that shit go. It will eat at you until there's nothing left. Trust me. You can't carry that forever."

"How the fuck do you know? You have your life up in Denton with your garage bar and your wife and your dogs, and you've never seen something so heinous from the inside. You don't know shit about what I carry."

"Fuck you I don't. Let's go back in time a few hours. The very bad phone call. Remember that?"

"Tragedy and guilt aren't the same thing, Harlin."

"You want fucking guilt—I'll give you fucking guilt. So, I'm supposed to be a writer. And I'm not even sure I know how to do that. So all I can keep doing is writing every possible scenario, ever fucking imaginable outcome, in my mind. Constantly Rubix-cubing equations in my head. And you know I was never any good at math."

"What the fuck does that mean?"

"It means that good news doesn't stay good forever. And when you come home one day to a whole mess of unexpected good shit, the first thing you do is start pulling threads. One good thing leads to another and another and another. But eventually you run out of the good, and the scenes you write in your head turn ugly. Real fucking ugly. And before you even know what you're doing, you've written a Very Bad Fucking Phone Call. Then all of the sudden you're in Austin with the red tide and murdered cousins and your wife calls to tell you there's nothing alive inside her. All because you imagined it real."

Sinclair threw himself at me. He didn't say a word. Just wrapped his arms around me and pressed his head into my chest and held me.

"Listen to me, Sinclair. We both got dark corners that keep us up at night. Everyone does. The secret, as far as I can see, is to tell whatever's skulking in those dark corners to fuck right off. You can't atone for the past any more than you can live in it. You got Dawn in there and your friends and a shiny new truck for trips to the beach, and trust me when I tell you that you'll piss it all away if you go through life hating your mistakes and beating the hell out of yourself for not being perfect. You'll wake up one day, and all you'll have left is that dark corner."

It was past 1:00 AM. A day's worth of drink and an hour's worth of emotional upheaval had exhausted us. We had a plan to cruise down to Port Aransas and sleep on the beach the next day. If we didn't get to bed soon, it would be just another failure in a weekend of fucking disasters.

"Let's go in, Sinclair. We'll get breakfast in the morning. Watch some football and figure out if we still think the beach is a good idea."

Sinclair hugged me again. There was power to his embrace. Fury.

"I'm sorry, Harlin."

"So am I."

CARS ON BOATS

I was fading by the time we hit the ferry. The Very Bad Phone Call and a day spent drinking across Austin had taken their toll. The sun was gone, and I felt hollow. Afraid.

A dozen years ago, I loved the night. Stayed inside all day just waiting for it to arrive. It held endless possibilities, and I lived in fear of missing any of them. But now I crave daylight. Warmth. Shady hideaways. Even the fickle Texas wind is a comfort. The night is no longer an irresistible mystery. It's just an end to a day—the bittersweet part of the story where everyone goes home before the drunkenness creeps out of the darkness and drops the final curtain.

We hit a liquor store right before the ferry and picked up a couple of six packs and some whiskey. I impulse-bought two prepackaged Jell-O shots from a bad-idea bin next to the register. Why the hell not? I was gonna need a pick-me-up eventually. Hotel pillows and cable TV were starting to sound a helluva lot better than sleeping in a chair on the beach, but that was not why we'd made the trip. Maybe some high-octane gelatinous snacks could fuel one last night of adventure.

The ferry lurched forward, and a cool blast of ocean breeze slipped through the sunroof in Sinclair's pickup. It was a short trip. We hit the other side, they dropped the gates, and it was two quick turns before we hit the main drag, a garish stretch of bars, restaurants, rental outfits, and stores that sold every type of beach crap imaginable. Boogie boards, flip flops, vials of sand, floppy hats, and stoner hoodies. We cruised the strip with the windows down while Tom Waits screamed at us to "hoist that rag."

The blur of billboards and shop signs made me think of Vegas and its never-ending neon battle for attention. Port Aransas is smaller and lacks the electric lure of gaseous light, but it follows the same model. Every spot to get a bite or a brew offered some spectacle out front to draw the eye. Giant sea creatures or big-ass shark heads were the most popular. I snapped a photo of a gnarly set of jaws and sent it to Leah in a pathetic attempt to cheer her up. She responded using end punctuation that suggested excitement or at least modest enthusiasm, but I could tell it was a front. Maybe I should have gone home. Fuck. There were no maybes about it. But I'll never be able to describe the sense of relief when she let me off the hook.

What I learned on my trip to the beach was that Port Aransas has a Tiki problem. We passed bout five of them before Sinclair caught the fever and busted a u-turn into a combination Tiki bar and steak house. It didn't seem like a terrible idea until we walked through the door. The joint was carpeted except for a small dance floor. It felt like someplace stashed in the corner of a mall so husbands could catch a buzz while their wives shopped for work shoes.

There was a birthday party going on, and I almost took out a kid when I accidentally stepped onto the dance floor. Fuck dancing. I didn't even want to get a drink at this place. There weren't enough windows. I couldn't see driving all the way to the beach to drink in a damn box.

Sinclair and I were in the midst of a hasty escape when a big dad joker of a motherfucker charged out the front door and stopped us in the parking lot. The old dude was in the friendly phase of drink, so we decided to talk to him.

"Where you boys headed?"

"Just got into town," said Sinclair. "Checking things out. Looking for a place to get a drink and some food."

"Y'all are more than welcome inside. We got a patio in the back."

"We saw y'all were having a birthday party, and we didn't want to intrude."

"Hell. There's all kind of people in there. Everyone's welcome. The restaurant is still open next door if you need food. Or there's Moby Dick's down the street. If you don't see Moby Dick's—you missed the island."

"Really?" I asked.

"Shit yeah. That place is three thousand square feet of every kind of nautical antiquity you could imagine. Got pretty good burgers, too. It's a must-see. Cool stuff all over the walls and stashed in every corner. I'm telling you. Miss it—and you miss the island."

"Might have to check that out."

"Ain't no might about it, son. Where y'all from?"

"We drove down from Austin," said Sinclair.

"Austin? Oh god. Y'all didn't hear?"

Moby Dick's biggest fan got theatrically quiet in a way that gave me a pretty good idea of what was coming next. Sinclair didn't pick up on it as quick as I expected.

"Hear about what?" he asked.

"Shit. It must have been damn near exactly one year ago today. Two fellas from Austin came down here to camp on the beach. Y'all camping out?"

"That's the plan."

"Well, these boys tried camping on the beach and nobody ever saw them again." The big fella paused deliberately. "The way I heard it was," he crept closer toward us. "Damn *chupacabras* got 'em!"

Sinclair and I couldn't resist laughing because this dude was straight-up roaring he was so pleased with himself. His torso shook, yet he still managed to hold open the door to the steak side of Tiki land as a welcoming gesture for some newcomers.

"Come right on in, folks," he said, chuckling his way through a little half bow. "All kind of people inside. Every kind of people welcome."

Sinclair and I waved goodbye and turned to leave.

"Remember what I told you boys. You miss Moby Dick's—you miss the whole goddamned island. And watch out for them *chupacabras!*"

His final warning tailed us through the parking lot, caroming off a giant squid before breaking up in the sound of the ocean.

LARRY'S SPOT

"This is a fireman bar," said Sinclair.

He was excited, but I was stuck thinking about whether or not it was a good idea to leave my luggage in the back of his truck. I'd been wearing the same shorts for three days, and I had no interest in wearing them for another. But fuck it. Everyone's got their own baggage in a tourist town. Why the hell would they want mine?

Sinclair was right. This was a fireman's bar. There were helmets hung on the wall next to yellowed posters of centerfolds with Jan and Dean curves. A full suit of fireman armor was strung up from the ceiling. Charred in spots, it loomed over the proceedings, which were scant. There was a couple hunkered down at table near the center of the bar. She was old now, but once upon a time, she might have been the best-looking girl on the beach. The smile was still there. Time could not fade that glory.

A broken-down old beau with a raspy laugh was sitting across from her. He had a cart next to him that I originally figured for an oxygen tank, but when he went to leave, I saw that I'd been wrong. It took a couple of fellas to hoist him from the chair and ease him onto this little knee-crutch-scooter-walker contraption. By the reverence shown to him by his handlers, I took him for someone important. Maybe the owner of the joint. Maybe a different kind of importance. Maybe that was his fire suit hanging over our heads. And maybe everyone in that bar knew him from before. When he was young and strong and pulled kids out of fires two at a time. Years ago, before their music was re-cataloged as classic rock, he and his flame-dousing brethren drank together in that bar, celebrating life and death and the all-too-short time in between.

The fireman bar was a quieter place these days. Instead of bellying up for beers, the forgotten heroes waited patiently at their table for the kindly bartender to serve them white wine from a plastic pitcher. At their night's end, the man and the woman exchanged cheek kisses and went their separate ways. It was about a twenty-minute adventure for the bartender to get the man up, out the door, into the car, and return to his post. While he was gone, I listened to the proprietor of the little food shack next door take an order.

"How do you take your bacon, sir? Some folks like it chewy. Some folks like it burnt to a crisp. I can make it any way you want it. You just gotta say how."

I appreciated his attention to detail. You can make yourself into a damn good cook just by giving a shit. My first ever rack of ribs came out tasting like salt dipped in salt, but I cared enough to get better. Fish Stand Man was eager to please and willing to hustle. I silently wished him the best.

Sinclair must have heard the same conversation because he leaned over and gave me the nudge.

"Man, I could start thinking about some food."

"I'm already closed out, brother."

"Whatcha think?"

"Word on the street is that Moby Dick's is the spot."

"I wouldn't mind seeing me some of those nautical antiquities."

"Let's do it then."

We passed Fish Stand Man on our way out the door. He'd seen us coming and held it open.

"How y'all doing tonight?"

"Not too bad," I replied. "You?"

"Could be worse, I guess. Be a lot better if I were busy."

"Good luck with it."

I thought for a minute, a very hard minute, about calling a dinner time audible. I had a hunch about the kind of menu we might find at Moby Dick's, and I didn't figure it'd have as much love put into it as Fish Stand Man put into his. I didn't say anything, though. I was thinking like some shitwit host of a cable travel show. Looking for bright lights and crowds instead of the bona fide real deal shit. That kind of thinking can be dangerous.

MAGELLAN

"It'll be a twenty-minute wait."

That's what the teenager working the hostess stand at Moby Dick's said. She wasn't particularly interested in seating us. Maybe it was a lie. The place was only about half-full, and from the looks of the joint, we shoulda turned tail and run. That's what I wish I could go back in time and tell Sinclair and me. Or maybe that's a damn lie. Stories are only stories because something happens. You'd have already stopped reading if all I had to say was: Sinclair and I had a perfectly adequate meal at a reasonably clean restaurant with a highly average gift shop, and nothing at all out of the ordinary happened whatsoever. So, yeah. Fuck it. I'd tell us to get our asses there a little earlier. Drink more enthusiastically. Stay a little longer.

Ain't nobody want a normal life. We want that Circus Circus shit so people pay some fucking attention and make our stories matter somewhere outside our garages and hometown bars. Obscene. Lurid. Bizarre. Strange. None of us are happy with a thick slice of meatloaf, a cocktail, and falling asleep in front of the television. We want the story nobody's ever heard about the crazy shit that's getting harder and harder to find on our whitewashed town squares because that's the shit that reminds us we used to have a pulse before it went fucking faint somewhere along cubicle row.

This is one of those fucking stories.

Sinclair hit the pisser while I settled in to get the lay of the land. There was a big patio off to one side populated by the tipsy leftovers of some late afternoon shindig. Drunkards straggled in and out to smoke cigarettes out front. They spoke in labored grunts and struggled to make eye contact from under droopy lids. I took a couple big steps toward the gift shop to give the inebriates a wide birth. A gullet packed with fried fish and diabetic Tiki swill is a cauldron of ugly just waiting to erupt. I wasn't about to be the victim of a lurch-by wretching.

Like a coward trying his best not to feel like a coward, I texted Leah again. She responded, but barely. Not that I blamed her. I was in a strange haze where nothing seemed real. Like I could reach out and try to grab something, and it might slip right through my fingers. Ephemeral. Dust in the fucking wind, baby. I couldn't even imagine how she felt. The great trickster Loki shook our lives up like a cosmic snow globe, and now we had to deal with the fallout. Except we were at opposite ends of Texas, and I wasn't there to give her what she needed because I had an excuse not to be. Besides, it wouldn't have done any good. Very Bad Phone Calls have to run their course.

"Dude."

Sinclair pulled me out of the darkness.

"An old drunk lady just said some nasty shit to me."

"What the hell are you talking about?"

Sinclair was looking down and sorta shaking his head.

"She never took her eyes off my dick, man. I just got propositioned."

"Seriously?"

"Dead. It was fucking blatant. Everyone at the table was fucking cheering her on."

I looked over toward the bathrooms where two separate bachelorette parties were waging a raging battle of who could get obnoxiously blind drunk the fastest. The party closest to the men's room was made up of a bunch of thirty-to-forty-somethings and one gal on the wrong side of fifty-five.

"Which one?"

"The old cougar. The slow one with stretched-out sinews and shrunken muscles. The one that doesn't get to eat until the younger, faster cougars have feasted. The one just hanging on and hoping for scraps."

"That's the most dangerous kind, Sinclair."

"How so?"

"Young cougar got sharp teeth. Kill you quick. Old cougar got old teeth. Death comes slow."

"She had the evil in her eyes. It was hard to spot through the lust and the booze, but I saw it."

"C'mon. Let's get you out of the Serengeti for a bit. Maybe check out that gift shop."

It's funny how fast things change. Just a couple hours earlier, Sinclair and I had been laughing with Chupacabra Man and thinking what a great guy he was. But now, as we wandered the aisles of the shitty gift shop, his story was already being re-written. No longer was he the friendly local who dished the inside scoop on can't-miss attractions. He would now forever be the devious old bastard who sent us to Moby Dick's. Nautical antiquities, my ass. Unless you were looking to add to your sea shell jewelry collection, on the hunt for a floppy hat, or just had to have a plywood boogie board adorned with a Corona logo—there was nothing at Moby Dick's worth paying for.

And that probably went for the food, too. Quality dining joints don't usually have machines that charge you a buck to stretch out a penny and stamp it with the imprint of a cresting wave or a pelican or some other maritime bullshit. We tried our best to kill the twenty minutes laughing at all the tacky crap, but we couldn't even make it ten. Sinclair, I honestly believe in my heart, was just about to suggest we bail when a couple of seats opened up at the bar. We dropped our vibrating LED coaster off with the hostess and claimed two spots at the bend of the giant horseshoe.

Sinclair ordered a margarita, and I was looking at the beer list when I felt a presence invade my personal space. I turned to my right to find a massive Tongan-looking fuck slumped over the bar top. Dude was decked out in beachwear made by some company called Magellan. He had the logo on his hat and right above the breast pocket of his vented, short-sleeve, button-up shirt. The bartender took my order and poured me a warm Miller Lite before turning his attention to Magellan. The exchange was painful.

"What can I get you, buddy?"

Magellan responded with a lot of grunting and nodding and finally slurred out an order for two beers. I think we all assumed he was ordering for him and his buddy—but no. Both drafts were for Magellan. And this dude definitely did not need two beers.

"You gonna be eating tonight?"

More grunting and nodding from Magellan, only this time he never managed to form words that added up to an actual sentence—let alone a menu item. His buddy, a little beach rat version of Freddie Prinze Jr., stepped in to save the day. He translated Magellan's grunts into an order for a giant platter of fried fish planks and steak fries. The scenario was growing sinister with a quickness. I was already pissed at myself for not demanding that we leave the second I looked at the menu. I'd spent enough time working in restaurants to know that the food was most definitely gonna suck. And cost a lot. Having Magellan's drunk ass looming over my shoulder was not helping.

The bartender came back with Sinclair's margarita. My brother leaned in for a big sip, but quickly aborted. I watched his face twist into a grimace as he choked down the radioactive liquid that should never have been freed from its glow-stick prison.

"This is the worst fucking margarita I've ever had in my life," he said, whispering his way through a high-pitched giggle.

"Too sweet?"

"It's like warm syrup. Take everything you've never liked about a margarita, put it in one glass, and this is what you get. And I just paid eight dollars for it, so I got no choice but to drink it."

We laughed and shook our heads because that's what you do when the surreal becomes your reality. Warm beer, Day-Glo drinks, the hulking beast Magellan, and his sidekick Ratty Prinze Jr. A Saturday night on the town in Port Aransas during the off season. I spent months dreaming up the perfect wintertime coastal expedition because I wanted sparsely populated beaches and a cottage filled with my friends. Bonfires and shrimp boils and maybe a boat ride or a little pub on a corner we could get to without driving too far.

In my perfect dream of that winter beach trip, I never would have ended up at Moby Dick's watching the gin blossoms erupt on Magellan's tanned cheeks and nose as he swayed haphazardly over his piss-warm beers. But, then again, that wouldn't have been traveling at all. It would have been something sad. Moving my friends and the things that make me feel safe to a new place—only to pretend we were still in our old place.

Somewhat shamed, I settled in for the slow grind through my seventeen-dollar plate of broken dreams. The heartburn was steadily creeping up my esophagus. I wondered if there were outhouses on the beach and if those outhouses actually had toilet paper. My mind was on the way to sad, scary places when, in a shocking display of life, Magellan bolted upright and swung his mighty head from side to side. A drunken sentinel surveying his tourist bar kingdom. He settled into a thousand-mile stare and paused—ever so slightly—before hocking a prodigious wad of phlegm and spittle and half-chewed fish bits. The vile clump hit the bar with a heavy thwaap, landing mere inches from my plate. His work done, Magellan collapsed back into a drunken slumber.

"What the fuck," said Sinclair?

"I got no fucking words, bro."

"You want to move to the other side of the bar?"

"I want to move to a different fucking bar, but I'll settle for that. Just get me as far away from Magellan as fucking possible."

We grabbed our plates and drinks and slid down from our barstools. Ratty Prinze Jr. gave us a quick, pleading look, as if to say *I'm sorry* and *Please don't leave me here*. A lady bartender on the other side of the horseshoe greeted us with a smile.

"You can't move, honey," she said to me. "I need you over there to keep him propped up!"

"That guy just spit on your fucking bar."

"Say what?"

"The big drunk dude you want me to keep propped up? He just spit on your fucking bar."

She looked like she still didn't understand for a second but there is no earthly way anyone could not understand what just had just happened.

"How bout I get y'all some fresh silverware," she said before disappearing, no doubt scurrying off to make some more shitty drinks with radical colors and very long straws.

REVERB, TX

ODE TO THE ANGEL OF THE SILVERLEAF

I've seen Sweet Kate raise hell over a motherfucker spitting on the floor at Dan's once upon a time. She came tearing ass out from the behind the bar and got straight up in the face of this mannerless slackjaw—she used her teacher voice and everything.

"Did you just spit on the floor in my bar?" She demanded.
"Um, yes."
"Why would think that's okay?"
"I don't know. I guess I wasn't really thinking."
"No shit. There's a trash can five feet away from you. Do you mop this floor at night?"
"No, ma'am"
"That's right. You don't. I mop this floor. Or my friends, who I love, mop this floor. So you don't get to spit on it. Got it?"
"Yes, ma'am."
"Good. Now, I'll fix you a drink," she said, throwing a handful of bar naps at him. "But you're gonna wipe that shit up before I do."

HE AIN'T DROOLING. HE'S MY BROTHER.

The next time I could stand to look back in their direction, Magellan and Ratty Prinze Jr. put on one of the most grotesquely endearing displays I've ever witnessed in all my days. Magellan was passed mostly the fuck out, and he was suckling at the back of his hand. At first I thought he was dreaming about kissing someone, but on second glance, it was clear that he was rooting. Like a puppy weened and separated from his momma way too soon. Only drunken Magellan wasn't as cute as a puppy, and he was slobbering something fierce, and it was drooling down all over the bar, and sometimes he'd turn his head and this trail of spit would stretch out thin and wobbly between his mouth and his goddamned hand.

Ratty Prinze Jr. was halfway trying to eat his food and halfway trying even harder to chat up this girl sitting next to him, but he never took his eye off Magellan for longer than a minute or two. He had this stack of napkins next to his plate, and the next time his buddy jerked his head up in a drunken stupor, the loyal little bastard slid a bunch of those napkins straight into the slobberzone.

I'm not sure what burning building Magellan had pulled Ratty from, but he must have done something big to earn that kind of devotion. Or maybe there just aren't that many people to drink with once the tourists leave town and the locals are left to their own devices. Magellan peacefully laid his head back down on his hand, the little bar nap serving as a pillow of sorts, and all was quiet until the beast kinda snorted and almost inhaled one of the napkins. He woke up with a start and toppled off his barstool. Only the quick reflexes of Ratty Prinze Jr. saved him from crashing to the floor completely.

The big man must have been in a bad way because he did the buffalo rumble straight to the men's room. I'd eaten all I could stomach and seen about all I wanted to see, so I turned to Sinclair.

"You wanna get out of here?"

"Hell yes."

We were waiting for the bartender to get back with our receipts when we heard a crash, and all the girls from the bachelorette party started going crazy. Sure enough, Magellan, without the steady hand of Ratty Prinze Jr., had failed miserably at maintaining verticality on his way back from the men's room. I looked over and saw him struggling to get up off the ground while all the girls catcalled him. Above the general din of chaos, a single voice called out louder than the others. It was an older voice. A voice filled with lust and hunger.

"Did you hurt yourself, baby? Come on over and sit on Momma's lap. She'll make it all better!"

I looked at Sinclair and said exactly what was in my heart.

"Fuck Chupacabra Man. Fuck him all the way to hell."

PARTY MANNY

A tall, tan woman with a long ponytail and a ball cap sauntered up to the bar.

"Hey, Manny," she called to the bartender. "We got us a six-seater for the night."

She was talking about one of the little all-terrain golf carts we'd seen zipping up and down the strip. The idea appealed to me. Beach cruising with the wind rushing past you. Next time I get down that way, I might rent one.

"You gonna come out with us tonight, Manny?"

"Why you wanna do this to me, girl? You know Party Manny is retired."

"Never, baby! Party Manny must live on!"

"Party Manny has to stay locked up, girl. He gets Regular Manny in too much trouble."

"Free Party Manny! Free Party Manny!"

"Not tonight, darling. Party Manny is locked up. For a little while, at least."

"You know where to find us if he gets loose, baby."

"Girl, you gonna have to survive without me tonight."

The tall woman slammed a shot of something brown, stuffed some cash in the tip jar, and waggled real nice all the way out the door. Party Manny wasn't fooling anyone. That motherfucker was gonna be at the beach an hour after his shift was done.

AFTERMATH

I didn't want to go to the next bar we went to so badly that I didn't even bother to remember the name of the place. Moby Dick's had hurt me. My chest was on fire, and I was tired, and Sinclair managed to hit a massive crater at the entrance to the parking lot that jolted me right up in the air. Lightning bolts of pain raced up and down my spine as I crashed back into the seat.

"Shit! Sorry about that. I didn't see that hole in the fucking Earth."

"That hurt more than a little," I said coldly.

I wasn't at all mad at Sinclair, but I'm a dick when I'm tired or not getting my way. It didn't help that we were at opposite ends of the spectrum. Sinclair was ready for adventure, but I was ready for bed. The last thing I wanted to do was stare at another wall full of bottles that were probably only gonna make me feel worse, but it's tough to stop Sinclair once he gets his mind set on something.

We snaked our way up a winding staircase leading to the back door. The restaurant was nearly empty, but it had a warm, friendly vibe. They'd managed to avoid the garish sea creature motif that dominated the island, and there was nary a hint of Tiki décor. Judging by the dirty dishes still sitting on the tables, the dinner crowd had only just departed. A pretty bartender with a thousand-watt smile came over to take our order.

"How's it going tonight? Y'all eating, or drinking, or both?"

"Just drinking," said Sinclair. "I'll have whatever IPA you have on tap."

"I can do that. How about for your friend?"

Nothing sounded good, but I could tell Sinclair was already halfway into that magic act where he becomes our dad at the peak of his garrulous, traveling-salesman years. Not quite door-to-door, but a salesman who spent his fair share of nights on the road. I was gonna have to drink up to keep up.

"Shot of tequila, please. And a Lone Star if you got it."

"No problem. Where y'all in from?"

"Came down from Austin this morning," said Sinclair. "Gonna try and find a place to sleep on the beach."

"I know just the spot. It's where all the locals go when the tourists leave and we finally get our beach back. I'll point you in the right direction before you leave."

She was the kind of girl men who spend too much time sitting on stools fall in love with every day, but all I wanted to do was shrink down so I could climb in her mouth and scrape the young off her teeth. Take it back to a dentist and have it implanted on my own. Yank the sweet bird of youth right out of her DNA and steal it for myself. Anything to feel fresh and new and not even the least little bit worn out. Because that's what we all crave. Most people trick themselves into thinking they want the girl behind the bar, but that ain't the case. We just want the thing they have that we don't. Possibilities as endless as the horizon over the ocean. More future than past.

An older man came in for a glass of wine and to see if they had any bread pudding left. He was a regular. A friendly face to our bartender. He knew she was studying marine biology and engaged to a young man in the oil industry that had just bought her a house on the coast. He called her by name and gazed upon her with grandpa eyes, but I knew. I could tell. If he could have flipped a switch and made her old and him young he would have done it faster than she could pour the fucking wine.

"They have the best bread pudding on the island here. What did you fellas have to eat?"

"Well," said Sinclair. "It's kind of a long story."

"Some local told us we had to check out Moby Dick's."

"Moby Dick's?" said the old man. "I'm sorry, son, but anyone who would tell you to check out Moby Dick's is no damn local."

DANGER

The prospect of a very long night weighed heavily on me as Sinclair attempted to navigate the darkness of Mustang Island. The restaurants and bars were all behind us now. A steady stream of timeshares marked off the increments of our journey. Massive fortresses with empty parking lots and an unsettling lack of welcoming lights.

I could feel Sinclair getting serious all of the sudden, and it snapped me out of my mental wanderings.

"You see this fucking guy?"

"What guy?"

"Look behind us."

I twisted my torso to the breaking point and strained my neck to look out the back window. All I could see were headlights, but that was enough. They alternated between bearing down on us—and then quickly fading as the distance between our vehicles increased. The driver was clearly having trouble maintaining a steady rate of speed. "Holy fuck!" said Sinclair, as the headlights swerved onto the shoulder, spraying sand and bits of driftwood into the road.

"I sure as shit hope that's not Magellan behind us."

"No kidding. I'm gonna put some distance between us and see if I can find someplace to turn off. No sense in taking chances with that kind of drunk."

Sinclair gunned it, and the pickup surged forward. The headlights turned to specs in seconds. The maneuver bought us just enough breathing room to find a safe spot to pull off and wait, but the headlights reappeared far more quickly than they should have. They were in the wrong lane when they passed us. Sinclair gave it a minute before pulling back into the road.

"If that wasn't Magellan," he said. "There's someone else on this island just as drunk."

"There could be a whole island of Magellans out there in the darkness."

"No shit," said Sinclair with a laugh. "Let's get our asses to the beach and away from drunk people in cars."

Wiser words may have never been spoken, but in the time it took Sinclair to say them, another set of headlights appeared. Coming right at us. In our lane.

"What the hell? Did Magellan pull a u-turn?"

Sinclair jerked the truck onto the shoulder. It probably wasn't as close a call as it seemed at the time, but I know for damn sure those taillights didn't swerve back into their own lane until after they'd passed us. Island dwellers live by their own rules, and it didn't appear that any of them had anything to do with not driving shitfaced. Or maybe those weren't enforced during the offseason.

EL DIA DE LOS MUERTOS

The 2015 edition of the Denton Day of the Dead festival was truly a halcyon day in this new chapter of our town. The weather was cool, a stark contrast to the insufferable heat of the previous year's event, and nouveau-local celebrity, Jason Lee, was spotted in the crowd snapping photos of all the coffin racers before they sped down the hill on a quest to be crowned the fastest casket in town. The coffin races, a spiritual cousin to the soapbox derby and the day's main attraction, were about to begin. Music blared and a troupe of zombies danced to Michael Jackson's "Thriller." There was a hint of rain in the air, but not enough to ruin anyone's make up.

I finagled my way onto the pit crew of Juan Verde's Evel Knievel coffin racer. Each team has three members, but it's really only a two-man operation: driver and pusher. The driver drives, and the pusher tries to get the coffin headed down the hill with as much momentum as he can muster. Back in the day, there used to be two pushers per team, but they knocked that down to one, so now the odd man out, which was me, gets to hang out in the VIP area drinking all the free beer they can hold.

Site lines, unfortunately, were shit from the VIP tent, where all you could see were the backs of people's heads unless you happened to be a very tall man such as Slobberbone bass player Brian Lane, who was hanging out behind the velvet ropes, or in this case portable fencing, with his faithful pup Louise. When the races officially started, I drained the rest of my beer and headed for a high spot on the hill. There were a couple of racers I was excited to see, and I just wasn't tall enough to do it from my previous elevation.

Every installment of the Day of the Dead Festival since its inception has drawn larger and larger crowds. Streets get blocked off, and the general rules of the road get ignored. It's not unusual to see an ATV towing racers back up the hill after they streak down Hickory Street. Juan Verde—in his red, white, and blue Evel Knievel coffin—is a legitimate threat to take home the trophy every year, but some of the coolest cars in Day of the Dead history belong to Daniel Vaughan, a hard-working father with two jobs and a talent for building hot shit on wheels. His entry this year was Mad Max-inspired, and, as always, his son Memphis was along for the ride.

Juan Verde and Daniel squared off in the second heat. The Knievel coffin smoked Daniel's radass Mad Max apocalyptic buggy, but it didn't matter because Memphis stole the whole damn show just like he always does. The kid sailed down the street with his arms tossed up in the air while all the shutterbugs fluttered. That Vaughan is a damn good dad. He busts his ass so his kid gets to play James Dean for the paparazzi every Day of the Dead. Judging by the smile on his boy's face, and the fact that the kid always ends up in a *Dallas Observer* slideshow or a city of Denton calendar, Memphis wouldn't trade a single minute of it for the world.

In a ghastly turn of events, this year's race was very nearly marred by tragedy. Some dipshit dad sent his kid hurtling down the hill in a piece of shit coffin rolling on what looked to be shopping cart wheels. The rig flipped, and the kid did a header into the pavement, fucking up his helmet and painting one cheek a faint shade of road rash. Evel Knievel coffin pusher and all around good guy, Eric Eisenmann, got up in the dad's face and read him the riot act. I didn't see it, but I bet there were little bits of spittle flying like a motherfucker. After they cleared the track, I caught up with Eisenmann and Juan Verde in the beer tent.

"I'm not opposed to sending kids down the hill, but send them down the hill in a contraption that works."

"No shit," said Eisenmann. "I called that before the race even started."

It wasn't the first time Eisenmann had a premonition of Coffin Race carnage. He predicted the Great Tardis Disaster of 2013, in which a massive blue hunk of danger with shoddy steering and no brakes went rogue mere feet from the starting line and slammed into a kid in a wheelchair. The sound of the collision was violent to its core—shattered glass and the collective gasp of the crowd. An ugly moment in an otherwise vibrant day. Somewhat inconceivably, all parties escaped without serious injury.

Another beer and a couple races later, Eisenmann started staring ugly over my shoulder.

"What the hell is that kid doing back at the starting line?"

"There's no way they let him run again," said Juan Verde.

Sure enough, the Shopping Cart Coffin Kid was back in action. It was a goodwill race, which meant no competitor, but the real threat was the kid's own racer. Could it possibly stay upright all the way to the finish?

"Fucking ridiculous," said Eisenmann. "This has to be stopped."

The starting gun interrupted my friend before he could act, but there was no need for intervention. He may have done it the hard way, but the kid's dad learned his lesson. This time down the track, he ran behind his son, holding onto the cart the entire time, ensuring that it would not, could not, spill his boy into the street.

"Problem solved," said Juan Verde. "Dumbass should have done that the first time."

He was right, of course, but later in the day he would endure his own moment of tragedy. I hesitate to even recount the incident for fear of permanently traumatizing a dear friend, but this ain't fiction, and I can't go ignoring the facts.

Between the craftsmanship of Juan's racer build and having a big dude like Eisenmann as a pusher, Team Verde breezed through their first heat. But the wheels came off in the second round, so to speak. Eisenmann built a full head of steam and, with a mighty heave, sent the Knievel coffin hurtling down the track. The crowd roared in excitement, and Juan Verde cruised through the finish line several lengths ahead of his opponent. They smoked the competition, but it would be their last race of the day. There were flags at the top of the hill. Foot fault. In his enthusiasm over their tremendous start, Eisenmann inadvertently stepped over the line that coffin pushers must not cross. There had been no illicit contact past said line, but the rules were clear. Team Verde was disqualified.

I spotted the heartbreak through the crowd. Juan Verde consoling Eric Eisenmann in the wake of their elimination. Juan was upbeat. Encouraging. Because as long as he had a few good runs and got to wear his Evel Knievel costume, it was a good day. But Eisenmann was taking it hard. Shoulders slumped. Head down. A sad little big boy dressed in red coveralls who'd just lost his birthday balloon. I was struck by the sudden urge to buy him a conciliatory ice cream cone.

In the end, Tex Bosley and the boys from his drum shop took home the trophy, and I ended up in the Oak Street Draft House beer garden with my old friend Littlejohn debating how it was that Jason Lee had come to dwell in the 940.

"I heard it was because his son went to school here."

"Does he even have a kid old enough to be in college?"

"How the hell would I know?"

"I always figured it was because of the Midlake connection, but fuck. You know how Denton is. The truth don't really matter. Everyone just makes up their own little story."

"That's sorta what I'm doing."

We laughed for a second until this motorized mule came hauling ass up the dusky street dragging a coffin behind it. The driver tossed up them heavy metal devil horns at the beer garden spectators while somewhere in the background The Cure reminded us all that "boys don't cry."

And just for a second I forgot that anything in Denton had ever been any different than it ever was before.

THE BEACH

Mustang Island goes straight Mad Max after dark. If we'd wanted to get away from drunks in cars, we'd come to the wrong place. A cavalcade of tricked-out trucks and jeeps prowled up and down the beach, spinning donuts as they sped from one bonfire to another. There was defiance in their recklessness. Drivers stared you down, daring you to get in their way. I felt unsafe. We were the outsiders here. We had no allies. If things turned ugly, we were just two brothers armed with a Styrofoam cooler and a couple of camping chairs. Sinclair probably had a piece somewhere in his truck, but it wouldn't be enough to stop a gang of aggressively drunk beachcombers. I felt again the yearning for the safety of four walls and a locking door.

My brother read the scene differently. He was wide-eyed with wonder, laughing at the antics of teenagers raising a little hell on the beach. I could tell he wanted to do donuts, too. I wished I could be like him. Fearless. But this was nothing to Sinclair. Not after surviving a year in the bitter hopelessness of Mother Russia, where they'll cut you for your growler of beer and a bit of dinner. Or his adventures in the Basque region of Spain. Or even his summer spent exploring South America on the Che Guevara trail. He was the traveler, and I was the homebody. My jealously was in no short supply.

Sinclair found a spot to his liking and parked the truck. He jumped down into the sand and busied himself setting up our makeshift camp. Step one was music. Music always came first. He plugged his iPod into his little contractor radio and cranked it up. Step two consisted of setting up a folding table, so he could move the radio closer to where we would actually be sitting. Chairs were the final piece of the puzzle, which was fine with me because I never sit down anyway.

Sinclair cracked a beer and took a pull off the whiskey he'd bought. I didn't have the stomach for it yet, so I wandered up the beach a little ways. Music rose from the various camps and then dissipated in the rhythmic crashing of the waves. Mostly rap. No Jimmy Buffet out here. They must have left that shit in the tourist bars. There was an eerie peace about the night that was nearly shattered a thousand times by roaring engines or drunken revelers. Sinclair appeared at my side.

"Have you looked up, yet?"

"What?"

"Stop worrying about what's happening on the ground and look up."

Fucking Sinclair was inside my head again. He knew all the things I'd miss if I didn't stop thinking long enough to notice them. I turned my eyes skyward and saw the alien yolk of a Fabergé nimbus. Jagged otherworldly shadows crumbling into the ocean so that the moon could shine down upon the beach and all its dwellers.

"None of this can be captured by camera," said Sinclair.

I wish I could say I didn't try, but I did because I'm an asshole. And that's exactly what I would have called myself if I'd had the mutant ability to walk behind the version of me foolishly trying to capture the vastness of all the worlds above with something that fits in your fucking pocket.

"C'mon," said Sinclair. "Let's have a little smoke and get you a beer."

The first beer was a hard sell. The second wasn't much better until I got it halfway down. It was my mistake for going the fancy route. Trying to impress Sinclair with a Dallas beer called Local Buzz that came in cool pop top cans. It was a good beer, but it hit me hard. Somewhere around beer number three, I trumped the Jell-O shots.

I should have known it was a bad idea, but I'd figured it might make for a good story someday. I guess that day is today. They were heavier than Jell-O shots should be, and they had the consistency of an ambrosia-like side dish that someone brings to Thanksgiving. Only that person can't really cook, so the dish is shunned in favor of more edible offerings. After that, it just sits in the fridge for a very, very long time. I used to think those dishes were eventually thrown out, but now I know they get sent to some sort of Jell-O recycling plant where the very cheapest of liquors are added before they are repurposed as prepackaged liquor-store Jell-O shots.

It wasn't so much the taste as the thickness of the alcoholic sludge. Homemade Jell-O shots wiggle free from their containers and slide down the back of your throat with relative ease. These heinous concoctions were far more stubborn. You had to really work to excavate them from their plastic reservoir, and choking them down was no less of a chore. I started gagging halfway through.

Sinclair found my distress amusing. He laughed harder and harder with each successive wretch until I started cracking up and alternating gags with laughs. The frantic kind where you try not to snort milk on someone across the table from you in Junior High. Sinclair was absolutely fucking loving it right up until the point I howitzered him with a mouthful of that shit. By the sound of the splat it was a direct hit.

"Dude! What the fuck?"

Heroically, I soldiered on, retching and gaging and laughing and projectile hurling chunky bits of Jell-O shot into the night. Sinclair took shelter behind the table, safely out of spewing distance. It was silly and undeniably disgusting, but it had us both breathless and gutstruck. And just like that, my mojo was back. All it took was a Jell-O shot facial.

RAGE

It's hard to pinpoint the exact moment the mood shifted. There had been many beers, and eyedroppers of liquid THC and, of course, the Jell-O shots. We must have been talking about food because I can sort of fight through the tiredness and the fog of alcohol and remember Sinclair saying something along the lines of "Old Bruns still says that for his money Chili's has the best burger in town."

I didn't expect them to, but things went straight fucking downhill from there.

"I swore a solemn vow to never eat at Chili's again."

"You swore a vow to never eat at Chili's again?"

Sinclair was not amused.

"I did."

"Why?"

So I told him as best as I could recollect.

"Well, there's a Chili's right down the street from the cartoon factory, and one day, me and my buddy Kerm wanted a good burger. We were in kind of a hurry, and like I said, Chili's was close. So that's where we went. Fast-forward to the end of the meal, which was passable—but nothing special—and the check comes. Me and Kerm were both on the hook for about 14-15 bucks before tip. No beers or nothing. Just burgers, maybe a couple strips of bacon, and some fries. Fifteen bucks each. We're talking almost forty bucks between us after tip. And you can't not tip just because the bill hurt your feelings. The waiter didn't set the prices, and he didn't force us to eat there. That poor bastard's just working a job. So we settle up and start walking towards Kerm's truck, and I looked at him and said, 'With that money we just spent, we could have gone to the grocery store and bought some real nice ground beef, some good buns, and probably a twelve pack of beer. Instead, we blew it on a mediocre meal with no beers at Chili's. Call me crazy, but I think I'd rather grill my own burgers in the backyard than ever set foot in a fucking Chili's again.' So I took a solemn vow right there in the parking lot and that was that."

Sinclair got serious as fuck.

"Did you keep your solemn vow?"

"Mostly."

"That's not an acceptable answer."

"Well, I did for about two years, and then my boss at the time made us go eat there for a work lunch."

"So you broke your vow and shamed our family?"

"I don't think you're following me, Sinclair. I only ate there because I had to. The boss picked the restaurant. I had no choice."

"You could have not eaten."

Sinclair has a way of being a real dick about the details. I was starting to sense that I'd offended his code, and he wasn't gonna let up til he'd proved his point. I got defensive.

"That's all fine and dandy, Sinclair, but I was hungry, and the boss was making a big deal out of having these bullshit morale-boosting lunches. I would have looked like an ass for refusing to eat."

"Better to look like an ass than to break a solemn vow."

"Fuck you, Sinclair."

"Fuck me?"

Things were on fire now.

"Fuck me?" he said. "Do you even know what would have happened to you in the old world if you broke a solemn vow?"

"Judging by your reaction, or your overreaction, I'm guessing it wouldn't have been too good."

"Of course you don't know what would have happened. You like to talk about Vikings, but you damn sure haven't done your fucking homework."

"Go to hell, Sinclair." I think it scared both of us how loud I got in the moment. "It must be easy for you to sit back and judge when you work with all your best friends and everyone watches out for each other. But I worked for a fucking paranoid, passive-aggressive asshole that constantly played us all against each other, and that meant sometimes I had to eat at fucking Chili's, solemn vow or not."

I was screaming at Sinclair now, giving the crashing waves a run for their money.

"So when the fucking boss picked fucking Chili's, what the fuck was I supposed to do? Make a stand on behalf of our ancestors and piss off the motherfucker who signs my checks? I've got fucking responsibilities, Sinclair, and sometimes they may get in the way of me living up to your precious fucking code. I was trapped, motherfucker! What the fuck do you want me to do?"

"I don't know. Maybe not swear a fucking solemn vow about fucking bullshit when you can't be bothered to keep it."

"Fuck off, Sinclair."

Pride kept us from stamping out the flames before they scorched us. We needed space. Some distance between us so we could quiver with the rage shame in private. It would eventually be all right, but the wounds were fresh. I wandered away from the truck and our makeshift camp. Too angry to acknowledge what an asshole I felt like.

Sinclair probably loved me as much as anyone in the world, and he'd gone to hell of a lot of trouble to make a nice trip for us. All I'd done to repay him was to piss all over something I had no business pissing upon. I was a dick. I wanted to tell him that, but I had to wait for the throbbing in my head to stop.

I walked even further away from the car, and that's when I noticed it. There was a pickup with a sketchy-looking methhead fuck hanging out the driver's side window headed straight for me. As he got closer, I could tell there was an equally suspect motherfucker in the passenger seat. I didn't know what they were looking for, but it wasn't gonna be good.

"Hey, mang. You wouldn't believe the shitty fucking night I'm having. My bitch old lady lost her damn mind and poured out all my beer. You got a couple cold ones we can take off you?"

Sinclair was at my side like a fucking watchdog before the fucker even stopped talking. We were still angry, but brothers don't abandon each other to face nocturnal misogynist beach villains alone. That would have violated the ever living shit out of Sinclair's code.

"No," said Sinclair.

"No?"

"No. We don't have extra beer."

"You sure you ain't got nothing?"

The dude was trying to stare us down but his eyes were messed up on something, and it's incredibly hard to squint someone down in the darkness.

"I can pour you a little whisky in a cup," said Sinclair. "But what beers we got left are our own."

"I guess I'll take whatever I can get. Crazy fucking wife didn't leave me much choice."

"What'd you do to get her so mad?"

"Shit. Ain't hard to make a woman mad. Especially mine. You boys gonna hang out for a while?"

"No," said Sinclair and then he handed over the little cup of whiskey.

The strangers didn't move. They just sat there and idled.

"Well fuck it," said the driver. "Better get back before she starts burning my shit. Thanks for the whiskey. You boys watch yourself now."

The headlights came on, and the tires spun sand up into the night as a couple of dudes we never wanted to meet circled back to where they came from.

MORNING

I woke up in the truck. Sinclair was still sleeping in a chair on the beach. There were a bunch of dudes in orange vests picking trash out of the sand. They were wearing regular clothes, so I pegged them for drunk-tank leftovers doing their mandatory civic duty. Sometime in the night, all the kids on the beach had been replaced by older folks or families surf fishing in the cool of the morning. They didn't seem at all alarmed by the vest wearers. They just handed over bags of trash whenever one of them wandered into their camp.

I walked over to where the water was eating the sand and watched a bunch of tiny little sea birds do a dance with the waves. They'd get brave and creep further out when the ocean took a breath only to dart back up the beach when the surf charged at them. Something about it made me a wonderful kind of sad.

Sinclair walked over to me, yawning.
"I been thinking about last night."
"Yeah?"
"About the solemn vow."
"Sinclair, we ain't got to—"
"No. It's good. I think I got it figured out."
"How so?"
"What you were trying to do is make a boast. Like a warrior saying he could kill twenty monsters. Big words, but nobody takes them as seriously as a solemn vow. There's no penalty for not following through. When you said you weren't ever gonna eat at Chili's again, that was a boast."
"A boast, huh?"
"Yeah. A bold statement that won't get you shamed if circumstances stack up against you."
"So I just had my terminology fucked up."
"Yeah. Neither of us was really wrong, we were just—"
"Drunk and shouting?"
"Exactly. You wanna grab some breakfast?"
"I could eat."

Everything looked sadder in the daytime. The Tikis didn't shine, and the fake sea creatures were even more ridiculous. We drove around for a while until we found a little spot in the back of a short strip mall. There were about a hundred things on the menu, and the radio blared at an uncomfortable volume. Sinclair ordered a mimosa, and when it came, he only needed one sip to proclaim it the worst fucking mimosa he'd ever had in his life.

PART THREE
THE JACKSON CLAN

NIGHT RIDERS

Jackson finally showed up around 8:00 pm. Being December and all, it was well past dark, but that didn't matter to me. Things were churning around in my head, and I was having a helluva time processing them simultaneously. I was excited about spending a couple nights under the stars at the Jackson Family deer lease. But I was more than a little freaked out about the possibility of actually killing a deer. I got no problem with folks hunting deer, and I'd shoot a motherfucking wild hog from a damn helicopter. If I only knew someone with a helicopter. But hogs are sons of bitches, where a deer is something wild and beautiful. I'll eat them, but I could never pull the trigger.

My gear was already in the driveway when Jackson pulled in. Dude's first name is Kody, but only his immediate family uses it—to the point that it sounds foreign to those of us who call him a friend. I threw my cooler and a sleeping bag and my old Ithaca Deerslayer shotgun into the back of his vehicle.

"Your CD player work in here?" I asked.

"Yup. You got CDs? All I got in here is me."

"I got a mix. Might even have a little Jon Spencer Blues Explosion on it."

"Sweet. My record is awesome, but I don't want to be one of those assholes that drives around listening to themselves all the time."

Truth is, driving around listening to yourself is a necessity for a guy like Jackson. Dude's got two rambunctious boys, a wife to be sweet to, and a business to run. An early morning commute makes for a good time to listen to studio mixes and master recordings and such. Denton is full of artists, and damn nearly all of them work a day job. But that's not a phenomenon unique to our little town. It's a badge proudly worn by artists and musicians and writers all over the world. Trying to be creative sure feels like a full-time gig, but it's a neat trick when you can make it pay the bills.

Jackson lit a smoke and pointed his old Nissan Xterra toward Decatur. A dark stretch of divided highway lay in wait. A giant church, some ranch land, and a shitty little lonely beer joint marked our progress. Signs of development were steadily on the creep. Cookie-cutter housing developments would be popping up before too long. Maybe they were there already. It was dark, after all.

We passed a billboard for Sweetie Pie's Ribeyes, a locally owned and operated business that was proud to serve steaks and fried pies on the Decatur town square.

"I tried to write a song about that sign once. Got about as far as the chorus."

Jackson sorta hum-sang the tune until we hit the next landmarks, two brightly lit restaurants that appeared to be thriving despite their remote location. Catfish O'Harlies and Bono's Chop House.

"You ever eat at that catfish joint, Jackson?"

"Nope. But my dad loved that place."

RELUCTANT PASSENGER

I tried like hell to weasel out of it by offering to cook, but big Welch sat me down and shot me straight.

"Jackson don't need any more food, Harlin. You've met his family. They'll have plenty of food. What he's gonna need are his friends."

"You're not wrong, but man, I'm bad at that sort of scene."

"You ain't gotta be good at it. You just gotta be there. When it's your time, you'll damn sure want Jackson around. Because he'll understand."

"Fuck, man. I can't argue with that."

Darin did the driving. I was waiting for him on the front porch of this shitty red rental house Leah and I lived in for a couple of ugly years. The neck hole of my dress shirt had mysteriously shrunk, making it impossible for me to button the top button, so I had to cinch everything in place with my necktie. It was sunny outside, but I remember it being windy.

It's funny how much you don't remember about trips like that. I couldn't tell you what we listened to on the radio or recant any of the stories Porter told about Jackson's old man. Hell, I can't even say with any certainty if Porter even told any stories. I just feel like he did on account of him going further back with Jackson than any of us. He and Jackson met while they were both working at the mall. They became buddies, started making music together, and the rest is Denton history. Only seems natural he would have had at least a little something to say about the patriarch of the Jackson clan.

I figure there was probably the usual chatter along the way about how much the area had grown up over the years. There may have even been a forced chuckle when one of our party, most likely Porter, made the obligatory attempt at busting up the tension that ratcheted ever tighter with each passing mile, as though we were on our way to a doctor's appointment where a diagnosis hung in the balance. By the time we reached the church, no one was talking much. We got out of the car and lit cigarettes without thinking before squeezing into our jackets and heading toward the entrance.

We hooked up with Eric Eisenmann somewhere in the parking lot. I was a little surprised because I didn't know he and Jackson were that close, but I shouldn't have been. Eisenmann is one of the genuine good guys of Denton. He can live the rock-n-roll life as good as any of them, but when push comes to shove, he's a dude you want to have your back. Good drummer, better dad, and all around dependable motherfucker. That's Eisenmann.

I teared up pretty up pretty quick once we got inside. I always do at funerals, no matter how well, or little, I knew the deceased. I catch the sadness from those left behind, and I drop salt for them. All it took was one look at Jackson trying to be strong and brave for his family. His father. His hero. The man who taught him to hunt and fish and be a good person was gone. My friend was crushed. There could be no joy on a day the world pays its last respects to a man like David Jackson.

The service was beautiful. Jackson's adopted sister said many wonderful things about the kindness of the man who gave her a home and a family. It's strange to suddenly learn so much about a person after they're gone. When you know you'll never get to discover any of those things for yourself. It's too late. You've missed your chance, and now the only thing you can do is hold tight to those stories in an attempt to honor the man who shaped the lives of the people that share yours.

When it was over, we met our friend outside. Other than his wedding day, I'd never seen Jackson so dressed up. He was wearing a new suit and dark, aviator sunglasses. They failed miserably at hiding the pain in his eyes. We didn't get to talk much because he had a lot of hands to shake and condolences to accept. We tried our best to say good things—to somehow make it easier—but those words were beyond our reach.

"Your dad was a good man, Jackson."

"I wish I'd gotten to know him better."

"Brother, your dad fed me and looked after me like I was one of his own," said Porter. "I know how bad you must be hurting right now, and it kills me. Just know I'm here for you."

Jackson just nodded and tried not to say too much. You can't blame him. He didn't just lose his dad—he lost a grandfather to his children and a companion for his mother and the protector of his sisters. The same way our little band of friends was hurting for him, he was being drug through the coals by the gaping hole left in the lives of all who loved and depended on Father Jackson. Maybe it's selfish, but when you share that pain with a brother, a little of it becomes yours and yours only—a flashforward to a day you know you cannot escape but hope never comes.

I didn't ride back to Denton with Darin and Porter that day. Instead, I made the return trip with Eisenmann. It felt wrong to make someone fly solo after something like that.

It wasn't long before we had to do the same thing again, and I hitched another one-way ride to a funeral with Darin. Only this time I rode home with Jackson after Porter said his last goodbyes to his own dad in a sprawling, lush green cemetery somewhere in Ft. Worth. I didn't bother with any pretense of staying home to make food. I simply cinched that tie tight around that button that still wouldn't button and prepared myself for the tears I knew would be coming.

WIZARDS AND WINDMILLS

Not long after we passed Catfish O'Harlies and Bono's Chop House, Jackson got to talking about some of the crazy shit you can find in the mostly empty parts of Texas. Our state has lots of people and plenty of big cities, but this territory is so vast that it never takes too long to find the country.

"If you turn there," said Jackson. "And go down the road a ways, you'll run into Wizard Wells. You don't want to be there after dark. That's why I never turn there."

"What's wrong with Wizard Wells? It's got a pretty kickass name."

"That ain't nothing but a little meth community outside of Mineral Wells."

"A meth community?"

"Yeah, man. Bunch of folks cooking that nasty shit."

"The cops don't try to stop it?"

"It's country folk in a small town. They either got the police on their side—or they don't give a damn. Probably use some sort of redneck Paul Revere shit to warn each other when someone's in the area that ain't supposed to be."

"That's fucking crazy, man."

"Ain't nothing good going on in Wizard Wells, Harlin."

Of course, I immediately wanted to visit Wizard Wells. How could I not? We were decked out for adventure. Sleeping bags, camo gear, a cooler full of beer, and guns. We had everything we needed to take down those meth heads. It would have made a helluva chapter for the book, but one, or both, of us probably would have gotten shot or taken prisoner and used as some meth lab guinea pig. Plus, Kurtis Jackson and his famous chuck wagon were waiting on us at the deer lease, so we stayed straight on the road to Windthorst.

The night was black and cold, and Jackson's Xterra was rattling like hell.

"Not sure how many trips the hippie wagon has left in it. I'm always afraid I'll get stuck in the clay out at the lease. Might be time to start looking at trucks."

Texans gotta be the most truck-lovingest people on the face of the Earth, and I'd recently caught the fever. Been driving a minivan for about the last ten years, and while the utility and convenience of the vehicle can't be questioned, I was about ready for something a little more manly. Something like the poor, neglected 1978 International Scout that's been sitting dormant in my driveway a helluva lot longer than I can bring myself to admit. But that's a whole other story.

One of the mix CDs I'd brought was dialed into that Phil Ochs track where he's talking big about doing what he has to do and saying what he has to say. Only it's not just big talk because the man backed it up. I've listened to that song about a million and a half times while working on this damn book. It's honest and inspiring and if Phil can risk going to jail to make the world a better place, it makes it real difficult for me to excuse my way out of logging a few hours of writing time in the garage because I've had a long day at work. Artists and shit got to get used to the suffering.

I was listening hard and thinking deep when suddenly, the sky flashed red and lit the night with a preternatural glow.

"What the fuck was that?"

"Those are the windmills. They flash on and off, so low-flying objects will know to stay clear."

Jackson's tone was gentle. The same one he uses to teach his boys the things they'll need to know in life. Respect fire. Every gun is always loaded. Be kind to old dogs. I'd come out to discover a little part of Jackson's world, and he was sharing it with me just as he would his own offspring. The night was full of wonders, and my friend clearly took great pleasure in acquainting me with the land from which he'd sprung up.

"Do they do that all night?"

"All night. All day."

"That's fucking amazing."

"Wait til we get there. You can hear them *woosh*."

Jackson's "woosh" came out in a low, brain-rattling baritone. The kind of sound you hear from the inside out. A row of windmills stretched out across the horizon like extraterrestrial Christmas decorations blinking daggers that pierced the darkness of the country. It scared the fuck out of me in the most exciting way.

LOCAL CONGESTION

Getting where you need to get during Christmas time is always a booger bear, but shit's getting ridiculous in the not-so-humble burg of Denton town. It took me a Wandervan and two Ubers just to make it the two or three miles from my house to the square during the Holiday Lighting Festival this year. Some of that was my own fault. I made the tragic decision to cancel my first Uber and bank on the fact that my eighteen years of 940 citizenship would help me sniff out the secret parking spots. Only those don't exist anymore. You can pay fifteen bucks to park at the mega church next to the Wells Fargo, but fuck that.

Leah had warned me that the square was gridlocked, and after forty minutes of driving at about 2 mph, I decided she probably was right. Only took me thirty minutes to get home. I dialed up a Wandervan, Denton's vintage answer to Uber, but the driver called almost as soon as I booked it.

"Harlin?"

"Yeah."

"This is your Wandervan driver. Man, I just wanted to warn you that it might be an hour, hour and a half before I can get to you. You wanna wait?"

"Not even remotely."

"I don't blame you. Good luck."

There was a part of me that wanted to call it a night and just drink some tequila in the Barage, but Leah is on the Holiday Lighting committee, and I'd promised her that I would make an appearance. So I turned to my Uber app for the second time that night. A dude named Mark showed up in a busted-ass Mercury Cougar about ten minutes later.

"Is it cool if I sit up front?"

"I don't give a shit, man. They say we should make passengers ride in the back because it's safer, but I'm not sure who in the hell it's supposed to be safer for."

"I guess it all depends on whether the driver or the passenger is the axe murderer."

"That's what I'm saying."

Mark didn't exactly inspire confidence in his professional abilities, or even his interpersonal skills. But he looked like a harmless little guy, and all I needed was for him to get me close to the square.

"Can I ask you a question, man?"

"Sure."

"Are long johns just a Yankee thing?"

"I'm not sure I follow."

"You know. Long johns. Are those just for Yankees?"

"Like the donut or the warm underwear?"

"Not the fucking donut, man. Long johns. Wear 'em under your pants. Are those just for Yankees?"

"I'm pretty sure we got those down here, too."

"I just never hear anyone talk about them. You know what I mean? And long johns would come in handy on a cold night like tonight. You know what I'm talking about?"

We were closing on walking distance to the square, which was good because Mark was one weird dude. He seemed harmless, but you never know when weird is gonna go crazy on you."

"You can let me off anywhere you can pull over for a second. I'm just going about a block up that hill."

"No way, man. I think I can get you closer."

Mark hung an abrupt left and drove me about three blocks down the hill we'd already nearly summited. To his credit, he looked like he was about to try and make a right in an attempt to maneuver a little closer to where we'd just been, but the traffic started closing in on him.

"Fuck, man. This is a goddamned nightmare. I'm just gonna let you out right here."

Mark slammed on the brakes three-quarters of the way into an intersection and threw the car in park.

"Have a good night."

Cars were honking and whizzing by in every direction. I scrambled out of the car and jumped a storm drain into the parking lot of a corner gas station. Took me about another twenty minutes of walking in the cold to get back up the hill and find Leah.

"You finally made it!"

"It was an adventure."

"Traffic?"

I looked around at all the lights burning up the Denton grid. *Humming* instead of *wooshing*. Luring the masses to our town to clog our streets and guzzle our wassail.

"Among other things. Looks like y'all already lit the tree."

"Yeah. You missed it."

"Well, that's fucking awesome. You stuck here for a while?"

"At least another hour or so."

"Guess I'm headed down to the Silverleaf."

I kissed Leah goodbye and started high-stepping my way through the packed streets. Only I ain't no fucking running back. I got jostled and bumped and spun around and splashed with wassail from every direction. Fifteen minutes and three hundred feet later, I was in the middle of the wrong fucking street.

"What the hell?" I said to myself. "Did I just take a wrong fucking turn in my own fucking town?

I let my shoulder slump and began the sad trek down a back alley past horse-drawn carriages, pre-teen dance troupes and elementary school choirs, and a couple other bewildered motherfuckers trying to figure out when their town got so popular they could no longer shuffle instinctively through the crowd in the direction of their favorite bar.

CHUCKWAGON NIGHTS

The first thing I saw when we pulled into the clearing where the Jackson clan set up their hunting camp was the Chuckwagon. Backlit by fire, the beast called to me. Some old timer out West had it custom built, and Kurtis Jackson bought it off him a few years back. It was feat of rustic engineering the likes of which could never be found in a Bass Pro Shop.

When it's all battened down and ready to roll, the Chuckwagon appears to be nothing more than a big ass box on a two-wheel trailer. But look a little closer, and you'll discover an intricate system of doors and secret compartments that lead to a host of culinary wonders. Two large panels on one side fold down to reveal a cast iron cooking stove and what can best be described as a camping pantry. S'mores fixins, boxes of mac-n-cheese, coffee, and whatever Kurtis needs to pull off his latest cookout masterpiece.

The top of the Chuckwagon is covered by a custom-built awning and can be used for storage, or as legend has it, for two brothers to cuddle up in and take shelter from freak ice storms. I've burned up the internet looking for tow-behind smokers and cook rigs of every imaginable style, and there ain't nothing out there quite like the Chuckwagon. It makes you feel Grizzly Adams manly just standing next to it. After his kids, his wife, and his guns, Kurtis probably loves the Chuckwagon more than anything. And I might have some of those out of order.

In true big brother fashion, Kurtis had some sausages waiting for us on the stove and an extra helping of shit talk on the back burner. He laid into Kody almost immediately.

"Not everyone can show up for a hunting trip with a half case of beer, a pack of smokes, and borrow a gun."

"Jackson's got a gun in his car."

My friend looked sheepish in the face of my defense.

"That's actually Kurtis's gun."

Big Brother kept right on riding Little Brother as Jackson tried to get his tent set up. The wind was not interested in cooperating. He eventually got it erected just long enough to enjoy a bit of whiskey and a cold beer before a big gust tore it all down again.

"It supposed to rain tonight, Kurtis?"

"Not til late tomorrow. If y'all got some tarps, we can get you set up under the Chuckwagon awning. Should be good for the night, you know."

Jackson started breaking down his crumpled tent, and I wandered off to grab our tarps and find a place to make some water. Out in the darkness away from the crackling fire and the brotherly banter, I got my first chance to be alone with the sound of the windmills. It went something like a jet plane buzzing the tower before crashing into a dolphin song. High-pitched and unsettling. More alien than mammalian. A shiver ran the length of my spine, and I looked up at the sky almost expecting to see a pod of dolphins swimming through it like a cornfield in a Bryan Adams video. But there were only stars. So many fucking stars. Like a planetarium in real life.

As I made my way back to camp, a massive pair of headlights appeared in the distance.

"Looks like Kyla's here."

The arrival of a third Jackson completely changed the dynamic. No more brother sniping on brother. Kyla was running the show now, and she could fill any silence. From the moment she bounded out of the hulking pickup, she spun yarns endlessly. A cyclone of storytelling.

"What y'all boys doin?" she asked as we worked at turning the Chuckwagon into a bed and breakfast. "Y'all ain't got no tent?"

"Wind blew it down," said Jackson.

"Ah! So y'all gonna do the Chuckwagon Snuggle again! Boy, you should have seen it," she said turning to me. "These two come out in the middle of a damn ice storm to do some hunting, but the ground was too damn cold to sleep on. So they get the bright idea to climb up on top of the Chuckwagon and cuddle their way through the night. Sweetest thing I ever seen."

"Both of y'all squeezed into that little space? How'd you even climb up there in the middle of an ice storm?"

"It wasn't that bad. Close up the stove and the storage area, and you can get up pretty easy. Beat the hell out of sleeping on ice, you know."

"They must have been nice and comfy. Slept through a damn deer jumping over them in the night."

"Ain't no deer jumped over that Chuckwagon," said Kurtis. "I think you made that up."

"You don't know. You and Kody were too busy cuddling and snoring to notice. I was the only one still up. Deer came running right through the ice and sleet and cleared y'all by a foot."

"It'd have to be one big-ass deer to jump over the Chuckwagon."

"It looked big as hell to me, but maybe deer just look bigger when you don't sleep. Alls I know is that I saw a deer jump over the Chuckwagon right before I went to sleep in the Chalet."

The Chalet was an old camper that used to be on Kurtis's truck. He and Jackson got it fixed up pretty nice, took it on one badass trip, and then Kurtis rolled it. After that, it was put out to pasture, so to speak, at the deer lease. It's become rat-infested and generally nasty as shit since its retirement. Kyla was a brave woman to have spent a night in there with the rodents. Or maybe it was just that damn cold.

"I still can't believe you slept in there."

"I'm surprised you made it out alive, you know?"

"Barely! I crawled in there and felt all these tiny little eyes just a-watching. Tried to fall asleep real fast, so I wouldn't feel nothing creeping on me. Woke up that morning with an ugly cough. Kody said I got the viral ratingitis."

"Viral Ratingitis?" I asked.

"Rat cough. Kody said it would probably kill me. Between the cuddling and the rat cough, we was laughing our asses off. It wouldn't have been so funny if the rat virus had got me, though. Guess it's a good thing I'm tougher than a rat."

It was fascinating to watch the stark contrast between the Brothers Jackson, calm men who went about their camping business and beer drinking with few words, and Kyla's frenetic energy. Once she hit the scene, we were all just trying to keep up.

JACKSON SPLASH

We were searching for firewood under the intermittent glow of the windmills when Jackson unleashed the anguished wail of a big man realizing that not even his bigness can shield him from certain offensive scenarios, intentional or inadvertent as they may be. Kurtis and I went straight-up dog-eared and snapped our necks in Jackson's direction. Kyla was considerably less concerned.

"What the hell's all that about?" she said.

"KYLA!"

I wish there were a typographical way to express the manner in which Jackson called out his sister that night. It started low, like a growl, and built with alarming tenacity into a furious, tooth-rattling thing.

"What was in your water bottle!?"

"What water bottle?"

"How many water bottles you got in your car?"

"Oh, you mean the one in the console?"

"Yes. What was in it?"

"Vodka."

"Vodka? Why in the hell do you have vodka in a water bottle?"

"Because the vodka bottle was almost empty, and I didn't want to be driving around with an empty liquor bottle in the truck. So what?"

"So I went in for the Jackson Face Splash thinking it was water and ended up with damn vodka all over my face and in my nose and my eyes."

"I bet that burns."

"Hell yes it burns."

"Well, what the fuck is the Jackson Face Splash anyway?"

"You know exactly what it is. Ever since I was a kid and I'd be playing outside or doing chores and I would get hot, I'd go inside and splash water all over my head and face."

"What the fuck for?"

"Because it cools me down."

"Well maybe you should ask before you go dumping out other people's water because it might be vodka. Now what the hell am I supposed to drink?"

MORNING IN THE BLIND

Sleep is a fleeting thing when on you're on the hunt. It's damn hard to drag your ass away from the comfort of a warm fire and an open bottle of whiskey to go sleep in a bag on the ground. So you stay up later than you should, which is fine because your tent-mate will be snoring, or you'll be snoring, or some guy in the next tent will really be snoring all night anyway. And there ain't nothing comfortable about sleeping on our red Texas clay. Sometimes I think the reason people like to get housed around a campfire is because passing out's your only chance at getting any sleep. But it's all good because you're not out there to get your beauty rest. Step one of hunting is having your ass up and in the blind before the first light of day.

I woke up feeling pretty not bad considering all the beer and whiskey and cheesy sausages and pickled quail eggs I'd consumed the night before. No churning in my gut, and no aching in my back. It was still dark, but the sky was definitely teasing that light would be coming soon. Kurtis was standing by the fire drinking coffee and wearing a Jones Cap that fit him as perfectly as the trademark "you know" he tacked on to the end of seemingly every other sentence. Old school country boy. That's Kurtis for you.

"Would it be bad form to have my first beer at 5:30 AM?"

I needed something to chase of the light fog in my head, and I never could stomach coffee.

"Early beers are just part of hunting, you know."

So I cracked a keystone and lit a cigarette. The smoke, that early, was revolting, but I stuck it out because it felt like the thing to do. Being out there hunting with the Jacksons was a little like playing grown up, which is odd for a nearly forty-year-old man to say, but I don't always feel my age. Right about then, Jackson came lumbering out of the woods, and just like that, the morning pleasantries were over. Kurtis and Kyla packed up and disappeared. It was time to hunt.

Jackson's brother and sister use manufactured, elevated deer stands, but Jackson hunts from a mesquite turret fashioned out of indigenous rocks and gnarled branches of the thorny wood. There are bits of bone and scrub brush and other debris that he adds every year. Anything to keep it looking like a natural feature on the horizon. Set the deer at ease.

We crept behind it in camo onesies. The sun wasn't even up yet. My pant legs were too long, and I couldn't see for shit. Jackson led the trek with his rifle carefully slung over his shoulder in a way that it would never, ever fall into a position where the business end was pointed at me. I had a plastic grocery sack with beers in one hand and a couple of camping chairs in the other. Every step was a concerted effort to be quiet. The unseasonable warmth made the onesies a stuffy affair.

Daylight had begun to dispel the darkness by the time we got into place. We set up our camping chairs and, very slowly, eased into them. Jackson prepped his gun and leaned it up against the blind in exaggerated slow motion. Then he took about five minutes to turn his head toward me.

"Deer can see and hear better than us," he whispered. "Move as little as possible. Say nothing. If you think you see a deer, tap me on the leg. No sudden movements."

It took me an hour, but I reached into the grocery sack, grabbed a couple of beers, and handed one to Jackson. The muscles in our necks and shoulders strained and stiffened as we tried to stifle the sounds of cans being cracked. Our eyes darted quickly across the land to be sure we hadn't spooked anything. I settled back in my chair. Every damn thing I could see, and there were so many things, was absolutely beautiful. Windmills were spinning on the right, looming over the little deer feeder Jackson had set up. On the left, a long, tall ridge stretched straight and true toward the end of the horizon. The sun was high enough now to make the hunt legal.

"What now?"

"Now we wait."

Wonderful things to say about all the majesty that surrounded me raced through my head. I wanted to remember everything and write it all down so I could better tell you all about it, but my eyelids began to get so heavy. I felt my head start to topple. I dared not yank it back into a conscious position. I could hear Jackson slowly sipping on his beer, his breath coming and going even slower. Nothing for what seems like too long, then a contented rising and falling of the shoulders and ribcage. Slight. Covert. I knew I would not last much longer.

A GOOD TEXAS MAN, PART II

Brenda used to be one of the neighbor kids. The way Jackson tells it, she got two handfuls of bum tickets in the parent lottery. I never even knew she existed until I saw her speak at David Jackson's funeral, but she's damn sure part of the family now. Time was, that was a hotly contested issue. But that time is long gone. David Jackson made sure of that.

"We never thought much about it when we were little," said Jackson, sitting at the bar in my garage while my little Beagle tries to scramble up his leg into his lap. "She was always just playing in our yard. Then she starting having dinner with us sometimes. Then it was most times."

"Where were her parents?"

"Not exactly sure," he pauses for a long drink and a pull off a smoke. "Might have been in some trouble or just poor and not able to take care of her. I just know it pissed my dad off.

"Mama Jackson feel the same?"

"She did and didn't. We didn't exactly have a hell of a lot of money at the time, either, and there were hungry mouths to feed at our own table."

The beagle is still after Jackson, begging for attention with a flurry of paws against his denim shins, but my friend doesn't even notice. He's talking family, and he don't get distracted easy when it comes to family.

"I remember I heard them arguing one night. Dad was fed up, and he was gonna do something about it."

"But, David. We can't. We're poor. We're poor as shit."

"I don't care. This just ain't right."

"I don't know if my mom actually said 'poor as shit,' but that's how Brenda came to be a Jackson. My dad saw something wrong, so he fixed it. That just how he was. How he lived."

Jackson bends down now and gently scratches my seventeen-pound, old lady beagle on the neck and head with a man paw big enough to crush her like a fat grape. She ever-so-slowly eases into a careful roll and ends up on her back. Jackson gives her a good brisket scratching and says something kind to her in a low, low voice. His head is turned away from me, but I can feel him smiling at the little creature through his big black beard.

IN THE BLIND, PART II

"How long was I asleep?"

"About as long as we were supposed to be hunting. You're just like my kids. Actually, I think Barret lasted longer than you on his last hunt."

"Damn. Sorry, buddy."

"I'm not. I love it when my kids fall asleep in the deer blind. I get to be quiet and still and not worry about anyone fucking that up."

"You see anything?"

"Nothing but a real pretty sunrise."

Judging by the fact that Jackson hadn't hushed me yet, I figured we were about done with the morning hunt. Deer are nocturnal, so you can only really catch them on their way in for the day—or their way out for the night.

"What comes next?"

"We gotta check my feeder before heading back to camp. Then we hop in a truck and fill all the other feeders. After that, I'm probably gonna take a nap."

"A nap?"

"Yeah. A nap. We got up early as shit. Naps are good when you get up early."

"But I just had a nap."

"Well, then you can drink beer with Kyla. Try and keep her out of trouble."

THE IN-BETWEEN

True to his word, Jackson crashed out after we got back from filling all the feeders so the deer could get their fix and wander into shooting range. He drug a cot over near the smoldering remains of the campfire, changed his socks, and went lights out. Me and Kyla were drinking beer, and she was nipping at the Beam in between stories about a lot of people I've never even met. Kurtis was being Kurtis. Quietly going about the business of preparing the night's meal. I usually get roped into helping with the food, but not on Kurtis's watch. He's got everything he's gonna eat, and exactly the way he's gonna prepare it, planned out before he ever hitches the Chuckwagon to his truck.

"You know," said Kyla. "Kurtis looks more and more like my dad every time I see him."

"Yeah?"

"Not in the face so much, but just the way he moves around. His walk. The way he carries himself."

It was the first thing she'd said to me all weekend that didn't end with a punch line or a wicked burst of laughter. We must have been enough beers in to start getting emotional because I felt my throat catch and the corners of my eyes started to sting.

Kurtis went right on working. He rebuilt the fire and got the ball rolling on his chicken fricassee. It wasn't at all what I expected out of a hunting meal, but it sure looked like the man knew what he was doing. First he tossed the chicken in a skillet to sear it. Then everything went in a cast iron dutch oven, which was set to rest on a cinder block in the fire ring. And that's where it would stay until we got back from the evening hunt and cracked it open for a first whiff.

Jackson got up from his nap and started drinking beer with me and Kyla.

"Get some good rest?"

"Yup. Rested and ready."

"You looked so cute sleeping all peaceful. I had to put your picture on the Facebook."

"Asshole."

"Say, little brother. I think we need to make a run into town. Get some more beer and a cheddarwurst down at the general store."

"Hell. Yes."

We checked with Kurtis to see if he needed anything from the store and then piled into Kyla's truck. I had a nice beer buzz going, and the sky was getting dark like it was gonna storm soon. I loved everything. The windmills. The grey clouds. Kyla's stories. The feeling of being in a big truck that was moving fast.

Across the street from the General Store sits the St. Mary's Grotto. The little half-dome structure is similar in shape to a band shell. It has statues and religious artifacts and candles you can light. Jackson says that they built the Grotto because 64 citizens of Windthorst went off to fight in World War II, and all 64 of them made it home alive. It's a peaceful spot and a good reminder to be thankful whenever you get the opportunity.

The Windthorst General store, according to the sign out front, was established in 1892. It's a small building packed with everything from work boots to pickled delicacies. Walking through the front door, you'd almost swear you'd slipped far, far, back in time. We bought beer and ordered our cheddarwursts from the man behind the counter. I could have spent an hour wandering around the little store, but there was no time. Daylight was running out, and the deer blind was calling Jackson's name.

THE BLIND AT NIGHT

The sky over Windthorst turns an impossible shade of blue right before sunset. Jackson and I watched as a narrow wall of storm clouds began to roll toward camp.

"That don't look good," he whispered.

"Where the hell are we gonna sleep tonight?"

"We'll figure something out."

I managed to stay awake longer than I did for the morning hunt, but there were still plenty of groggy moments. It had been a long day of drinking beer and lugging sacks of deer feed over rough terrain. For the second time that day, Jackson had carried his rifle to the blind only to set it down and not pick it up again until it was time to return to camp.

"I'm calling it," he said. "Let's head back."

I was comfortable sitting in the blind in my camo onesie and not overly inclined to move. We still had three or four beers in our grocery sack. There was no need to relocate. Except that Kurtis had given us very-important jobs. Time-sensitive tasks that could make or break this, and all future, hunting trips. I was supposed to start a pot of rice for dinner. Kurtis's blind was further away than Jackson's, and if he got a deer, he would not be back in time to do it himself. Jackson had a far greater responsibility. He had been charged with entertaining the Lessor of the land.

It was starting to sprinkle a bit by the time we made it back to camp. I fumbled about getting the rice started, I'd never actually cooked rice before, and Jackson pulled out the special bottle of scotch Kurtis brought to give the Lessor as a token of their appreciation. The man showed up a few minutes later. He was a fast-talking good old boy who laughed with his whole body. I liked him immediately.

"You boys get anything today?"

"Nope," said Jackson. Didn't see a single moving thing."

"I seen me a big old buck the other day, but it was too close to dark to take a shot. Wife wouldn't let me hear the end of it. I tried to go back out the next day, and she says, 'Why bother? You ain't gonna pull the trigger.'"

Jackson made a show of laughing. The Jackson family lease was about to expire, and if they could not agree to terms on a new one, they would lose their place to hunt. Kody and Kurtis did not want to explore that scenario. It would mean moving deer blinds and the wreckage of the rat chalet when what the Jackson boys really wanted to do was build up on the land they already had. Them Jacksons are dig-in kind of people. They had a plan for their little piece of wilderness. Losing the lease would ruin it all.

"Where you boys from?" asked the Lessor.

"I live in Denton, and we got a family business over in Grapevine."

It's no accident Jackson dropped a mention of the family business. People trust families. Family-owned. Family-operated. Family-friendly. It makes you feel safe. Jackson was telling the Lessor that he could be confident that his family would treat the land with respect. Bring their children and nieces and nephews out there and teach them to love the land.

"I don't get off the ranch much. Danged old Garmin saves me and the old lady's ass when we get into the Metroplex. That 121 is a bitch."

"You ain't lying."

The old dude cut loose a barrage of stories about hunting coyotes with a pack of greyhounds and tracking wounded deer after his wife hit them with the car so he could make the insurance pay out. He must have had a thousand crazy stories, but you got the feeling they all had some degree of truth to them.

Kurtis returned to camp, and Jackson and I fell back to let them talk in private a while. I was glad not to have to worry about being extra polite or maybe saying the wrong thing. It's best to let Jacksons handle Jackson business.

Darkness was upon us, and it was no longer a question of "if" it would rain. The only guesswork now involved when and how badly we'd get drenched. I was slipping into that not-quite-drunk but very, very tired stage of all-day drinking. Dinner was ready. There was a young beagle that belonged to a friend of Kurtis's sniffing around the camp. I tried to pet him, but he'd been trained to track, and that's all he wanted to do. Every so often, he would disappear into the brush, and the only proof that he still existed was a faint, mournful bay from somewhere deep in the trees.

CRAMPED BEDFELLOWS

The rain showed up right about bedtime, drenching the little spot under the Chuckwagon where we'd slept the previous night and creating a situation wherein Kody Jackson and I were about to get closer than we'd ever been before. When the ground is wet and your tent won't stay pitched, sometimes all you can do is bed down in the back of a Nissan Xterra. It don't matter if one of you is six foot and the other is six foot three and you both weigh in at over 220 pounds. You will fold the seats down and sleep in the cargo space of that import SUV because at least it's dry.

When you wake up in the night with a fierce need to piss, you will stubbornly test the limits of the human bladder because it's cold and water is still falling from the sky, and crawling out the car door with the seats folded down has a high degree of difficulty. You can either slither out headfirst—or try to spin around like a turtle on its back until you can get your feet out the door. Even then, there's no good way to get your shoes on so you end up trying to sleep the rest of the night in wet socks.

There will be bad smells and loud snores in the small place you are sharing with a big man. And that big man might try to cuddle you and steal your warmth when the night reaches its coldest point. You will have no choice but to let him because he is, after all, the bigger man. If you sleep, you will sleep poorly and wake to fogged-up windows and doors that are still tricky as shit to crawl out of. But you will be glad. Because you did not sleep in the rat chalet or in the wet grass. Glad because you stayed dry. Glad because you were willing to cram yourself and another human being into a place where luggage goes and now you have a story to tell.

A GOOD HAT IS YOUR BEST FRIEND

It was snowing at the Wal-Mart in Bowie, Texas. We were standing in the parking lot smoking cigarettes and waiting for Tex to show up. Some of us were starting to think that this camping trip that had almost been canceled should have been canceled after all. Jackson was antsy to get to the lake, so he dialed up Tex on the phone.

"Where you at, buddy? Seriously? We've been here for about twenty minutes."

Jackson cupped the phone and looked at us.

"Tex was in the parking lot the whole time we were inside. He took off about five minutes ago."

Jackson shrugged and went back to his conversation.

"You're gonna see a gas station on your right in about ten miles or so. Hold tight and we'll meet you there."

The snow was starting to taper off as we pulled into the gas station about fifteen minutes later. Everyone scattered once we hit the front door. Tex started looking at pickled foods, Jackson and Porter ordered slices of pizza from a little counter next to the register, and I checked out an aisle filled with trail mixes and various dry snacks. Everybody shopped at their own pace and then wandered out the door.

It was still chilly outside even though the snow had mostly stopped. I was shivering a little bit and worried that I didn't have enough cold weather gear. Right about then, a couple of our buddies came out of the store sporting new hunter's caps, the kind with the furry ear flaps you can fold up or down depending on the need. Whoever owned the store should have hooked them up with a couple free slices or at least an employee discount because those dudes had just unknowingly kicked over the first domino in a hat-buying frenzy.

One by one, we went back into the store to pillage the three racks of winter hats next to the door. Jackson and I ended up with the exact same model because it had extra room for us big-headed folk. It was a camouflage number, which I typically can't stand, but the faux fur flaps and cozy fit suggested it would be a good friend in the cold weather.

Twenty minutes later we were scavenging for firewood and setting up BB gun targets on Jackson's family land at Lake Arrowhead in Scotland, Texas. The sun came out from its cloudy lurking spot and threw down some heat. Like clockwork, earflaps started flipping up all over the campsite. I was chopping wood, and chopping it well thanks to either my nifty new hat or my Viking heritage. I damn near broke a sweat.

Fastforward a couple of hours, and the sun disappeared and everyone started dropping their flaps and would have been happy to throw down double whatever they paid back at that gas station. I remember waking up the next morning and finding Warden shivering by the fire. He'd passed out early, then woke up late, and must have passed out all over again drinking whiskey by the fire. The flames were all gone, and the wood was ashy and smoldering, but he had one of those hats on his head bottling up all the warmth and keeping him from freezing to death in the night.

Sometimes an impulse buy will straight-up save your life.

PARTING SHOTS

Jackson and I skipped the morning hunt. Our thoughts were already halfway home, and neither of us wanted to deal with the aftermath of shooting something. I know the deer population has to be controlled or they'll wreak all manner of havoc. I just don't want to be the one to have to kill something beautiful.

I asked Jackson if his boys had any trouble the first time they saw him bag a deer.

"Not really," he said. "They were young, and I explained it to them. This is how we get food to feed our family. We don't shoot more than we can eat, and we don't waste anything. They could understand that."

The Jackson boys were on their second cups of coffee when we heard the rifle shot.

"Somebody's shooting at something."

"Or they're just shooting. I didn't hear it hit anything."

"You can tell that just by the sound?"

"Yup. It makes a kind of a thumping noise, you know."

The man who owns the beagle showed up back at the campsite a few minutes later. He was smiling real stupid.

"Was that you shooting?" asked Kurtis.

"Sure was. I was over in Kody's blind, and I saw a doe way the hell up on that ridge. Lobbed a shot up there and knocked it down."

"You kill it?"

"Nope. I think it got back up and ran off."

"You didn't track it or anything. Just left it?"

"It was a long shot, man. By the time I got up to where it was when I hit it, she'd have been long gone. Waste of time."

Kurtis didn't look too happy, but the Beagle Daddy was oblivious. He went over to his truck and opened up the back door, revealing two little kids and that beagle all wrapped up in blankets. Dude pulled out a rifle, went over to the little makeshift shooting range, and started firing off rounds real obnoxious-like and generally fucking up a peaceful morning. Lucky for us, dude had zero to no attention span. It wasn't long before he was digging around in the back of his truck again and speaking harshly to child and beagle alike.

"Well, Kurtis. I better get these kids home. When you coming back out here?"

"Not real sure yet. I'll let you know."

The dude started walking toward his truck, but Kurtis wasn't done with him just yet.

"Say. Where on the ridge was that deer when you hit it? I might go up and see if I can track it."

"I don't know exactly. Way up there. About a quarter of the way down maybe."

"All right."

"I guess I'll see you next time."

"I guess so."

Dude got in his truck and drove off exactly like you'd expect someone who's got no sense of just how annoying they might be to drive off. I hardly knew him, but I was glad to see him go. He was the type of dude that buys a dog for hunting and then treats it like an employee. I don't trust anyone who could have a perfectly good beagle and not be sweet to it.

"So let me get this straight," I said. "That dude winged a deer and just left it out there to limp around and bleed until it dies? Ain't that against the rules or something?"

"That's not how we do it, but I don't think he actually hit anything. I think he sat out here for two days and didn't see shit. Same as us. Probably just wanted to shoot his gun so he'd have something to say, you know."

Departure time was rapidly approaching, and Kyla was nowhere to be found. The brothers Jackson speculated that she probably headed home sometime after the rains came. One night in the rat chalet is more than enough for anyone. You can only dodge the viral ratingitis for so long.

I was ready to be home, but there was work to do before we left. Kurtis had fed us all weekend, and now it was time to help him break down the camp. First we did the tent, and then we moved on to the Chuckwagon. When everything was packed and battened down, we hitched the beast to the back of Kurtis's truck. What had been a campsite just hours ago was now back to being mostly wilderness. I took one last look at the windmills and wished that it were dark so I could see them glow again.

Jackson and I folded the seats back up in the Xterra and climbed in for the drive home. As we approached the edge of the clearing we gathered speed for our last adventure of the trip.

"Hold on, Harlin. There's an ugly stretch of clay between here and the gravel. We won't make it through if we're going slow."

Jackson never let off the gas. The back end of the Xterra slid sideways as we hooked a right and made the transition from grass to clay. Big chunks of red blitzed past the back window. We shimmied a bit but stayed straight and true until our wheels hit gravel.

THE VASHTI MYTH

"We're passing through Vashti right now," said Jackson. "You know who's buried out here?"

I had no fucking clue who'd been laid to rest in this tiny little Texas town located somewhere between his family's hunting land in Windthorst and our neighborhood in Denton. But that was all right because I could tell Jackson was looking forward to educating me on all the things he'd grown to love about the country roads on which he was raised. Like the broken-down stone house on the way to Windthorst. The one he snuck up to and photographed. A photograph that eventually ended up on the back cover of *Minding Days*, his second solo album.

"I couldn't guess who was buried out here if you gave me a hundred chances, buddy."

"C'mon. You gotta at least try."

Jackson was way into it, so I threw out a couple names that were so far from hitting the nail on the head they weren't even worth remembering. When he was satisfied with my effort, he shared his secret knowledge.

"Vashti, Texas is the final resting place of Hoss Cartwright."

"How the hell does a famous actor end up buried in Vashti? He from here or something?"

"Nope. Not from here. My dad always said that he passed through town once and thought it was so pretty that this is where he wanted to be buried."

"No shit. That's an interesting bit of trivia. Probably not gonna forget that anytime soon."

And I didn't. In fact, a few months later—after the calendar flipped and the weather started to get warm again—Jackson and I were sitting in his backyard drinking beer and telling stories. Or rather, he was telling stories, and I was trying to remember as many details as I could. I didn't want to put a family like his, and a man like David Jackson, in my book and then fuck up all the specifics. A writer should do no harm unless someone's got it coming.

Anyway, we were talking about his family and the old days and Vashti came up again.

"The place where Hoss.is buried, right?"

"Not exactly."

"But you made a big deal out of pointing that out to me on the way home from hunting?"

"Turns out I fell victim to a Dad Myth, Harlin. Hoss is buried somewhere, maybe even in Texas, but it is definitely not in Vashti. He might not ever have set foot in the town for all I know."

"Why would your dad lie to you about something so fucking random?"

"No idea. Maybe he heard it from someone else and just assumed it was true. Or maybe he thought it was funny to make stuff up, you know?"

"Was this a regular thing for him?"

"Looking back, there was definitely a pattern. He got Katha real good one time."

"I think I need to hear this story."

"So, we're on a family vacation to Colorado, and we stop at the Grand Canyon. That's where Dad decides to tell Katha that Indians built the Rocky Mountain with five pound buckets of dirt—and the hole where they got the dirt is what we know today as the Grand Canyon."

"She believed him?"

"She didn't just believe him. She got in a fight with a teacher who told her it wasn't true. My parents got called in for a teacher conference, Dad had to come clean, and that's the story of how Katha became a skeptic. Dad Myths ruined her forever."

Part Four
High Desert Waltz

PREAMBLE TO A RAMBLE

My friend Dan Mojica loves the desert. And his friend Joe Pat Hennen loves it, too. Joe Pat's a music lifer. He's been singing for family and friends further back than he can remember. Forty years ago, his wife Susie bought him a Guild F20 guitar at the Denver Folklore Center, and he's had the fever ever since. He used to host a show out in Marathon, Texas called Joe Pat Hennen's Campfire at The Gage. It was a popular event until the economic collapse of 2008.

"The hard times hit live music hard," said Joe Pat. "Our fans and friends would lament the loss of this event, but the Gage Hotel lost interest due to low response, and I didn't have the personal resources to keep it going."

That's where Dan enters the picture. Joe Pat and Dan have known each other since their kids played T-ball together almost thirty years ago. Back then, Dan was refueling jets at DFW Airport, and Joe Pat was working for the state. Dan eventually ditched the airline gig and opened the original Dan's Bar, which quickly became Joe Pat's favorite place to play. When he got the itch to take the band back to Marathon, he reached out to Dan to partner with him on a two-day party they would call The Big Bender.

I'd be going along for the ride to get my first taste of the high desert and chronicle the trip, as best I could, for this book. Dan and I were gonna roll out west in a van that used to be the tour vehicle for Denton's own musical heroes, Slobberbone. We'd spend a few days at the Marathon Motel and RV Park, and once the show was over, head down to the *hacienda*, a little spot in Terlingua where Dan likes to go and put some distance between himself and the rest of the world.

I'd heard many stories of desert adventures, and I couldn't wait to get out there and start making some of my own. It was sure to be a hell of a time.

EMBARCADERO

Mine and Leah's bed was a wonderful place full of softly snoring warm bodies. Wife on my right, Jakey on my left, and old Earl stretched across the bottom. I didn't want to get up, but Dan had told me about a hundred times that he'd be in front of the house at 4:45 AM. Sharp. My excitement over the trip, and not going to work for a full week, got the best of me the night before, and I'd stayed out too late. Now it was a heavy blinking morning, eyes burning from too much fun and not enough sleep. Upon resolving myself to the inevitability of the act, I slithered out from under the covers to avoid rousing my bedfellows.

The steam from the shower scalded me awake. I tied on my favorite green bandana—headband-style, not do-rag. Next came my blue Dickies shorts and my red shark hoodie, and my maroon New Balance 574s. I jammed my toiletries and a bath towel into my duffle, in the process busting one of the two remaining functional zippers. Poor bag. It had been good to me over the years, and now this would be its last trip.

Jake lifted his head to peer at me through the darkness, huffed, and then sunk his snout between his paws. I went over and scratched him good behind the ears. "Try not to be an asshole," I told him. Then I picked up my bag and crept down the hallway toward the light of the front porch. I'd show Mojica 4:45 in the damn morning.

I lit a cigarette on the front stoop and started ticking off items on my mental checklist. There ain't no fucking Walgreens in the desert. No Walmarts, either, for that matter. You better bring what you need because shit ain't cheap out there. When I was mostly satisfied with my preparedness, I lugged my gear from the porch to the curb. An easy load-in is the best way to start a road trip. Dan would be chomping at the bit. Sure enough, his big white van pulled up to my mailbox ten minutes early. I smiled. We were on schedule to be ahead of schedule. Before we knew it, we'd make the turn at Monahans and crack our first beers. The high desert was out there just waiting for us.

Things were going great until we hit Weatherford. We were cruising along all peaceful-like and generally excited about what lie ahead. And then out of nowhere there was this king hell sound like someone shot the engine from the inside out. Dan said "whathafuck" and started looking around and trying to figure out what to do because the van was sounding a lot like a fucking go-cart, and we had no idea how far we could get before it gave up the ghost. It took him just a second to get his shit back together.

"I think we blew a plug, buddy."
"Like a sparkplug went bad?"
"If by bad you mean it blew right out of the engine block."
"That don't sound good."
"It's happened before. Down in Terlingua."

"Fuck, man. Where do you find a mechanic out in the fucking desert?"

"It's a long story, Harlin, but when you do, he's the kind of guy that drives around with a fucking AK-47."

"No fucking shit?"

"Brother, you don't even know."

Mojica eased the van off the highway at the next exit. Even in the dark of the morning, in the midst of a crisis of currently undetermined severity, it felt like he knew exactly where he was going. We looped a backroad into the parking lot of a trucker motel. There was a greasy spoon next to the place that would make a fine spot to figure out our next step while we waited for the local mechanics to open up shop. Breakfast in Weatherford, motherfuckers. Where our travel plans were just as scrambled as the fucking eggs.

A sweet, but scared-of-her-own-shadow, waitress met us at the hostess stand.

"Just the two of y'all this morning?"

"Yes, ma'am," said Dan. "Say, would you happen to know a mechanic around here that opens early?"

"A mechanic? I'm not really sure. Y'all having car trouble?"

"Busted down on the way to the desert. Trying to get back on the road as soon as we can."

"I can ask the other girl if you want."

"That'd be real sweet of you."

She led us to a table and took our drink orders before rushing off. When she returned, she put a coke in front of me and carefully placed a cup of coffee in front of Dan before pulling a small, white card from her apron.

"I found this behind the register. Sometimes people leave business cards. Just in case, you know?"

The card was for a place called Boss Shop.

"It's just on the other side of the highway. I don't know if they do good work or not, but they open at seven."

"Thank you so much," said Dan. "This is a huge help."

She smiled real big at that and then asked if we were ready to order. We rattled off the thigs we wanted to eat. She wrote it all down with the same care she poured coffee. The grub came out fast and hot. Nothing spectacular, but solid. All you could hope for in an emergency breakfast scenario. We ate quickly and tipped well.

"How do you figure a girl like her ends up working the ass crack of dawn shift at a no-name diner behind a shitty motel, Dan?"

"Probably made a wrong turn somewhere. Hell, maybe more than one."

I knew it would start to depress me if I thought about it too much, so when Dan hit the bathroom, I distracted myself by browsing through all the Texas-themed junk for sale at the front of the restaurant. I wondered if anyone actually ever bought any of that shit. Like maybe some sad fuck in Iowa has a Texas room decked out with all manner of tacky roadside crap. Someplace he can go and sit and pretend to be in the greatest state in the nation when it's colder than hell outside and his deck is covered in snow. I don't reckon I could blame them if there were such a person. If you can't live in Texas, you might as well pretend.

The Boss Shop didn't open for another thirty minutes, but we headed over anyway to make sure we were first in line. We climbed down from the van into the brisk morning air and smoked cigarettes in the parking lot.

"I hope Boss can get us fixed up, brother. I want to be back on the road and in the desert by sunset."

"I'm sure it'll be fine, Dan. They got like five bays decked out with all the tools. Can't imagine they couldn't fix a sparkplug."

"It takes a special kit. If you don't have the kit, you're fucked."

"Have a little faith in the Boss, buddy."

Fifteen minutes later, a big guy carrying a Herman Munster lunch pail showed up for work. It had to be Boss. Dude sorta looked like an old lesbian, and he didn't seem at all happy to see us.

"Howdy, brother." Dan greeted him warmly. "Van blew a plug."

"That's not good."

"Sure isn't. We gotta get down to the desert today. Think you can get us fixed up?"

"Nope."

"No?"

"Nope."

"So . . . are you too busy? No room on the schedule or something?"

"Only work on big trucks."

"Like semis?"

"Yup. Big trucks."

"Well. Do you know anyone in town that works on regular cars?"

Boss grunted out a snarl.

"I don't know anyone in this town."

"Hold on," I said. "You don't know another mechanic in the entire town?"

Boss tossed his head back and to the right, exhaling heavily. A fat old mule trying to drive away the flies.

"You might try Christian Brothers."

"Where are they located?" asked Dan.

"That way."

Boss tossed up a steak finger in the direction we'd just come from then unlocked the front door to his shop. The big bastard never said another word, or so much as took a second look at us, as he pulled the door shut behind him. Boss was finished talking to us. He had no time for the drivers of little cars. If you ain't in a big truck, leave Boss the fuck alone.

Dan and I got back in the van.

"Dude," I said as we sputtered along in search of hope. "Boss is kind of an asshole."

"Yeah, brother. He's a real cocksucker."

We were entering the forty years in the wilderness portion of our journey. Light was creeping across the sky, but it was still mostly dark as we made our way to Christian Brothers Automotive. Dan was cautiously optimistic.

"If they've got the right kit, it should only take a couple hours to get us up and running. That's how long it took the guy in the desert."

"Hell, maybe it won't even take that long, Dan. I'm not trying to question the mechanical skills of a man I've never met, but your desert mechanic sounds like a machine gun-toting madman. We might get better service at a reputable, gun-free repair shop."

Dan just laughed and kept on driving. Up ahead, we spotted Christian Brothers on the opposite side of the highway, so we hooked back around at the next overpass. The Christian Brothers' office was a stark contrast to the Boss Shop. Bright and welcoming even though they didn't open for another ten minutes. I noticed, with no small amount of concern, that nearly every bay in the shop was occupied by some manner of broken vehicle. Nevertheless, the man behind the counter greeted us warmly as we walked through the door.

"Morning, fellas. How y'all doing?"

"We were doing all right until about an hour ago," said Dan.

"Yeah?"

"Van blew a plug while we were driving down the highway."

"Ford van?"

"Yessir."

"They'll do that."

"Think you can help us out?"

"I can, but it won't be today. Booked solid. Soonest I could get to you would be late tomorrow or Monday morning. Y'all got time to wait?"

"Not that much. We need to be in the desert by tonight. Tomorrow afternoon at the absolute latest. Got anyone you'd recommend?"

"There's a place not far from here that does solid work. Get back on the frontage road and take a left at the light. Go down about five or six miles, and there will be a shop on your left."

"Thanks, brother."

"Good luck, fellas."

The next shop wasn't open yet, so Dan parked out front, and I started looking up mechanics on my phone. When I found one that was open at seven in the morning, I'd give the number to Dan, and he'd get them on the horn. We must have called about eight places before we made contact with a Firestone that had a mechanic on his way into work and an opening on the schedule.

"We'll be there in five minutes," he said.

Almost as soon as Dan located the tiny button to disconnect the call, he let out a quick "Fuck," and started redialing. I heard the phone ring once before someone on the other end picked up.

"Hi. I just got off the phone with you. The guy with the busted van. Where exactly are you located? Where are we? Shit, brother, I don't even know. It's kinda been one of those mornings."

Eventually, we figured out how to get to each other, which allowed the Firestone guy to give us some directions that more or less got us to where we needed to go. Eventually. As we limped into the parking lot, we were encouraged by a long row of empty bays. The waiting room was a ghost town, too. Either we were lucky, or we were at the worst mechanic in Weatherford.

A tall man, the guy Dan talked to on the phone, got a quick rundown of our situation and told us his mechanic should be there in about a half hour. Dan and I sat down to wait. There was a *Vikings* marathon on the television.

"You ever watch this show, Harlin?"

"Used to. Got pissed off when Ragnar dumped his kick-ass shield-maiden wife for that skinny, no-ass princess. Fell behind after that and never caught back up."

Dan looked up at the TV.

"Which one is his wife?"

"The one riding on the horse next to the younger guy. That's Ragnar's kid. He went to live with his mom after his dad cheated on her."

"She left him?"

"Viking shieldmaidens weren't known for taking a lot of shit."

Dan laughed, and I went out to smoke. The sun was rising higher, and it was getting warm. I didn't want to be in Weatherford anymore. I was ready for the desert.

We were on our second episode of *Vikings* when a husky dude wearing a work shirt and a hangover came lurching through the door.

"I think that's our dude, Dan."

"About fucking time."

Tall Firestone guy gave Hungover Mechanic Dude the rundown on the van. Instead of hustling his ass to work, he groaned and yawned and hit the coffee machine on a quest for early morning clarity.

"Seriously," said Dan.

This mechanic didn't work like any master of the wrench I'd ever seen. There was no investigation. Dude just kept taking things apart. I'm no expert on Ford cargo van engines, but this guy was pulling shit out left and right and just piling it up on the ground. Maybe he had to go that deep to get to the root of the problem, but it sure seemed to me like he was caught in some fugue state that he might not snap out of until he got all the way to the transmission.

Dan was getting twitchy. He'd watch Ragnar axe some fools on the television for a minute and then start squirming around in his seat to try and see what was going on out in the bay. I understood. You get that far down into the engine, and you could be talking serious money. Not to mention that folks were depending on us to be in Marathon come sundown.

About a hundred years later, Mechanic Dude stuck his head in the door and motioned for Firestone Guy to come outside.

"That don't look good."

"Not especially, Dan."

When he got done talking with Mechanic Dude, Firestone Guy stared down at the ground and rubbed the back of his neck. He lingered in the garage area for about ten minutes, kicking tires and wiping clean stuff with a rag. When he ran out of things that didn't need to be done, the man took a heavy breath, came back inside, and walked over to us.

"Dan."

"What's it look like?"

"Well, you were right about blowing a spark plug."

"Can you get it fixed? I know you need a special kit."

"I don't think it's gonna be that easy. My guy says something inside the engine actually hit the sparkplug to knock it out. So you could put a new plug in, but it would just happen again."

"What does that mean?"

"He thinks you're looking at major work. Maybe have to redo the heads."

"How much does that cost? I mean, can you guys even do that?"

"We can, but it's not cheap. And once we get inside, it might be you need a whole new engine. "

"So we're talking in the thousands?"

"Unfortunately, yes."

"That van might not even be worth what it'll cost to fix it. I wish this would have happened before I spent a couple hundred bucks getting the brakes done."

Firestone Guy laughed.

"Doesn't it always happen that way?"

"You're telling me, brother."

"I'll give you guys a minute to figure out what you want to do."

There are times in life where you need to figure out what to do next, but try as you might, no amount of figuring will add up to a solution. This was one of those times. I half-expected Dan to lose it any minute, but he just kept plugging.

"We don't have a lot of options, Harlin. People bought tickets. The bands have been booked. All of that goes straight to hell if we can't get this gear to Marathon."

"Shit, Dan. We know enough musicians that somebody has to have a van they aren't using."

"Didn't you say Tex was renting one for the trip?"

"That was his plan last I heard. But I don't think he's leaving until tomorrow."

"Can you call and see if he has any extra room? We might have to wait and go with him."

I didn't want to wait until tomorrow, and I sure as hell didn't want to backtrack through Fort Worth only to end up in Denton. My mind was set on Marathon. That's where I wanted to be. Besides, Tex would have his drums, Mama Tex, probably his dogs, and who knew what else. He'd want to help, no doubt, but I was afraid we'd be trying to cram two loads into one van.

"Hah-lin. How you doing buddy? Y'all already down there?"

"Not quite, Tejas. We hit a snag in Weatherford."

"Uh oh. What's going on?"

"Dan's van died. We're stuck at a Firestone with no way home and no way down."

"I'm having some transportation issues of my own. You know that van I was gonna rent?"

"That's sorta why I was calling."

"Well, that's not gonna work out the way I thought."

"You got a backup plan?"

"Hell, I might have to rent a minivan and get creative with my packing."

"You can fit more than you'd expect in a minivan."

"I know, but I got Mom and her friend and the dogs and my drums. It's gonna be a tight squeeze."

"Good luck with it, buddy. I'll keep you posted on what we figure out."

"Do that. And let me know if I can help. If you need someone to come pick y'all up or something."

"Will do. Talk you later, bud."

I hung up the phone and looked over at Dan. He'd been watching me real close and trying to follow along with the conversation. I just shook my head.

"No go?"

"Nah, his travel plans are almost and fucked as ours."

"I guess we're gonna have to rent something. We don't have any other choice."

However much time we spent looking for a mechanic, we tripled that trying to track down a rental that would fit our significant needs. Dan called Avis and Hertz and Budget and Enterprise and some of them twice. They tried to sell him on trucks and trucks with camper shells and minivans and a couple other things that wouldn't come close to hauling our load.

We found salvation in half a funky shoebox of a U-Haul office filled with scores of creepy-ass dancing "Solars." Four-inch tall gnomes and kitties and elves and such populated every window and bright spot, ticking and tocking back and forth on the sun's dime. Their eyes watched you, daring you to purchase one and suction-cup it to the back window of your car, royally weirding out or pissing off everyone that would ever have the misfortune to get stuck behind you in traffic ever again. And the smell. Dear god, the smell.

Some unholy bastard had just microwaved his lunch, which as far as I could tell, was bad curry poured into a dirty diaper stuffed with five pounds of ground chuck and left sitting the sun for a two and a half weeks in August. The stench violated your nostrils and left a rancid sheen on your skin. I tried not to breathe unless absolutely necessary, but things weren't exactly moving fast.

Dan was haggling with the clerk, a sad man who looked like a beaten-down, grown-up version of Paul Williams if Paul Williams had been an adorable child star instead of a full-grown actor.

"I don't know how he came up with this price," he said. "I'm gonna have to try and do something in the computer to make these numbers work."

"That's what the guy on the phone told me," said Dan.

"I know. I know. I'll find a way to make it work. How many miles are y'all travelling?"

"A lot."

"Where you headed?"

"Marathon."

"Where's that?"

"Down in the Big Bend area."

"How far is that?"

"I'm not exactly sure, but something like four hundred miles."

"Oh boy. I'm really gonna have to work that computer. I might even have to call someone."

"Whatever you gotta do, brother."

U-Haul Paul started punching away at his computer and muttering to himself. Sure enough, he got someone on the phone and started rehashing the gist of what he'd been saying ever since we walked in the door. That whoever Dan talked to on the phone gave him a lower price than he should have, but the price had been given, and now our new friend was going to have to do some computer magic to make it work. It was a big production. In the end, he succeeded in making what would have felt like a full-on fiscal corn-holing feel like merely half a corn-holing.

Dan started signing paper work while U-Haul Paul peppered us with questions about our trip.

"What y'all headed all that way for?"

"We're putting on a show."

"Like a music show?"

"Yeah. It's called the Big Bender."

"What kind of music?"

"Country."

"Y'all musicians?"

"Nope," said Dan. "We're the roadies."

"I know a guy that was a roadie for the Eagles. Used to travel all kinds of places and come home with the craziest stories. One day he just stopped going on the road with the Eagles. The stories ran out after that. I never could figure out why."

"Seriously?"

U-Haul Paul shook his head.

"My friend's a carpenter now. Never thought a guy like that would have ended up a wood cutter. But then again, I never figured I'd end up working in a place like this."

I felt small for having judged this man by his Solars and his smells. One glance was all I needed to paint my own pathetic picture of his life and reduce him to a caricature when, in reality, he was just like me and everyone I love. Holding on to stories and wondering how it came to be like this. Working a job you don't love to pay for all the things that keep you from being free.

U-Haul Paul eventually handed over the keys, and we walked through his shop to a small lot crammed full of trucks. Dan climbed behind the wheel and fired up our new rig. It didn't exactly purr, but it would have to do. I went to the back of the truck to signal Dan on how much room he had before crashing into something. It was tight, but we got her out. All we had to do now was head back to the Firestone, transfer our load, and get gone. It was almost noon. Sunset in the desert was becoming a fairy tale.

HOLY SHIT, COWPOKE

The good people of Weatherford hold a special place in their hearts for riders of bulls and the son of the big man upstairs. I feel confident tossing this speculation out into the world on account of an advertisement I saw while Dan and I were cruising the main drag in our sweet U-Haul. It was a poster for a showing of a film by the name of *Cowboys & Jesus The Movie*. Sure as hell feels like there should be a colon in the title, but I ain't found it yet. Even checked the Facebook page. Damn thing's got over sixteen hundred likes.

PROJECT HABAKKUK

During the Second World War, a man called Geoffrey Pyke somehow managed to sell Winston Churchill and his advisors on a plan to build a massive aircraft carrier out of ice. Project Habakkuk, the code name of this top-secret project, was technically to be constructed out of pykrete, a mixture of wood pulp and ice, but

I'm gonna take a little poetic license and just call it a ship made of ice. It just sounds a hell of a lot better that way.

What does this have to do with the general exploration and enjoyment of Texas? Not a damn thing, really. Except that the U-Haul Mojica and I ended up in had a big-ass picture of Project Habakkuk on both sides. I'm no stranger to U-Hauls. I lived in thirteen different places during my first twelve years in Denton, and every time I schlepped my shit, I did it in a U-Haul. I've seen moving trucks adorned with everything from alligators to space shuttles, but I'd never before seen or heard of anything like Project Habakkuk.

Dan and I didn't even notice the picture on the side of our new rig until we got back to the Firestone station to pick up our gear. Had it been a snake made of ice, it would have bitten us on the nose or the ass or whatever came into striking range first. I remember moving one of Joe Pat's massive speakers from the van to the truck and catching a glimpse of the Habakkuk out of the corner of my eye.

"Holy shit, Dan. You see this?"

"What is it, brother?"

"This crazy-ass aircraft carrier made of ice on the side of our truck."

Dan stopped what he was doing, walked over to where I was standing, cocked his head and stared at the U-Haul while he read the little blurb about the ice boat. Pretty quick after that, Firestone Guy noticed we'd stop moving our junk out of his garage so then he came over and started looking at the side of the truck.

"Project Habakkuk?"

"Top-secret project," said Dan. "Aircraft carrier built out of ice and wood pulp."

"How in the hell does something like that even work?"

Without even knowing it, Firestone Guy had perfectly summed up the story of Project Habakkuk. Old Geoffrey Pyke's U-Boat battling aircraft carrier had plenty of promise, but the practicality of the beast was sorely lacking. By the time they'd finished construction on the scale model, it measured sixty feet by thirty feet and weighed in at a cool thousand tons. They revamped and reimagined a few times, but ultimately, it would have been far too expensive—and would have required more steel than a traditional ship just to build the refrigeration housing—for them to ever complete the full-sized version. And so, somewhere in Canada's Jaspar National Park, the story of Project Habakkuk slowly melted away only to be remembered by weary travelers and folks who just happened to catch a glimpse of the U-Haul that carried its name.

LONG (U) HAULING

"Do you like talk radio, Harlin?"

"Depends on who's talking. I used to listen to the Ticket when I had a commute."

"I love Mike Rhyner. That is one cool dude."

"I'm a Norm guy myself. I like it when he's gets pissed and starts yelling at some idiot."

"I mostly listen to talk radio when I drive. After enough years in the bar business, music is the last thing I want when I'm not at work. Give me a baseball game or just someone talking."

The Ticket faded not too far out of Weatherford. I tried bouncing for a good station, but out in that neck of the woods it was all red-dirt, country bullshit, crappy pop music, folks calling in to talk about their financial turmoil, and super conservative assholes trumping up the Donald as a potentially viable candidate for the presidency. I got mad listening to them talk shit about reason and logic. Bitching about immigrants and refugees and rabble-rousing about building a giant fuck-off wall on the Texas-Mexico border.

"Goddamn it, Dan. America is supposed to be the melting pot. How can a state that loves chili as much as Texas not realize that it takes all kinds of different ingredients and flavors for something to be good?"

Dan kind of chuckled, but he didn't say anything. That's not unusual. Mojica can tell a story as good as anyone, but he can also be a real quiet motherfucker. A man who loves the desert as much as he does seldom feels any obligation to fill a perfectly good silence.

In the absence of chatter and music, I had plenty of time to watch the shifting landscape. These parts of Texas were unfamiliar to me. I'd been to Lubbock once as a kid with my dad, but the town itself and the drive there is barely a memory. My bachelor party was a BBQ cook off at the Rattlesnake Round Up in Sweetwater, Texas. That was almost ten years ago, and I really only remember the park where we camped and how a diet of meat, chili, and beer is less than ideal when the only facilities available to you are portable. This was my first grown-up ramble to the Big Bend area. I was desperate to remember everything I could.

The world out there is harsh. Eruptions of cactus-covered rock jut from the landscape. The twisted wreckage of a burned-out cedar forest sprawled along for miles outside my window like something Tolkien would have spent about thirty pages describing before getting some hard-luck hobbits lost in that shit. We saw a castle on a small mountain in the middle of nowhere. Not an ancient castle, but a castle nonetheless. Probably built by some desert baron, so they could look out over all the hardscrabble and laugh in its face as they lived like kings in a wasteland. I began to fall in love with how you could stare at nothing and everything simultaneously.

Signs in the Permian Basin advertised water sales in front of massive tanks in vast, empty fields. There were oil derrick graveyards, the final resting place of violent apparatuses built to rape the land and steal its power. Rows of tiny houses, prefab and identical, littered the horizon in active drilling zones. None of the things I saw belonged where I saw them. They could not have occurred naturally. Cities like Midland and Odessa exist because there is oil in the ground, and someone has to be there to take it.

We stopped in Midland at the very worst Walmart I've ever had the misfortune to enter. The parking lot was pure chaos, especially for two dudes in a U-Haul. Dan parked near the back of the lot to avoid accidentally flattening the children darting out from behind cars or the people riding rascals because they hadn't lived right. We split up the grocery list. Dan went in search of vegetables and canned goods, and I picked out the meat and the bread and the condiments. We reunited in the beer isle, combined our hauls, and headed to checkout.

There was a guy in line in front of me who was a real asshole. Probably a roughneck. He was verbally whooping the clerk's ass something fierce, but she kept a smile plastered on her face.

"There ain't nothing to do in Texas but get drunk and do meth. I guess that means I'm out of luck because I don't drink. And I don't do no fucking meth."

"That's good, sir."

"I don't do meth because I'm not from Texas. I'm just here for work."

"Yes, sir."

"Texas ain't nothing but meth heads. But I'm not one of them because I ain't from here."

"That'll be thirty-seven fifty today, sir."

"Gimme some Camels, too. I'll smoke some cigarettes, but I don't mess with the meth like you Texans."

"I'm sorry, sir. You'll have to go to that line over there to get cigarettes."

"I can't just get them here?"

"No, sir. I'm sorry."

"All right, all right. You watch out for them meth heads, lady. Goddamn place is full of them."

Methy the Roughneck gathered his bags and headed over to the cigarette isle. I looked at the checkout lady, and she smiled and shook her head.

"What the hell was all that about?"

"I have no idea, sir," she said.

"I'm no expert, but if you make a point of telling a perfect stranger three or four times that you aren't on meth—you're probably on meth."

She laughed politely and kept on scanning our items.

Dan and I split the tab and headed back to the truck. We packed the cold stuff in the cooler and left the rest in bags in the back of the U-Haul. In a true stroke of genius, Dan had purchased a small bathroom trashcan that he loaded up with ice and beer and stashed between our seats. It was almost that time.

"I usually go all the way to Monahans and turn off there, but I'm thinking about taking 1053 this time. That good by you?"

"It's your party, Dan. I'm just along for the ride."

"Groovy."

The early morning wake-up and all the day's excitement started to get to me a little. I was feeling tired, my eyelids heavy. There wasn't much to look at outside of Midland, and my hamstrings were starting to cramp up from all the sitting. I was reaching the point of being bored or wanting to be someplace else when Dan spoke.

"Here's our exit, Harlin. Get ready."

We picked up 1053 and shot south. The sports radio station we'd been listening to choked to death on static. As we left the highway and the oilfields behind, the high desert sprawl unfolded before our eyes.

"You can look for some music if you want, buddy. Or I think there might be an NPR affiliate down here."

I fiddled with the radio, and Dan started fishing in our trash-can cooler. The world around us was transforming. There was sand instead of rock, and the hint of mountains loomed in the distance. I found a music station, and Dan handed me a cold one. The long, sad opening to Metallica's "One" crept through the speakers. We cracked our beers and cruised the dunes.

SCENESHIFTER (WE NEED TO TALK)

Denton, we have a problem. It's Friday night, and I've just returned from the City of Fountains. Your streets are crowded. Too crowded. Traversing the town square is more of a challenge than getting from one side of Kansas City to the other. Used to be, I could glide through your streets to the soundtrack of my latest mix CD. These days, I've got to start and stop. Bob-n-weave. Dodge the swarms of motherfuckers doing their goddamnedest to Denton the fuck up. It's more aggravating than a gnarly scratch on your favorite record because your favorite record is now full of gnarly scratches. The good dudes at Mad World on the square would never even let you in the door, old friend. You're bad for the rep. Immovable inventory.

MAPS AND STRANGERS

Getting a good look at that big, fuck-off Texas sky is not an easy thing to do when you're sailing a U-haul across the desert. I was a cloudstruck twelve-year-old wiggling in my seat and craning my neck in every imaginable direction for a better view. Dan was kind to me. Patient. Even when I started motormouthing, he never complained about me wrecking the precious silence. Just like Kody Jackson in those windmill fields, Dan was genuinely excited to share one of his favorite places in the world with someone who'd never been there before.

The sky was changing color by the minute, and all the stories Dan and Sinclair had ever tried to tell me about the desert were suddenly becoming real. My point of reference was expanding. I understood now. Dan and I were small things in a vast space. Insignificant. Texas will make you feel that way. Like you shouldn't be able to survive in a state so massive and full of wildness. But something, be it audacity or blissful ignorance, keeps you shuffling along, stumbling in and out of moments of wonder.

Dan put me on map duty. Like an honest-to-god, physical map that you can hold in your hand and you don't have to charge. It reminded me of the map my dad used to carry on family vacations. Directions to all the places you'll ever need to go all in one big book. A map that maintains its utility even outside of signal range.

My navigation skills must have gone to shit in the modern world of connectivity because I either steered us wrong or missed a road sign in Fort Stockton. That's the town where Dan and his wife Pam had to ride out the great desert blizzard of 2014. They got stuck there on the way back from Terlingua. Snagged the last hotel room in town that allowed dogs. Dan made trips to a bar across the street to watch football until they lost heat on the second day. After that, they just stayed in their room, drinking and smoking while the outside world froze.

Dan pulled into a gas station to get directions after he realized we missed the turn. A friendly old dude at the pump next to us struck up a conversation the minute he got out of the car.

"Whatcha hauling?"

"Music equipment. Van broke down outside of Ft. Worth, so we had to rent this."

"What's the story on that aircraft carrier?"

"Top secret project during the war. Apparently, it was made of ice."

"No kidding?"

"I only know as much as the truck told me. You live around here?"

"I do."

"We missed a turn a couple miles back. You think you could help us out with some directions."

"What road you need to find?"

Dan looked back through the driver's-side window at me.

"What road was it, Harlin?"

"Forget the road," said the man at the pump. "Where you fellas headed?"

"Marathon," said Dan.

"Let me pay for my gas, and I'll get you where you need to go. It's on my way home."

"So we'll just follow you?"

"Yessir."

Our gas station buddy pulled his truck around the back of the store and picked up a country road. We followed behind and kept our beers low. After a couple minutes, he pulled over. Dan stopped the U-Haul, and I rolled down my window.

"Y'all just stay on this road for about another mile or two until you come to a T. Hang a right there and you ain't gotta do nothing else the rest of the way to Marathon. You'll be there before you know it.

"Thanks, buddy," I said. "You have a nice evening."

The man waved goodbye and drove off. Dan and I kept on keeping on until we got to that T in the road. We hung our right like the man told us to do and set our sights on a belated happy hour in Marathon, Texas.

WRITING

I was gonna write some more yesterday, but I checked my word count, and it was 666. Can't fuck with that. My metal friends would never forgive me.

HOMESTRETCH

The mountains had us surrounded before I ever saw them coming. It's an odd thing to say about wonders a thousand years in the making, but that's how it happened. One minute they're a streak of color on the horizon. You're looking at the sand and the abandoned pumpjacks and maybe thinking how nice it would be to take a dive into one of those dunes and just lay there and listen to Billy Thorpe slay an electro prog rock jam about the future that was supposed to be the future only now it's the past. Then you look up, and a satellite zooms across the sky, and all of a sudden the mountains are on top of you and the sun's sliding down them in a smoky blue colorwash that makes you loathe every minute you'll have to spend indoors for the remainder of your days. Eventually, you remember to start breathing again.

"Dan. Have we even seen any cars since we got on this road?"

"I think maybe two."

"This is a one hell of a wide open spot to be all alone in."

"That's why I like it."

We chugged along toward Marathon, all the while the pressure was building in my bladder. I wasn't sure if I'd make it, and I knew we wouldn't be seeing a gas station or any other place to stop until we got there. I breached the subject real casual like just in case emergency maneuvers were necessary.

"I bet you could just stop right on the side of the road if you needed to take a leak. No one passing by to catch you with your pants down."

"No doubt."

Neither of us said anything for a minute.

"Do you need to me to stop, Harlin?"

"I'm probably good for now."

"We're about fifteen miles out, and brother, I plan on getting there in ten minutes. But you just say the word if I need to pull over."

"Roger that."

The sun had already set on our dreams of watching it do just that by the time the first lights of Marathon came into view. It didn't look like much in the heavy dusk from the inside of a U-Haul moving truck. Just a quiet strip no longer than a city block. Maybe not even that. But as we got close enough to actually see the buildings, everything changed. A small, friendly-looking liquor store offered welcoming light to weary eyes. There were a couple of funky shops with folks inside and a bar with a patio out front.

But the real jewel was the Gage Hotel. It's the dominant structure on Marathon's main drag. Rich adobe walls and heavy wooden doors that make you feel safe from the hazards of desert life. A long courtyard with fire pits and comfortable places to sit and look up at the stars. It's a swank-as-fuck joint that no doubt stocks many fine whiskeys and impressive cuts of meat.

"My brother and his fiancée stayed at the Gage last time they were out here."

"We can go check it out tomorrow," said Dan. "I wanna have a drink at their bar. But just one. I doubt it's a cheap drink."

It doesn't take long to get from one end of Marathon to the other. We barely had time for a couple of sips of beer before we arrived at the Marathon Motel and RV Park. Dan pulled into the parking lot and swung a left around the courtyard. Up ahead, we could see Joe Pat Hennan's van in front of one of the cabins. We slowed to a crawl and parked in a big empty field next door to them. Dan greeted his friend and Big Bender partner-in-crime with a hug. I didn't say shit to anyone because I was bolting for a dark spot in the field in search of someplace to be alone for a minute. In the midst of sweet relief, I saw lights popping up like dragon flies and hunched-over figures scuttling across the desert floor, so I zipped up quick and got the fuck back to the truck.

I was still hustling away from whatever was behind me when I looked up and fell into my very first high dessert waltz. Head tilted, leaning back, spinning slow circles trying to see all the stars. Like I could fall backwards without ever crashing into the Earth. It was the kind of shit that makes you feel all right about getting up at 4:00 in the morning and spending ten hours in a U-Haul.

SCENESHIFTER, PART II
(I DIDN'T MEAN IT, BABY)

Maybe it's the Lone Star and tequila talking, but I think everything is gonna be all right. I'm at the Silverleaf, and James McMurtry has the stage, and it's a packed house. Jackson is there with his lady. Sweet Kate is relaxing on the patio after her shift. Somewhere near the back, my neighbor Hank is drinking beer from a frosty mug. We're both dog tired after a long week, but the music keeps us going. It will continue to do so for nearly three hours.

When James and the boys finally decide that they're done for the night, the audience disagrees. We whistle and shout and clap and stomp until McMurty gives us what we want. This time around, it's just the man and his guitar and the "Lights of Cheyenne." A slow burner of an encore, but we hang on every word. Some of them, we sing along with him. We laugh when he gets to the part about the daughter with the cowboy problem, and I almost get misty when the antelope start grazing.

I look over to my right at Jackson. I want to talk to him, but I can't afford to miss a minute of the music. Besides, he's hugging on his lady, and that's not something I should interrupt. McMurtry nails the final note, and despite our vociferous protests, there will not be another song.

I retreat to the patio to smoke with Sweet Kate and her husband, Slobberbone's Brent Best. There's a buxom, older blonde lady all over Cornbread, the bass player from McMurtry's band. He's grinning and loving every minute of it. Ma and Pa Goliad walk up to me and we just look at each other like *Goddamn, what a badass show that was!* I mean, McMurtry is always good. But tonight he was real good. I order another beer even though I shouldn't because I'm too tired to finish it. All I want is to stay until they turn on the lights and kick me out, but I know I'll never make it. The music is still lingering in the cool, post-rain breeze. The night is too perfect to give up on. I am happy. There is no place else I would ever want to live, and I can't think of a damn thing that could ever make me leave. I love the Denton of the moment, and for the moment, she's enough to get me past all the other shit that isn't like it used to be.

UNDER THE STARS

That first night in Marathon was a dream played out at double speed. Dan and I checked into a nice half a cabin with two soft beds.

We changed into warm clothes to protect us from the desert cold. Beanies and scarves and fingerless gloves. Tall socks and zip-up jackets with insulation. We joined Joe Pat and Susie Hennen and their family for pizza on the front porch. Ballast acquired, it was now safe to resume drinking beer.

Joe Pat led us over to the courtyard that's the heart of the Marathon Motel. Strong adobe walls surrounding a little oasis with a fireplace and its big wooden mantle. On the far end, a beautiful fountain stands as the last line of defense before you hit the highway and then the desert after that. There are picnic tables and a fire pit and a patch of grass that shouldn't even exist. Standing in that courtyard is the safest you'll ever feel in a place where the storms come quick and the sun wilts the will to live and the plants and animals cut you with fang or thorn or quill.

The owner of the motel was drinking wine by the fireplace with some guests. Joe Pat went over to say hi and work out some final details for the show. Dan and I just stood there drinking it all in. The massive emptiness of the place was overwhelming. The sky full of stars—the darkness consuming everything else, even shrouding the mountains looming silently all around us.

Joe Pat returned with news of our of fellow Marathon Motel guests.

"There's an astrophotography convention that's been camped out here for the last few days. Marathon has some of the lowest levels of light pollution in all of North America."

"So there's literally dudes out here taking pictures of galaxies?" asked Dan.

"Galaxies, constellations, anything that's up there."

"Where are they?" I asked.

"Out in the darkness," said Joe Pat. "They move away from the motel lights, so they can get better pictures. This is their last night in town. By morning they'll all be gone."

"I believe I ran into a couple of those dudes right after we got here."

"You talk to them?" asked Dan.

"Not exactly."

We told stories and laughed as the night grew old. The stress of travel had dissipated in a glorious haze of pizza grease and beer and smoke. All that was left to do was fight the onslaught of sleep until defeat was inevitable and we surrendered to our warm beds with their soft pillows.

A GOOD HAT IS STILL YOUR BEST FRIEND

Bandanas won't cut it in the desert. They'll always be my go-to headwear, but I wasn't even halfway through my first day in Marathon, and I already needed more coverage. Skin's gotta be protected so you don't go lobster and end up looking like a saddle bag or get the fucking cancer.

Dan and I stopped in at the French Grocer because I'd somehow managed to forget my toothbrush. Had plenty of toothpaste, but no brush. The store was a little stretched-out rectangle near the center of town. I loved it immediately. In addition to having everything a traveler could possibly forget, it was the only source of supplies in town. If you needed it, and the French Grocer didn't have it, you'd be headed to Alpine with fingers crossed.

I was looking at pickled quail eggs or jerky or something like that when I noticed the back wall of the store was lined with straw hats. My eye caught on this real beauty with a Robert Duvall in *Lonesome Dove* look to it, even though this was straw and Mr. Duvall's was felt in the movie. I wanted that hat. Bad. But here's the thing. My head is shaped kind of funny. It's big and tall, and if the hat has any sort of fine, fedora-like crease down the middle, the damn thing is gonna sit high on my skull and make me look like a pinhead. No offense to pinheads.

I was cautiously optimistic as I plucked the hat off the rack and placed it atop my head. It felt good as it slid into place. Like it belonged there. I couldn't find a mirror, so I pulled out my phone and tried to gauge the fit by the reflection in the blank touchscreen. Didn't look half bad.

"Dan," I called out over the top of the small bread aisle. "Whatcha think?"

Mojica spun his head around and sized me up for a second.

"It's you, brother."

"Yeah?"

"Absolutely. And you're gonna need a hat like that in the desert."

I checked the price tag. Seventeen bucks. A steal for such a handsome, wide-brimmed provider of shade. So I bought it. That and a six pack of beer from the Big Bend Brewery. And a toothbrush, too.

Dan and I rolled back out onto the streets of Marathon, but they just as easily could have been the Streets of Laredo. I snatched off my bandana and shoved it in my bag, then I flipped on my new lid and enjoyed a shady stroll back to the motel. Under the awning in front of the main office, I snapped my first selfie and sent it to Sinclair, my dad, Leah, and some of my friends in Denton. The signal was still shit, but every once and while I'd get a text from someone back home. A couple of "hell yeahs" and a "badass" or two. I don't mean to brag or anything, but it really has been a struggle trying to find a proper hat to fit this fucking melon.

A handful of months after my trip to the desert, I was looking online for land to buy in Marathon, and I noticed the French Grocer was for sale. Believe you me, I've spent more than a few sleepless nights trying to figure out how to scare up about four hundred grand. I'd miss my friends, but I could sure get used to running that wonderful little store.

DESERT FRIENDS

Her name's Lucinda, but that don't matter because I call her Saint. The Patron Saint of Desert Wanderers and Honky Tonkers to be exact. Never seen her drink a drop, but we've sparked a couple in various backrooms and walk-in coolers around Denton. Take a quick break from the show, get a bit lifted, and then wade back into the crowd to quench our thirst for more music. Sometimes she sits in the back corner of the club all incognito-like. Other times, you'll find her front row, center stage. The only constant with the Saint is that she never ever bitches about paying cover. That's more than I can say for a lot of current Dentonites or Dentonians or whatever the hell they're calling us these days.

Leah and the Saint are good buddies, but I always felt my connection to her veered toward tangential. Shit tends to turn out that way when you're typically mixing it up in public with a head full of clouds and wrapped in the warm blanket of alcohol. You get to wondering exactly who you talked to and what you talked to them about. Did you ramble on way too long and become an ass-beating bore or accidentally blast someone with a face-full of cigarette smoke. Sometimes, you're not even sure you got all the names right. You wake up feeling guilty about not remembering everyone and everything, so you stay in your shell. Stick to old friends. Keep your mouth shut and stand in corners until the next time you catch a buzz and go pinballing around the bar.

That's sorta how I felt about me and Lucinda. At least until we ended up in the desert together. Dan and I were drinking beer, and she came walking right out of the darkness and said "Howdy, friends." But not in a bullshit, disposable-greeting kind of way. It was reassuring. Like she truly meant it. Next thing I knew, she was rolling up a joint and we were laughing and looking up at the stars and this old Basset Hound named Buster was laying at our feet getting enough good scratches and pets for an entire lifetime. Everything was fine and wonderful and warm despite the cold, and I almost believed that nothing in the world could ever make me feel sad again.

But sometimes, in the empty spaces between stories or laughter, the desert can be a very quiet place. And right when it gets the quietest, you start to feel yourself disappearing in the roar of all that nothing. That's when it's good to have a Saint. Every time I felt lost, Lucinda was my beacon.

I remember she found me wandering in the parking lot one night after dark.

"Harlin, what are you doing out here?"

"It's fucking cold."

"Well, no shit. It gets that way at night in the desert."

"I'm hungry."

"Come inside, and I'll make you something to eat."

She took me in and gave me a bottle of water and a ham and cheese sandwich. I offered her my stash, and she rolled us up a little joint.

"Hang out in here for a while," she said. "When the music starts again, we'll go back by the fire and listen to Joe Pat."

We sat in her warm room and smoked while I ate my sandwich. She taught me the right way to pronounce Marathon, so the locals wouldn't think I was an outsider. We talked about her place in the desert, and she told me stories of the history of the people of Big Bend country. I stole some of them for this book.

Back in Denton a couple months after the Big Bender, I ran into Lucinda at the Silverleaf. She was sitting there sipping a club soda and watching some cowboy with a pretty voice do his thing on stage. She looked good, like she was getting strong after some illness I probably heard tell of—but never asked about. My laptop was open, so I could try and reconstruct adventures that happened under dubious circumstances.

"You look like you're working hard, buddy."

"Hey, Lucinda. I was just thinking about Marathon."

"There are a hell of a lot worse places to think about."

"You know, you're in here," I said, nodding toward my laptop.

"Don't you fucking put my name in a book, Harlin."

I was stung.

"You don't wanna be in my book?"

"I like to do my own thing whenever I want to do it, and nobody needs to know about what I'm doing unless they're along for the ride. I don't want people on the lookout for me, and I don't need anybody else knowing about me."

"But I say a lot of really nice things about you."

"I don't doubt it, but you can say them to my face, or say them about someone else."

"All right, Lucinda. Whatever you say."

And that's how Lucinda who ain't really Lucinda became the Patron Saint of Desert Wanderers and Honky Tonkers. It may not be the name she was born under, but it fits.

THE BIG BENDER, FRIDAY NIGHT EDITION

I broke out my oldest shirt for the first night of the Big Bender, a hunter plaid flannel I got for a trip to Germany when I was in junior high. I bought it big then, so it still just barely fits. There are holes here and there, and the cuffs are tattered, but it's good for an extra layer of warmth when the weather gets cold. I knew from the night before that the temperature drops considerably in Marathon once the sun disappears behind the mountains.

Butch Hancock, a certified West Texas badass, was the first act of the night. The original plan was for him to headline, but he was gonna have to jet immediately after the show and head down to the Ghost Town in Terlingua to perform at SlimFest, a memorial for the late, great Slim Ritchey.

Butch was gigging that night with this son, Rory. My first impression of the kid was that he was born to raise hell on stages all across Texas. Before the set started, he was running around shirtless, hopped up on energy drinks, and spinning knobs on the PA. Dan watched him for a while and got this expression on his face that only a parent wears. It said, "This kid's gonna be a handful, and someone is gonna lose sleep over it." Kid comes by it honest, though. When your daddy's a bona fide legendary songwriter-philosopher-artist and you grow up in the desert, you're bound to develop at least a bit of a wild streak.

The Hancock boys launched into their set, and the crowd ate it up from the start. Classic West Texas tunes. Guitar chords strung together in a way that make you wanna throw on some boots and a pearl snap, and lyrics that could make even good songwriters feel like throwing away their pens. But it wasn't just the music. Butch had professional stage banter. He worked the crowd into an aw-shucks frenzy.

"Did y'all ever stop to think about what reality really is—as opposed to what it appears to be?"

No one said anything for a second, like they expected a softball toss and got a word problem instead. Then someone in the crowd shouted "Marathon!" Butch just laughed and moved on to the next song. Couple numbers later, he was back at it again.

"Anyone ever been to Lubbock?"

"Yeah!" came the reply from about half the audience.

"Why?"

Butch kept right on weaving his spell. He'd blow us all away with some beautiful piece of writing and then get everyone working together to nail a song with an audience participation part. People were sitting around fires and at picnic tables and on blankets in the grass. Smiling and drinking beer and wine and mysterious concoctions in big gas-station cups and generally loving exactly where life had taken them at that point in their existence.

And then just like that it was all over. Butch and Rory did their last number, packed up their guitars, and headed south to Terlingua. I must have gotten caught in some sort of desert time warp because it all seemed to happen so fast that, except for some notes I scrawled in my little Moleskine, I wasn't even sure it happened at all.

Next thing I knew, Joe Pat and his band had jumped on stage and they were absolutely letting it rip. Denton national treasure and multiple Grammy-winner Jeffrey Barnes was throwing down on two saxophones at once like it wasn't even shit. Susie Hennen was right there next to her man belting out harmonies, and Tex Bosley, the hardest working drummer in Texas, was keeping the beat while warming his backside by the courtyard fireplace. A small faction of Denton had invaded Marathon, and we were making ourselves feel right the fuck at home.

WHEN IT'S TIME, IT'S TIME.

Joe Pat and the Industrial Street Jug Band were still doing their thing, but I was about out of gas. It was cold and getting colder. Even by the fire, the chill had teeth. It probably didn't help that I was wearing shorts, but it's also just an old desert trick. One minute you're sweating and the next you're shivering.

I found myself sitting by a fire, surrounded by strangers, grappling with whether to call it a night or stick it out. A warm, well-lit place sounded nice, but I hated the idea of being all alone. I didn't want the night to end—I just wanted it to keep going someplace else. Someplace with lights and food and nice places to sit.

Our cooler was on the other side of the courtyard over near the band. Like a drunken ninja, I snagged an empty twelve pack box and loaded it up with some beers and a few club sodas. I was about to shut the lid on the cooler when I spotted the five-pound chub of bologna we'd picked up in Midland. Yeah. I was gonna need that, too. I snuck out the back gate and vanished into the night.

You don't always realize how drunk and exhausted you are until you have to walk a long way in the dark. That's when it hits you: the realization that this should be a very simple task, but due to circumstance of your own creation, it's become a mammoth undertaking.

I had to leave the confines of the Marathon Motel and RV Park and travel some distance down a gravel road to get to where I was going. I did the Boracho Two-Step for what seemed like miles. Two quick shuffles forward. Pause and Sway. Stumble one step back and repeat. The terrain was uneven, and the bigger chunks of gravel were motherfuckers.

I was freezing and wheezing by the halfway point, or at least what I estimated to be the halfway point. I had no real way of knowing for sure. The trek seemed even longer because I was walking toward nothing. I would be alone in the house while everyone else enjoyed the fire and music. Best case scenario, I'd crash out in a comfortable chair while obsessing over all the unknown fun I was missing. But it was too late to turn back. I'd already passed the lights of Joe Pat's place. Our cabin was just up ahead and to the left.

I kicked my drunken shuffle into double time at the sound of a pack of coyotes making demon noises in the darkness. Something told me they were after my bologna, and I was in no condition to do battle with wild animals. Finally, I reached the turn-off to the house. The driveway was a twisting, turning road a few hundred yards long. Take one step in the wrong direction, and you were likely to find yourself standing in a cactus or a yucca plant.

The sharp shit was kind enough to stay out of my way as I lurched towards the porch lights. I sighed heavily at the door, elated to have finally reached my goal. Before I left the fire-lit courtyard, it was possible that I harbored delusions of returning after putting on some warm socks and having a quick snack, but I was now certain that I would not venture down that road again until morning. My night was over. The sooner I accepted it, the better.

I barreled through the front door and dumped my messenger bag and battered box of provisions on the dining room table. There was a noise to my left. I looked up and saw none other than one

Dan Mojica warming up a can of beans and grinning like the cat that was about to eat a can of beans.

"Dan! What are you doing here?"

"Making beans."

"You going back out?"

"Brother, I did the hundred-mile zig-zag just to get here. I am in for the night."

"Been down that road myself. And lugging five pounds of bologna."

I held up my prize like a proud papa so Dan could see it.

"That'll go real nice with these beans, Harlin."

WHISKEY BEANS

The very best thing about the Big Bender was getting to know folks in the vacuum of the desert where the affiliations and affectations of everyday life cannot survive. You are who you are, and there's no use in pretending otherwise because there's no one around to care.

Within the confines of the Marathon Motel and RV Park, I connected, for the first time, with people who'd orbited my existence for the entirety of my life in Denton. The blurred edges of Silverleaf snapshots came into focus. Background music took center stage. The dude sitting two stools down at the bar was suddenly sharing a pizza with me next to a fire. Without all the bullshit like cell signals and mobile Facebook apps, strangers turned into friends.

The biggest of these new friends, and perhaps the one I most look forward to seeing back in the real world, is a man named Jimbo.

Tex and Jimbo rolled up on us while Dan and I were eating beans and bologna. The first thing I noticed about Jimbo was his bigness. Dude was huge and decked-out in cowboy clothes. Not ostentations, but he was rocking boots and a hat. Mojica was real happy to see him.

"Hey, buddy," he said as a genuine grin took over his face. "Thanks for making the trip out here."

"You kidding me? Thank you for putting it all together. This is gonna be a blast."

"Harlin," said Dan. "Have you met Jimbo?"

"I don't believe I have."

"He's one of my favorite regulars. Comes to the bar for most of the big country shows. I'm sure y'all have crossed paths when James McMurty or someone like that was playing."

"It's entirely possible. Stranger things have happened than me meeting someone in your bar and not remembering it."

Jimbo laughed. "He makes a good point, Dan."

I figured Tex was probably hungry after his set with Joe Pat, so I got out the bologna and started fixing up plates for him and Jimbo. I cut chunks of meat into little triangles and sprinkled them with my homemade BBQ rub so every bite would have just the right amount of flavor. Jimbo saw me working and came over to the stove to keep me company. He had a bottle of whiskey with him.

"You like cooking, Harlin?"

"Stove cooking will do in a pinch, but I'd rather be hanging out by the smoker with my dogs and a cold beer."

"I feel the same way, buddy."

We made small talk while I put the finishing touches on the food. I was trying to get a feel for the big man, figure out what kind of character he'd turn out to be. I figured him for a country boy. Someone who works with his hands for a living. An electrician or a rancher or something like that. I was so blinded by his hulking stature that I'd missed a few important clues. Jimbo's hat and boots were quality, as was his whiskey. He wasn't bringing no bottle of Evan Williams to the party.

I finished up the first plate, passed it to Jimbo, and then threw some more bologna in the skillet for Tex. My new friend tore into the food with the appropriate enthusiasm for a man who'd driven many, many hours only to start drinking in the high desert altitude.

"Damn, Harlin. You ain't messing around with this bologna."

"I never mess around when it comes to bologna."

Jimbo passed me the bottle, and I pulled deep to try and impress him. Not sure why I thought guzzling whiskey would make me seem like a big man in the eyes of a bigger man, but it probably had something to do with how that bottle looked like it belonged in a mini bar when Jimbo held it in his massive paw.

Tex's plate was just about ready, but the whiskey was giving me bad ideas. Little voices in my head were trying to convince me that the beans were thirsty. "Whiskey," they said. "The beans need whiskey." The plate was sitting on the counter right damn next to the whiskey. Jimbo was watching me. He could see the wheels spinning.

"Harlin. You sure you wanna do that?"

I looked him dead in the eye as I turned that bottle horizontal and flooded the beans with a river of brown.

"Nope. But it's not like I can unwhiskey them fuckers now."

In a futile attempt to absolve myself of culinary transgressions, I made like one of those pretentious chefs on cable cooking competition shows and ran a kitchen towel around the outer edge of the plate and then handed it to Tex. He took one bite, chewed twice, and did the heart attack stop.

"That's . . . that's an interesting flavor profile, Harlin. The beans, in particular, are unique. This isn't so much a whiskey sauce, but it's more like you poured actual whiskey, and a substantial amount of it, directly over the dish."

Jimbo and I were laughing our asses off like we were old friends retroactive to the respective dates we both started hanging out at Dan's bar. And now we even had a story to tell the next time we ran into each other and needed a laugh.

The night had taken a fine turn. I'd expected to stumble back to an empty, dark house, but instead I found bright lights, Dan and his can of beans, and, once Jimbo and Tex showed up, all the makings of an after party. Beer. Whiskey. Bologna. Freedom. We had everything but a bedtime.

I put on Sinclair's world-famous Late Boys mix, a sampling of Beach Boys tracks from when Carl took a larger role in the direction of the band and they were doing crazy shit like recording albums in Holland, only all the songs ended up being about how bad they missed California. I knew Dan loved the Carl Wilson era, and I figured it would sound real nice in such a serene and starlit setting. We went out to the patio to smoke cigarettes feeling good about the world and all it had in store for us over the next twenty-four hours.

Jimbo and Dan started to talk about how Charles Manson used to hang around the Beach Boys, while I tried to find a spot to text myself some notes that might not ever make their way out of the desert and into my email.

"That's the thing about Manson," said Jimbo. "Dude could sell. You don't convince people to do that kind of evil without some skill. That fucker could straight-up sell."

Jimbo knew more than a little about a lot of things. I've read some, and I couldn't throw out the name of an author or a book that he didn't know. Same went for movies and music. The dude could probably work with his hands, but I was sorely mistaken in thinking that was the extent of my new friend's talents. I learned a couple of valuable lessons late that night as I wandered around the house looking for a signal. First off, never judge a dude by his bigness. Secondly, don't go walking off the beaten path at night in the desert because you can get a shinload of cactus quills and not even know it until you go back inside and Tex asks why you got blood on your leg. And believe you me, those suckers are hard as fuck to pluck out when you're seeing two for one.

ONE ALPINE MORNING

I was the last one up in the morning. Dan and Jimbo were already showered and drinking coffee. Tex was rousting about the kitchen. I swung my legs out of bed and noticed that there were still some cactus quills stuck in my shin.

"Shit," I said. "Forgot that even happened."

"Harlin! How you doing this morning, buddy?"

"Still pulling these prickly motherfuckers out of my leg. How bout you?"

"Just fine, buddy. Managed to unfuck those whiskey beans after you went to bed, which by the way, was a damned impressive maneuver. One minute you were drinking beer and talking about the Beach Boys, and then all of the sudden you was tucked in and snoozing before anyone noticed. Even had your shoes and hat and belt all stacked and rolled up and ready to go for the morning."

"I do my best."

"You up for a little trip? Jimbo and Dan were talking about heading into Alpine for a bit. Poke around and see if we can't find a bar or something."

"My dad's been telling me to check out Alpine for years."

"Well, today is the day, motherfucker."

"I got time for a shower?"

"Make it fast. Train leaves in thirty."

The trip from Marathon to Alpine is a quick, thirty-mile jaunt on Highway 90. Traffic is virtually nonexistent, so you can haul ass. Civilization is an afterthought. It's just mountains and the high desert flora and fauna. Occasionally, you'll see a homestead carved out of the harsh territory, but they are few and far between. Cruising along in Jimbo's pick up, we may have been headed to Alpine, but we were singing about San Antone and Phoenix, Arizona.

Doug Sahm was still ringing in my ears when it struck me that someday this wondrous, remote part of Texas might get developed into cities and suburbs. One too many magazine articles or top ten lists or assholes like me writing down stories in books, and it could all be over. Folks get emboldened by tales of the must-see spots in Texas and venture out to Big Bend country. Hell, I'd only been there for a day and a half, and already I'd heard folks turn on Marfa for being full of hipsters and tourists. Marathon is the place to be, they said. It's still got that small-town feel.

KOKERNOT FIELD

Herbert Lee Kokernot Jr. built Kokernot field in 1947, and he built the goddamn shit out of it. It's a fortress of a stadium. Native rock for the walls. Beautiful iron gates adorned with intricately painted baseballs provide a touch of flourish for this temple to the national pastime. It was one of the first places Dan and Jimbo took us when we got to Alpine, and it instantly reminded me of Paul Richard's Field in Waxahachie. But even my hometown stadium doesn't begin to measure up to the diamond in Alpine. For starters, mountains surround Kokernot while Richard's Field is in the middle of a cemetery. They've both got their homefield advantages, but Kokernot is something out of a Ken Burns documentary. It feels historic. Hell, the great Satchel Paige once played an exhibition there.

Jimbo found a baseball in the parking lot, a fouled-off relic from the ghost of batting practice past, and tossed it to me. I put it in the center console of his truck and planned to keep it as a souvenir, but it disappeared somewhere during our adventures. Even though it was an old ball with a shitty imitation leather cover, it would have had enough sentimental value to earn a place on the mantle or in the garage. I could have had Dan and Jimbo and Tex sign it so as to always remember that morning at the ballpark.

Sul Ross and Alpine High School and a couple of independent league teams still play games at Kokernot. If my big dreams of owning land out between Marathon and Alpine ever become something more than dreams, I will watch a game there one day. I'll get a hot dog and a Dr. Pepper, and if there is any justice in this world, they'll have nachos for my wife. It doesn't take much to be happy when everywhere you look you find one of the most beautiful sites you've ever seen.

KILLING TIME IN HOLLAND

The historic Holland Hotel in downtown Alpine is a fancy joint. There are animal heads on the lobby walls and antique paintings and exposed beams and everything else you could ever want in a swank rustic getaway. It's got a real man's man vibe, but there's also a hint of the romantic that would appeal to our better halves. On that particular Saturday, men and women alike filed through the lobby, having their pictures made in front of the artwork or taxidermy marvels and inquiring about room rates and reservations.

The bar at the Holland has a real obnoxious mirror that makes you look yourself in the eye when you're drinking before noon. Or any other time for that matter. All the liquor is stashed in a secret compartment down below. I saw the bartender climb down there in search of tequila for someone to mix with orange juice. It would probably make a good place to hide out from the apocalypse, considering it's fully stocked with booze and cocktail olives.

We ordered a couple of Bloody Marys and a couple of beers, and Tex jumped in to do the honors. It was something like 37 fucking dollars for the four drinks. That's damn near a whole goddamn night at the bar in Denton. Out in the parking lot, there was an old white four-door sedan with "Food Shark" spray painted on one door and some strange symbols and gibberish on the other.

"What the fuck is that?" asked Tex.

"Hell if I know," I said. "But I like that motherfucker's style."

PLANTAINS AND SMASHING PUMPKINS

Harry's Tinaja looks like a desert shack some hermit from a Cormac McCarthy novel would have built out of whatever he could scavenge, and the inside is done up with antlers and skulls, license plates, guitars on the walls, dollar bills stapled to anything that would hold a staple, cowboy hats, and a bunch of other random shit thirsty wanderers felt inclined to leave behind.

It was a cash-only kinda spot, but the beers were cheap and cold as hell. Harry's is the place to go if you want to drink and be left alone. Sorta like my Barage, only with mountains and big-ass, wide-angle skies and none of the folks from back home that I usually invite over for a few rounds and some laughs.

Dan grabbed the first round, and I picked up the second about five minutes later. It was warm enough out to awaken our beerlust. Some dudes on the patio were playing guitar and sorta singing a little bit. Live music, sunshine, and bottle of Lone Star. It was shaping up to be one sweet fucking day. I sat down at a picnic table next to Jimbo and Dan.

The Tinaja didn't sell any liquor, but no one seemed to care about us pulling straight from Jimbo's traveling bottle. The Smoking Cuban, a food truck with a logo designed by way of an internet collaboration with an anonymous Ukrainian, had most of my attention until I started getting ugly phone calls and texts from

Leah. It seems the Barage had sprung a mysterious leak, and she was dancing towards frantic.

Being nine or ten hours away, I did the only thing I could. I ordered another drink. Then I pulled out my phone, and hoped like hell I could sneak a text message through the mountains to Juan Verde. After that, I went back to drinking beer and thinking about that food truck because I knew beyond the shadow of a doubt that if my S.O.S ever made it to him, my friend would pack up baby Green Bean and drive over to our house without a moment's hesitation. Once there, he would calm my frazzled wife while simultaneously identifying and eliminating the source of the mysterious puddle so that I would be free to resume partying in the desert and pretending the rest of the world didn't exist. That is, after all, the entire reason we are so drawn to the desert. It's the ultimate disconnect from a world that so often feels so ruined.

Maybe something like that was running through Harry's mind when he traded a perfectly good life in Germany for one in Alpine. Legend has it, he was traveling across Texas by train. Alpine was not his ultimate destination, but he disembarked there in search of new glasses or something similarly mundane. Harry liked Alpine, and so he opened a microbrewery, which was successful enough until a hybrid of entrepreneurial and domestic inconsistencies led to a divorce and the dissolution of the business. The Big Bend Brewery got the tanks, and eventually, Alpine and the all the rest of us got Harry's Tinaja.

We spent the remainder of our time in Harry's bar munching on these fried plantains called *tostones* from The Smoking Cuban, buying rounds, occasionally sitting very stoically and gazing at the mountains, and in the end, singing that song by the Smashing Pumpkins where there's a killer in you and a killer in me and they're both the same killer and one of us used to be a little boy.

Eventually it was time to return to Marathon. Dan had to get back to preside over the last night of the Big Bender. There were ribs and chicken and bologna in our cooler, as well as a couple of smokers near the chuck house, which needed my attention. Tex had two gigs to play, and Jimbo had a long night of drinking beer and listening to music ahead of him.

We hit the local grocery store on the way out of town to pick up charcoal and other supplies. Tex grabbed a six pack of Tejas Lager made by the Big Bend Brewery for us to share on the ride home. He had big plans for the cans, so he asked us to drink gently.

Jimbo handed his iPod to me for the ride back, and I went straight for the Dwight Yoakum. It was a fine fucking afternoon. I hope to have another like it someday.

THE BIG BENDER: SATURDAY NIGHT EDITION, PART 1

Night two of the Big Bender promised to live up to the high expectations set by its predecessor. An encore performance by Joe Pat Hennan and the Industrial Street Jug Band would no doubt feature some choice cuts from a musical outfit with a seemingly limitless catalog. And Cornell Hurd, a country OG of varying degrees of infamy and renown, was slated to headline the show. I would end up missing every minute of the whole damn thing because someone wisely decided that the music-craving masses needed ballast to make it through the night. The responsibility of providing that meaty, smoky ballast toppled down the pecking order until it landed squarely upon my shoulders.

Resigned to my impending solitude, I turned my attention to the meat. The meat was the key. People would get drunk, then hungry, then they would find me. I would be lauded as a hero for sacrificing my own enjoyment just to feed my fellow desert travelers. It was my only shot at sharing the spotlight with those who could pluck, sing, fiddle, or keep the beat.

I feel at home next to a smoker, where life slows down and you measure time in cuts of meat. A pork loin is roughly three and a half hours. KC style ribs take five—two hours open, two in foil, and that last one with the tin sheets peeled back so the smoke can get at them. Chicken is somewhere between two and three hours provided you can get the smoker hot enough. And Brisket, well, that's none of your fucking business because each and every smoker of meat has to solve that riddle their own damn self.

MOTORCYCLE CHRIS

Motorcycle Chris is a metal magician who just happened to have a pile of wood we could use for the smoker. Dude goes way back with Lucinda the Saint. They've been desert-running buddies for years, and they were something else even before that. He used to have a place in Denton, but he sold it and moved out to Alpine.

He lives in a sort of vintage junk shop museum shrine to the almighty motorcycle. You could spend a week there and not finish taking a visual inventory of all the treasures he's got. I'd wager there's at least a couple rolls of film worth of pictures in my phone. Old school stuff I snapped so I could show Juan Verde when I got back to Denton—or my Dad over the holidays. All that real-deal, priceless shit you can't buy on Amazon.

There'd been a fair amount of beer drinking going on, and I was starting to think how cool it would be to have this master craftsman build me a smoker. Not just any smoker. But my dream smoker. A vertical job like a silo with round racks on the inside that spin so you can get at the meat easier. I cracked another beer and pulled a notepad out of my bag, so I could sketch it out for Chris.

"See, you got the firebox offset over here. And this big-ass vertical cylinder is the smoke chamber. You follow me?"

"Yup."

"I was thinking there could be a metal rod that goes right down the middle of the smoke chamber and holds the shelves in place. Maybe drill some holes in it—or at least spots for cotter pins—so the distance between shelves could be adjustable."

"That wouldn't be too hard."

"So you could build it?"

"Oh, yeah. I've built something like that before."

"How much would it cost to have you make something like that?"

"Nothing."

"Nothing?"

"I only work on motorcycles."

"Like exclusively?"

"Exactly like exclusively."

"So even if an old friend of some old friends offered to pay good money to have a smoker built, you wouldn't do it?"

"Nope. I only work on motorcycles."
"What you got against smokers?"
"Nothing. I just don't want to build one."
"You get that much motorcycle work out here?"
"I get enough that I don't have to work anything I don't want to work on."
"Damn, man. What's that like?"
"It don't suck."

THE BIG BENDER: SATURDAY NIGHT EDITION, PART II

The party vibe shifted as we meandered toward sundown. Thick, noxious clouds belched from the smoker. Gray smoke. Not the fine blue smoke that infiltrates the meat without turning the rind bitter. People standing nearby coughed and moved away. Joe Pat and the band were mid-sound check, prompting further defections from the BBQ-producing outskirts of the Marathon Motel. The courtyard, with its fires and fountain and music, would soon take center stage. A part of me held out hope that Jimbo or Dan would stay to drink beer and tell stories while I cooked, but it was too much to ask. I would be alone in the night with the smoke.

Sometimes you get stuck running the smoker, and that turns into running two smokers because one of the fire boxes doesn't have a grate so there's no airflow and the coals are smothering themselves. Then you find an old shovel and transport your smoldering coals from the firebox of one to the belly of another, thus creating a grilling zone so you don't have to worry about serving raw chicken because at an event called The Big Bender, folks just might eat it. And that ain't good. When the flames start jumping and you can finally see that it's gonna all work out there's nothing left for you to do but dance to "Happy Day" by Taj Mahal while the coyotes sing backup. And sometimes you have to listen to it twice, so you can retrace the happy footsteps you left in the dirt the first time around.

THE BIG BENDER: SATURDAY NIGHT EDITION, PART III

The hungry masses flooded back to my realm during the break between sets. I could hear them coming before I could see them. It was a rowdy, tipsy mob, but we were ready for them. I had all the meat chopped and properly rested, and Mama Tex and her crew had put together a couple sides. I grabbed two beers from the fridge and got the hell out of the way. Eating wasn't on my list of things to do after spending so much time cooking, and I sure as shit didn't want to get trampled in the Big Bender Grub Rush of 2016.

The Saint was sitting at a table away from the crowd.

"Mind if I sit down?"

"Be offended if you didn't."

"Good, because my fucking feet hurt."

"They're supposed to hurt when you been working hard."

I handed her my little prescription bottle, and she rolled us up some medicine. She was good at rolling. Her joints were never too big. Just enough to take the edge off.

"What'd you cook tonight, Harlin?"

"Some ribs, chicken, sausage, smoked bologna. And a can of SPAM."

"You gotta be kidding me. SPAM?"

"Hell no, I'm not kidding. It was probably the first thing gone."

The Saint chuckled and took a slow drag off the joint. She was small, but she was tough. Tough as hell. We sat there saying nothing for a while. That's one of the great thing about her. If you ain't got nothing to say, you ain't got to say shit. It stayed quiet until Dan walked over to us.

"Harlin, these people fucking love you. Thanks for cooking, brother."

"My pleasure, Dan."

"A couple folks were asking if there were any vegetables or anything like that."

I looked at the Saint before answering.

"Hell no there ain't no fucking vegetables, Dan. Do I look like the kind of asshole who spends three hours in the desert cooking vegetables?"

I tried to keep a straight face, but I couldn't, and neither could the Saint. Dan looked confused for a second then kinda half-laughed and turned around and went back to the crowd. The break between sets was almost over. Cornell Hurd would be starting soon. Lucinda the Saint got up to leave, but then turned back to me.

"You know, Harlin. You're pretty all right."

"I can't argue with you on that, Lucinda."

"Asshole."

I gave my friend a big, drunk hug. I could feel her breathing. Maybe even feel her heartbeat if I stood still enough. It occurred to me that it was perfectly fine to love folks. Ain't nothing lasts forever.

JIMBO, DAN, AND ME

Joe Pat and his family and some of his bandmates were still partying at one of the swank houses just outside the Marathon Motel grounds, but the night was lurching to an end for Jimbo, Dan, and me. We were essentially homeless, Cornell Hurd and his outfit having supplanted our cozy digs from the previous evening. We milled about the commissary struggling to drain the last of our beers and shuffling cots around. Dan pulled the U-Haul next to the still-warm smokers with the remnants of their embers glowing faintly within. The temperature was dropping, and the coyotes raised hell in the darkness around us.

Where the fuck was I gonna sleep? Where the fuck were any of us gonna sleep? That's not the type of riddle you want to solve when the night's reached its end and exhaustion is crashing down on you in waves.

"Maybe we could camp out around the fire pit," I ventured. "Toss a couple logs in before we fall asleep."

"I think it's gonna be colder than that, brother."

"I'm with Dan," said Jimbo. "I want some walls around me. Lots of wild things out in the desert at night."

"I'm thinking the commissary is our best bet," said Dan.

"We just need to move around some tables to clear some space."

The commissary wasn't big. The thought of all three of us sleeping cramped like that didn't sound too appealing. Jimbo and I were big men, and big men are prone to snoring. Factor in drinking and smoking and the dry desert air, and it had the makings of one noisy-ass night.

"I think I might set myself up in the back of that U-Haul, fellas."

"You gotta be kidding."

"Why the hell not? It's up off the ground. It's got walls. I can leave the door open if I want to fall asleep watching the stars. Or I can shut it all but a crack and make it dark as shit. Bet I'll fall asleep quick."

"That's all you, brother," said Dan. "I'll be in the commissary. It's got heat."

"Heat is good," said Jimbo.

While I was haphazardly throwing together my U-Haul penthouse, a tender-ass, Waltons-esque, not-altogether-un-comedic scene was unfolding in the commissary. Dan and Jimbo shoved around some tables to clear the necessary space for two grown-ass men to lounge uncomfortably on a couple of cots. I was not there to witness what happened, so I'll rely on Dan's report.

"Jimbo never got horizontal. The second he tried to put any weight on the cot, his ass hit the floor. We took one look at the wreckage and said 'fuck this.' We were just too tired and wasted to do anything about it."

And so they went to bed. Dan on his fully functioning cot, and Jimbo on a ragged pile of what used to be a cot. Somewhere in the distance, a coyote screamed at something that was probably nothing at all.

ADIOS, BIG GUY

I got a little choked up when Jimbo and I exchanged numbers. Sunday morning had arrived, and that meant the ride was over. Dan and I were still headed down to Terlingua for a couple days, but I was gonna miss my new friend.

"Harlin, it was damn good to meet you, buddy."

"I can't believe it's over already."

"Doesn't seem fair does it?"

"Not at all, Jimbo. Not fucking at all."

"You and Dan be safe down there in the desert, and we'll hook up back in Denton."

"For sure. I mean, we've been hanging out at the same place for years. We might as well try doing it at the same time."

"Don't be a stranger."

"Vaya con dios, Jimbo."

That's mostly how it went. A little anticlimactic after our adventures together and sorta sad. I drifted into melancholy as I watched the big man climb into his truck and drive away. In another place and time we could have been Bruce Springsteen and Clarence Clemmons, but I don't play the guitar or sing, and I never heard Jimbo say shit about the saxophone. Plus he's white.

Dan was in the shower, and as soon as he was out, we'd make tracks for the little *hacienda* in Terlingua. A hangover was kicking in, and my world was about to get real, real quiet.

PETROL ORBIT

We stopped for gas on our way out of Alpine. Dan hopped out of the truck to work the pump, and I just sat there trying like hell to keep my head from exploding. Drinking all damn day and sleeping in the back of a U-Haul will make the next fucking morning a miserable endeavor.

Out of the corner of my eye, I noticed a woman in her early sixties running laps around her car. They were slow laps. I thought she might be speed-walking at first, but when I turned to get a better look, I could tell that it was her version of a run. The laps circled her vehicle, as well as the travel trailer she and her old husband were pulling behind it. She churned out orbits like a satellite. Watching her loop round and round and round again made me want puke even worse. The sun was getting bright, and I was about to start wishing I was somewhere else when I heard Dan call out to the woman.

"How many laps for a mile?"

A chuckle hit me like a little hammer in that spot in your knee, and I almost forgot to feel like shit.

FUCKING U-HALS, MAN

"Harlin, can you do me a favor, brother?"

"Sure, Dan. Whatcha need?"

"You got a side pocket down in your door?"

"Sure do."

"Can you take my beer and stash it down there? We got a cop behind us."

"Seriously?"

"Yeah. And I don't feel too good about it."

We were just outside Alpine near the Kokernot Mesa. I was more hungover than I'd been in a long-ass time. Maybe I was getting too old to marathon-drink and escape unscathed. Or maybe I'd just done a shit job of following Dan's advice about drinking plenty of water while we were out in the desert. Whatever the case, I could feel my guts churning as we rolled down the winding desert highway. And now the cops were following us.

"Fucking, U-Hauls, man. I should have known we'd attract negative attention driving this thing so close to the border. There's a fucking bullseye on the side of this truck."

"I don't know, Dan. Maybe they just want to get a closer look at Project Habakkuk."

We laughed, but it was hollow. I could tell Dan was nervous about the cops, so I kept my beer between my legs. It wasn't even that I'd wanted a beer. Dan had offered, and I accepted. Anything to maybe feel halfway human again. After about a half hour of silently looking in the rearview mirror to see if we still had a tail, I broke and took a quick swig. My mouth was full of cotton. I needed it.

"Sorry, buddy. I probably should have asked first. I can hide my beer next to yours, if you want me to."

"They don't care about you. Trust me. If they pull us over, I'll be the one they're interested in."

We drove on without saying much. The radio was starting to hop with news of the death of Chief Justice Anton Scalia. Dan was getting tenser by the moment. That cop was still right behind us, and there weren't many options in terms of other cars or other roads to distract him from the great white whale right in front of him. He was gonna be with us all the way to the *hacienda*. One look at Dan was all I needed to be glad as hell I wasn't driving.

After about a hundred miles of contemplating how easy it would be for a dirty cop to murder a couple of U-Haul transients and bury them in the desert, we finally reached our turn. I drank deep as soon as we got off the main road. Dan's spirits picked up. We were so very close to his favorite spot in the world. He could taste the freedom of the middle of nowhere. I offered him the rest of his beer, but he refused.

"Driving with a police escort for that long still has me rattled. Think I'll wait 'til we're on private property."

"Fucking U-Hauls, man."

TERLINGUA RANCH

Dan was trying to figure out how to sneak on to the Terlingua Ranch wireless network, so he could process payroll for the Silverleaf. I'd already given up on all that shit, so I decided to wander around a bit. There was a gorgeous pool you could float in and look up at the mountains all around you. Dan had told me there was nothing like kicking back in that cool water with a beer and shutting off your brain for a while.

Next to the pool, there was this big, badass grill under a little pavilion. I walked over and cracked the lid and tried to get an idea of just how much meat you could fit on it at one time. All of the sudden I got a real strange feeling. Like fucked-up kind of strange. So I shut the lid to the grill and took a step back like maybe I shouldn't be doing whatever I was doing. That's when I saw him. This crazy-looking old motherfucker sitting about fifteen feet away from me, camouflaged by cactus and scrubby brush. I nearly pissed myself. Neither of us moved for a couple minutes. Then real slow-like, the old dude kinda smiled this creepy-as-fuck, but-not-entirely-unfriendly, smile at me, ducked his head down, and fucking disappeared. I was done exploring.

A BREAK-THE-GLASS SCENARIO

"Pay attention, Harlin." Dan was using his dad voice on me. "This is important."

We'd just turned off the highway in Study Butte, so we could check out a couple of bars and watch the sunset.

"You see that building right there?"

"Yeah."

"That's an emergency clinic. If one of us gets injured or some kind of fucked up to where we need medical attention, that's where we go. You only gotta make two turns to get here. Just don't forget which ones they are."

"Got it, buddy."

Dan was playing it smart. Making sure all our bases were covered. You have to plan for the unexpected when you're out in the desert. Because along with all the beauty, there is a lot of bad shit that can happen to a person. When it does, there ain't no minute clinic on every corner, and your smart phone is a paperweight, so you can't be calling no ambulance. You better know exactly where to go if you get bit or stung or sick from the sun.

DESERT REVERB

Dan warned me ahead of time.

"The desert has a way of making you feel out there, Harlin. Spacey. It's hard to put into words, but you'll know what I'm talking about when it happens."

He wasn't lying. The spacey feeling hit me on our way to pick up supplies before heading into Ghost Town. The road curved between two mountains and then started a heavy decline on its way to what passes for civilization out there. All the angst and homesick hungoverness that had plagued me all day broke like a fever. My body became weightless. If I hadn't been buckled in, I would have floated up into the air and gradually dissolved in the reverberations of every living thing that ever roamed under the desert sun. All the stories of this place, told, untold, and yet to be written, invaded my DNA, rendering me permanently unfit for life in the real world.

I choked back tears. And by tears I mean sobs. Ugly devastating sobs. I was not prepared for the yin and the yang of desert life. Everything and nothing mingling in the great expanse. I thought to myself that this must be what the astronauts feel like when they leave their ship and float above the world with only a simple space rope maintaining their connection to all they left behind.

The tears stung hard as they fought to escape the captivity of their ducts. Thank god for sunglasses. I held my breath because I was no longer certain there was air to fill my lungs. Dan must have noticed because he broke the precious silence.

"You doing all right, buddy?"

"Remember that spacey feeling you told me about?"

"Yeah."

"I think I just found it."

Dan chuckled in a gentle, fatherly way.

"Right on, brother."

THE DESERT RAT

We found him at the Bad Rabbit, the only place to buy lunch or beer in Terlingua Ranch. Dan wanted to pick up a six pack, and he was still trying to solve the Wi-Fi mystery. This scruffy dude who gave me a bad vibe from the get-go was sitting at a table talking to his laptop. Saying something about science or some shit like that. He reminded me of a distant relative that no one really wants hanging around all that much.

"Excuse me, buddy. Do you know how to get on the wireless out here? I'm having a little trouble."

"It all depends on the network," said the Desert Rat. "Are you a resident—or a guest?"

Something about the way he turned his head to look at Dan when he said "guest" was more than enough for me. I'd already accidently rolled up on the old fucker in the cactus. This seemed like a good time to go have a smoke and maybe not meet a crazy dude who'd end up murdering us.

GHOST TOWN

If you want a taste of what life might have been like in the wild, wild west, go to Ghost Town. Anything can happen there, but as far as I can tell, mostly people just sit and drink and look at the mountains. It's a magical place to do all three.

Right before you get to Ghost Town you'll pass through Study Butte. There's an underground bar called La Kiva. And by underground, I literally mean underground. A man named Glen P. Felts owned the place for over twenty years until he was found murdered one morning in the parking lot of his own bar. A local river guide was arrested for the crime—but the trial failed to yield a conviction.

By all accounts, Felts was a central figure in Terlingua. A linchpin of the local culture. His death sent shockwaves through the community. La Kiva, being an active crime scene, was shut down for some time. New owners have opened it back up for business, but I heard at least a few locals lament that it's just not the same. Dan thought highly of Mr. Felts. He keeps a special bottle of Sotol from La Ciudad de Chihuahua on the top shelf at the Silverleaf in honor of his fallen comrade.

On more than one occasion, I've heard Mojica express great trepidation—that his life will end at the hands of some gun-toting asshole waiting for him outside the bar. I wonder if he thinks of that when he remembers Glen P. Felts. Maybe he even wonders when his time is coming. Or maybe that's just some shit all bar owners say. It's a brotherhood, after all.

We cruised into Ghost Town a few hours before La Kiva opened for the day, so we decided to hit a joint called The Boathouse. Ours was the only U-Haul in the parking lot. Big shock. There was a gal with a friendly smile working behind the bar. She was wiping things down in a way that suggested a shift change was on the horizon, but she stopped almost immediately to get us a couple cold beers. We took our drinks out to the patio to enjoy the view. Mountains and clouds and desert plants as far as the eye could see. Depending on the time of day, you might never find the same spot on the same mountain twice on account of everything changes color with every movement of the sun.

There were a couple of dudes on the patio breaking down sound gear left over from the night before. The Boathouse, for the last two days, had been the site of SlimFest, a tribute to the late great Slim Richey. Slim was a lone star music legend who rocked a long, white wizard beard and called himself the Most Dangerous Guitarist in Texas. A stone cold killer on the electric guitar, Slim could do everything from jazz to country to western swing. His memorial party was a raucous, two-day affair that was not to be missed. It's the same place that Butch and Rory Hancock had torn ass across the desert to get to after playing their Big Bender set. You can bet it was a real wild scene. The way I heard it, folks were grabbing handfuls of Slim's ashes, dancing into the desert, and tossing them into the void. If I ever die ... on second thought, fuck that.

Dan went off somewhere to see if he could find enough signal to make a phone call, so I wandered around and took pictures of stuff. Mountains, bar decorations, a wooden statue of Slim on the little stage outside, and a row of port-a-johns that looked permanent. The sun was out in full force, but it was a dry heat. If you found a bit of shade, you could still lounge comfortably in the outdoors.

I spotted a little box sitting on a table. I thought maybe there might be stickers or some sort of memento from the show inside it, but I was wrong as hell. The label on the top of the box clearly stated that it was filled with the cremated human remains of none other than Slim Richey. Apparently, the festivities had raged to the point that they forgot about Slim. Or maybe the box was an empty vessel and Slim was already part of the desert.

For reasons I will never be able to explain, I had to find out. There was a sickening weight to the box as I picked it up, and my stomach churned at the sound of bone fragments scraping across cardboard. I never dropped anything so fast in my life. It felt wrong for a man with such a mighty legacy to be reduced to ash and abandoned on a table on the patio of a bar in the desert. But maybe that's exactly what Slim wanted. It sure beats the hell out of rotting in a box in the ground until the worms find a way in.

When Dan got back, I told him about the box. We both walked over to the table and stared down at what was left of Slim. Dan made no move to pick it up. We went back inside for fresh Lone Stars, but the friendly bartender was gone, replaced by a very hungover young man who was only partially a bartender and mostly a river guide.

"What can I get, y'all?"

"I'll take a Lone Star and a shot of Tequila. Dan, can I buy you a shot?"

"No thanks, Harlin. I'm still a little weirded out by that cop following us all the way down here. I'm proceeding with caution until we're off the road for the night."

The bartender came back with two beers and a shot. He looked like he might puke just from pouring drinks.

"Rough night?" I asked.

"Rough weekend. It was SlimFest the last two days. Crazy-ass party."

"We know," said Dan. "We found a box of Slim on the patio."

"A box of Slim?"

"Yeah," said Dan. "A box of Slim."

"I'm not sure what you mean."

"A box. A cardboard box. With Slim inside. His ashes, at least. It's sitting out there on the patio."

"Well, that's fucking creepy."

A STRONG TEXAS WOMAN

That box got me thinking. Leah and I like to stop places when we travel. We stopped once for beef jerky at Duke's—one of those massive Texas gas stations complete with a BBQ joint, rustic home décor aisle, boiled peanut stand, dog park, and an assortment of ornate pocket knives—on the way to Louisiana. She headed straight for the jerky hut, where the friendly proprietor used pruning shears to clip samples of whatever piqued our interest. We tried prime rib jerky, turkey jerky, something jerkified in shrimp boil, and a few others. She bought me a hot dog and a Dr. Pepper Icee on our way back to the car. I could tell she felt bad that I was using up vacation days unexpectedly, but she didn't need to.

Leah took a turn at the wheel because I was tired. The heat and the general chaos of summer had worn me down in recent weeks. I kept thinking that if I could just make it to fall everything would be all right. But I knew it would take longer than that. The sun was warm on my face, and it felt good not to have to fight to keep them open. I've seen the hell that can bust loose at a moment's notice on I-20. That's not a battle you want to go into groggy.

In between little fits of sleep, I watched her work the radio. She kept the country music dialed in even though we were zipping in and out of signal range. When one station turned to static, she flipped right to the next one. It was an impressive feat I was unable to replicate when I rode home solo two days later. She's real proud of being a Louisiana Jew, but if you ever made that drive with her, you'd swear she was a Lone Star country girl at heart. She knows all the good old country songs.

The closer we got to the border, the deeper and more concentrated her breathing got. There'd be nothing for a minute. Then a real slow, serious inhaling followed by a labor-like expulsion of air through slightly puckered lips. I'm no dummy. I've spent years around this woman, so I knew exactly what all that was about. Leah was fighting off a panic attack.

We laid my wife's sweet, kind, magnificent Grammy to rest under the tall, tall trees in Shreveport, Louisiana the next day. It was brutally hot, so we got up early in the morning to tear our ribbons, say the blessings, and sprinkle that first shovelful of earth over the coffin. The rabbi said that we scoop the dirt with an upside down shovel because we do so reluctantly, and we tear our ribbons because a part of our heart has been torn and will never be the same. She was a good rabbi. Wise and prone to saying things that stick in your head and heart alike.

We moved to the temple for the formal service after we were done at the gravesite. Rabbi told a beautiful story about what she remembers most from the day Dot Kaplan passed away.

"The sky was full of balloons. They looked like little dots. And so I thought of our Dot. Now, that isn't to say that I believe Dot's soul floated from her body and entered a balloon, but I will never see another balloon without thinking of Dot."

When it came to the part of the service for my wife and her brother to talk, I braced for the worst. And by worst, I mean I expected to see her cry an awful lot. We'd even joked about it the night before.

"Jeffrey and I will get up there to talk, and I'll start crying that I miss my Grammy, and Jeffrey will have to do the whole thing himself."

"That's pretty much what I'm expecting," said Jeffrey.

But it didn't go down that way. Leah got up there and stood tall as she could next to her brother. Everyone could tell that they were both wrecked, but they never lost it. They told stories about watching movies and cooking with their Grammy and how she couldn't sing to save her soul, but she always made them feel a hundred-percent loved. It was a beautiful, sad thing. In the middle of it, I had to pass a tissue to Leah's stepdad, a big old Texas boy named Darold. I guess that's what kind of woman Dot Kaplan was. Someone so sweet and kind that even the biggest of men shed heavy tears on the day we all had to say goodbye. It made me proud to have known her, but nowhere near as proud as I was of Leah for making damn sure she got to say all the lovely things she ever wanted to say about her Grammy right when she was supposed to say them. My wife may be little, but she is fucking fierce.

GODDAMMIT, DAN

I was in the shower when I heard him, but I knew exactly who Dan was talking to. It was the fucking laptop dude from the Bad Rabbit.

"So I realized my knowledge of the physical sciences was insufficient. That's why I came to the desert. To complete my research."

When I'd left Dan at the U-Haul, he was hanging with the old dude from the cactus that scared the shit out of me by the BBQ grill. They were both staring at the picture of Project Habbakuk.

"That don't look like any aircraft carrier I ever saw in the war," said the Cactus Man.

"That's because it was top secret," said Dan.

"What made it such a secret?"

I headed to the showers at the Terlingua Ranch clubhouse because I knew how that conversation went, and I was starting to get a little freaked out by the locals. It being my first time in the desert and all. I figured I could get cleaned up and then maybe talk Dan into making one more trip to the Ghost Town. But from the sound of it, that wasn't gonna happen. Mojica had made a new friend.

I got dressed and brushed my teeth and headed out to the U-Haul. Dan and the Desert Rat were standing next to it talking. Or rather the Desert Rat was talking and Dan was standing there scratching his head and trying to keep up.

"Harlin, this is Richard. We're gonna go do a little something with Richard after I get a quick shower." Dan gave me a little half wink. "Didn't think you'd mind."

Richard just smiled real big and nodded his head. I was pretty sure we were gonna die out there.

THE HAPPIEST PLACE ON EARTH

With apologies to Walt, Disneyland can't be the happiest place on Earth because it's got no porch. It has trains, monorails, animatronic presidents, and aspiring thespians masquerading as world-famous mice—but no porch. The Terlingua Ghost Town, on the other hand, has the finest porch in all the land.

The Ghost Town porch is the epicenter of a couple shops and some abandoned buildings from the old, old days of Terlingua. At one end, you'll find the Twilight Theater, a drinking, dinning, and entertainment establishment that, until some renovations in the nineties, had no roof. Patrons could sit inside and enjoy themselves without ever having to forsake the comfort of a star blanket.

But the main attractions, for me at least, were the people of the porch. Friends and strangers conjuring up a spirit that permeated the wooden planks and nails beneath their feet. There were a lot of dogs and people smiling and hula hoopers. The gravitational pull of Tejano music assembled random musicians into a full-fledged jam session, filling the air with carnival vibes. Dan led me into a store with a little room that had a cooler stocked with a variety of brews. I pulled a bottle of Carta Blanca from the refrigerated air and took it to the counter.

"Is it like this all the time, Dan?"

"Maybe not this crowded, but there are people here most every night."

"Hanging out and playing music?"

"Sometimes they just drink beer and watch the mountains change colors."

"I love that the whole world stops at the end of each day to let the sundown do its thing."

"That's the whole reason for being out here, brother. Fuck everywhere else. The desert moves at its own speed."

CLOSE ENCOUNTERS

We drove to a little adobe church about five minutes from the Terlingua Ranch clubhouse. Richard was there waiting in an old Ford F-150 pickup. He had two dogs with him. The bigger one started barking like hell the minute I got out of the truck. I figured he'd knock it off once he caught my scent, but the little bastard wouldn't stop. Richard didn't seem bothered by all the noise. He just grabbed a beer out of the back of his truck and knelt down by his dog.

"He'll knock it off as soon as I let him smell this beer."

Dan and I just looked at each other. Richard cracked the beer, took a swig, and then held it in front of the dog's nose.

"Here you go, buddy. Smell this beer, so you'll know everything is all right."

The dog stopped barking and then jumped into the cab of the truck and laid down.

"See? He knows the smell of beer, man. He knows I like beer and my friends like beer, so if he smells beer, he knows it's all good."

"Smart dog," said Dan.

Richard reached into his pocket and pulled out a pinky sized joint.

"This a little something I concocted in my lab. A friend of mine ended up with eighty pounds of marijuana that wasn't cured properly. It wasn't good for smoking, so being a good friend, I told him I'd take thirty pounds off his hands."

"Holy shit," I said. "Thirty pounds of fucking weed?"

"Yeah. But it wouldn't get you high."

"So what'd you do with it?"

"I ordered a particular kind of alcohol, and I soaked the marijuana in it until it turned into a substance real similar to hash oil. What I have in my hand is the very last of that hash. This is something very special for a special occasion."

Richard sparked the joint and took a deep, deep drag before handing it off to Dan who puffed and then passed it to me.

"Does this place still operate as a church?" asked Dan.

"It does. The have service every Sunday, and some days it's open as a soup kitchen."

Richard hit the joint again then started telling us a story. He didn't even bother to exhale.

"Old Hat Bailey. The preacher here. Is way too militant and right wing for my taste, man. All these Tea Party conservatives are fucking up the country. They think they're smarter than everyone else, but I'm much better educated than them."

"Where did you go to school?"

"Private schools" said Richard. "I've studied the works of John Adams extensively. I know what those fuckers are up to, and its bullshit."

I was waiting for our new friend to pass that turbo-charged science joint, but he was busy waving it around and mostly just letting it burn.

"Can I tell you guys a really bizarre personal story that permanently altered the trajectory of my life from that point in time right up until this very minute in the right here and now?"

We didn't hesitate. Dan and I nodded motionlessly at each other out the corner of our eyes as if to say, "Buckle the fuck up, buddy."

"Hell yes, you can, Richard."

"Thank you, uh . . . fuck, man. I forgot your name."

"It's Harlin," said Dan.

"I gotta find a way to remember that. Let me think. There is an author I like that has "Harlin" in his name.

"Harlan Ellison?"

"No. That's not it. I can't remember the exact name, but it'll come to me eventually. In the meantime, I should be able to remember that your name is Harlin as a way of reminding me to remember the real Harlin. The one who writes books."

"Harlin writes books."

Richard shot razorblade eyes at us like he thought we might be fucking with him. He put that magic-homemade-hash-oil-hog-leg to his lips, but didn't puff. Head cocked in careful consideration, he made a scholarly type gesture with his getting-high hand that left tendrils of smoke dangling in the desert air like ghosts he couldn't shake.

"Interesting," he said. "But now back to my story. My parents were very well off. My father was a researcher, and my mother was highly educated and well respected by other educated people. We had this boat with a fifteen-foot keel. The boat was kept on a lake in Illinois, but we lived in Missouri."

"Why?"

"Because the keel was too long for Missouri lakes."

Dan and I nodded and made little sounds like we understood, but this shit was making less and less sense by the minute, and we didn't start off in a real sensible situation to begin with.

"One night, I was alone on the boat. The moon was out. I'd been topside doing some calculations and mind expansion exercises, and I remember suddenly feeling drawn to go down below deck. As I descended the stairs, I started to feel like I was not alone at all. Someone, or something else, was on the boat with me."

Richard paused to let the feeling settle in. Alone. On a boat. At night. In Illinois.

"Now, the fifteen-foot keel was attached to the boat with four massive bolts that must have been at least five or six inches across.

Directly above the exact spot where the four bolts attached the keel to the hull was the aluminum mast. I could sense an entity occupying the space between the keel bolts and the mast. Like an orb of energy. A cosmic sphere with jagged streaks of plasma running through it.

"What the fuck?"

"I asked myself the exact same question, man!"

Richard unleashed a stream of raspy laughter. He brandished that joint he'd been so proud of with no intent to pass or toke. More ghosts appeared as the last stash of Richard's reclaimed hash burned and burned and burned.

"What did you do?" asked Dan.

"I think I fucking blacked out for a minute, but I can't say with any certainty. I remember it got very loud in my head. I was afraid. And then nothing."

"Nothing?"

"Nothing. The next thing I can remember is waking up, sort of collapsed on the stairs."

"Was it still there?"

"The entity was still present, but I wasn't afraid anymore. I wanted to study it. Very slowly, I approached the orb. It allowed me to get much closer than I expected. But when I got too close, it would warn me."

"How?"

"I can't really explain it. There was no verbal communication. It was more telepathic. Like this warning would pop into my head that certain parts of the orb could harm me, and I needed to keep my distance.

"Jesus," said Dan.

"Not exactly," said Richard. "But we're getting to some very interesting shit, man. After studying the entity up close, I sat back on the stairs and stared at it for a long time. The orb itself appeared to be stationary, but I could see movement inside the thing. I tried to affect this movement with my brainwaves, but I just couldn't dictate the flow of plasma within the orb. I sensed, however, that it was responding to my attempts. This thing, whatever it was, wanted to communicate with me.

"Could you tell what it wanted?"

"Not at first. I had to learn how it communicated before I could understand what it wanted. Eventually, through some trial and error and basic experimentation, I figured out that it could answer 'yes' or 'no' questions. Like, if I thought of a question that you could answer 'yes' or 'no' to, the orb would flash if the answer was 'yes.'"

"What did it do if the answer was 'no?'"

"It didn't do shit, man. Not a damn thing. But that was okay because I knew how to ask the right questions now. I scanned my mental archives for some of the ancient texts I'm familiar with, and it started reminding me of the bible. So I asked the thing, 'Are you what Christians sometimes interpret as God?' And the thing flashed 'yes.' 'Are you the God that appeared to Moses?' 'Yes' again. 'So you know Moses?' The fucking thing flashed out another 'yes!'"

I don't know what the fuck Mojica was thinking, but my jaw was in the dirt. Every time this scrambled-up desert rat talked about some spherical energy source flashing out a "yes," I got the image of that little eight-bit trapezoid from Tron. The little floating guy that kicks it with the dude in the tank and can only say "yeesss" and "noooo." This shit was straight-up crazy, but Richard wasn't even close to being finished. He looked at me and Dan and got real serious for a minute.

"So it took me some time to process what I was experiencing. When it finally became real to me, I was like 'Fuuuuuuuck, maaaaan!' Look at the bible. Everyone who ever meets God has some seriously terrible shit happen to them. Here I was, seventeen years old, and I thought my life was about to be over. I couldn't decide whether I was having a psychotic break—or if I'd somehow forgotten about doing eight blotters of acid."

"Or it could have been both," said Mojica. "Maybe you did four blotters of acid and then had a psychotic break."

Fucking Mojica. I was absolutely certain Richard was going to kill us both. We were already in the desert. All he'd have to do was dig the hole.

"Exactly, Dan! You know what I'm talking about. Luckily, I didn't have to get swallowed by a whale or anything. The God entity had something different in mind. I was sitting there staring at the orb when this image of an old scientific magazine I had a subscription to as a kid appeared in my mind. On the back of the magazine and there was a full-page ad for a Tesla laboratory kit you could send away for. Make your own Tesla coils and shit. So I asked the thing 'Do you want me to continue my research into the work of Tesla?' Another 'yes' flash."

"Did you do it," I asked.

"In time," said Richard. "I woke up the next morning pretty freaked out. The thing was gone, so I tried to pretend it had never been there. But that didn't work. I spent the next few decades trying to be normal, making money and fucking up my life. I didn't want to accept that after seeing what I'd seen, I didn't fit in the real world anymore. But somewhere in the back of my mind, I always knew. I maintained a full laboratory set-up in storage, and I was a mostly functioning member of society until I had a breakdown, sold everything I owned, and moved my lab to the desert to continue my research in to the physical sciences. That was the key to solving the riddle."

"So you're saying you unraveled the mystery of God?"

"Yes and no. I know what Moses saw. And it wasn't God. The orb on my parents' boat was a result of microvibrations in the water traveling up the keel and interacting with the Earth's natural gravitational pull, which was being amplified by the aluminum mast. That's the God of Moses. The burning bush is the universe itself, man. The universe is alive—and it is intelligent."

"Groovy, brother," said Dan, finishing off a beer and looking around for an exit strategy.

"I think I can recreate the phenomenon if y'all want to come back to my lab. I live a few miles off the main road in the shadow of Sombrero Rock."

"Brother, that thing we smoked kicked in about five minutes ago. It was great to meet you, but I gotta get out of here while I still can."

"I understand, Dan. I'm sure our paths will cross again."

"Yeah, brother. I'll see you around the lodge."

Dan climbed into the U-Haul and fired up the engine. I got in his rearview mirror, so I could guide him out of the parking lot. Richard was hovering close by, pulling on a beer and still waving that joint.

"What's that on the side of your truck, man?"

Here we go again.

"Project Habbukuk"
"It looks like some sort of aircraft carrier."
"Top secret. Made out of ice. Canadian."
"Far out, man. I'm gonna have to do some research on that shit."

Dan was swinging the back of the truck around and trying to angle the engine towards the exit. One of Richard's dogs, not the one who likes the smell of beer, was sticking his nose where it was liable to get crushed.

"Watch out for your pup, buddy."
"It's okay. He's very good at not getting run over."

The truck shimmied down the little driveway out of the church parking lot and back onto the main road. Dan looked eager to roll, so I hopped into the passenger seat and pulled the door shut. Mojica laid on the gas, one eye on the road—the other on Richard.

"Jesus, Dan. How the fuck am I supposed to write that guy?"
"That's your problem, brother. I just wanted to get the fuck out of there before he pulled a Desert Eagle out of the back of his truck and wasted our asses.

Laughter like Texas thunder. Heavy, gut-busting howls. Relief. We'd had a desert adventure with a strange new friend and nobody had killed us. It was gonna be a helluva story to tell back at the bar. I was energized. Excited. Ready for whatever came next. Dan fished a couple of beers out of our trashcan cooler and handed me one. We drank, except for the crack of the pop tops and the rattling of the U-Haul on rough desert roads, in silence. I felt good. Five minutes down the road, I would be lost in my own head worrying about the dwindling supply of beer and cigarettes and trying like hell to outrun the silence that was bearing down on me. But all that shit was still four minutes and a couple dozen seconds in the future, so fuck it.

SOUNDS OF SILENCE

By the time Dan and I made it back to the *hacienda* after our encounter with Richard, I was in a state. The nonexistent walls of the desert were closing in on me. The more open my surroundings, the more anxious I felt. The idea that Dan and I could just disappear for any number of reasons, and no one back in Denton would ever know why was fucking with my head. And I wasn't even actually worried about disappearing. It was the busted link, the dead zone in the chain of communication. I'd become addicted to knowing what was going on in the lives of everyone I love, and now I was going through withdrawals.

I had six cigarettes left when Dan started cooking dinner. He was making chicken stew with our remaining provisions. I helped a little, but I mostly just wandered circles around the *hacienda* searching for cell signal or something to look at that would calm me down. I was afraid to smoke any grass, so I held a beer and forced myself to take the occasional sip. There was just so goddamned much nothing.

At least with Richard around there had been a story. A place with an alpha and omega and people and events and just enough space to let your mind wander. It's dangerous to do that in the desert. It might get lost.

Dan, on the other hand, was completely unaffected by the vastness of the place. He didn't seem to need anything. He was content to quietly sit in his chair, occasionally stirring the stew pot and staring holes in mountains. Were I to have suddenly vanished, he may have regarded it with no more than a faint, quizzical grunt and a long, slow pull from his lukewarm can of beer.

"What's the longest you've ever stayed out here, Dan? By yourself, I mean."

"Couple days. I usually got Pammy or someone with me."

"I don't think I could handle being out here all alone."

"Oh, man. I fucking love it. I plan on doing a whole week by myself sometime. Maybe two."

"Dude, I'd go insane. I already feel kinda strange. It's been like two and half days since I've even made contact with Leah. I feel so cut off from everything."

"Brother, that's exactly why I come out here."

"I guess maybe I'd eventually get used to it, but man, I sure wish we weren't driving a U-Haul, so we could go have a beer at that VFW. Watch the sunset and be around some people."

"Those might not be the people you wanna be around, Harlin. Been a rough crowd lately, especially since the dude that ran it got murdered."

"Fuck, Dan, how many people get murdered around here?"

"Technically, I think they ruled it a suicide. They found the dude burned to death in his trailer, but the autopsy also showed a gunshot wound to the head."

"So the dude shot himself in the head and then lit his trailer on fire?"

"Sounds fishy to me, but that's the story."

"I guess he could have started the fire and then shot himself, but still."

"Like I said, the crowd there's been rough lately. Dude started catering to bikers. I think he got mixed up with drugs, like heavy drugs, and he pissed off or ripped off the wrong people. Kind of a fucked up situation."

"No shit, man."

"But hey, we got beer in the cooler, so I think we're gonna be just fine. You wanna play some washers?"

I've never been much for lawn games. Sometimes, okay a lot of times, I forget to do all the fun stuff that goes along with drinking beer outside. I end up just drinking and watching everyone else do fun shit. I also hate to lose, and if I know I can't win, I usually won't play. Like horseshoes. I hate that game because I'm no good at it and I don't have the time or the patience required to acquire any horseshoe-chucking skills. But seeing as how I was on the verge of a king hell freak out and Dan was proposing an activity that might occupy my mind for a while, I was all in on some fucking washers.

Cigarettes five and four got burned down to their butts while I absolutely smoked Dan in three straight games of washers. It wasn't even close. To be fair, I was a few beers behind, so I probably had a slight edge in the hand-eye coordination department. The game was more fun than I expected, and I liked winning because it meant I didn't have to get down in the dirt to tend the pit. That's the loser's job.

"Dammit, Harlin. You're kicking my ass. You some sort of ringer?"

"I'm just a natural talent."

"Natural talent, my ass. You're getting lucky. I'll get you next time we're down here."

Dan went back to the *hacienda*'s outdoor kitchen to check on his stew. He took a taste with a plastic spoon, dumped in some spices, and fiddled with the knob on the gas burner. The blue flame beneath the pot kicked up a notch, breathing new life into the stew and encouraging the ingredients to mingle all friendly like. I walked to the other side of the *hacienda* to say goodbye to cigarette number three while I waited for the horizon's Technicolor slide show. Elephant Mountain was still out there, its gentle majesty a near constant companion since we hit the high desert. It was there before any of my people traveled by boat from Norway to America, and it will endure far longer than any of my bloodline walks this rock.

My anxiety rekindled by the realization that I was less than a blip in the annals of time, I smoked cigarette two, the next to last of its kind, and thought about how I was almost just like that guy in that Isaac Hoskins song, only without the Old Crow whiskey. Damn, that's a good song.

We ate in silence on account of the stew turned out damn good and there really wasn't all that much left to say. The sun was sinking quick, so there would be no more washers for the night. I sensed a shift in Dan. His mind was already on the morning, when we would have to pack up and leave this place that he loves so much. I knew the feeling. It's the same sense of dread I get on Sunday afternoons when the weekend is near extinction and the specter of the working week hangs heavy on your soul. No matter how brilliant and beautiful, every adventure comes to an end, and the expiration date for ours was on the flip side of sundown.

"We'll need to get up early, buddy. I want to repack the truck before we leave."

"Yeah?"

"I just want to make sure everything is neat and organized when we hit the border patrol checkpoint. I'd like to get through that with as little hassle as possible. Especially driving this motherfucker."

"It came through in a pinch, but a U-Haul ain't exactly the ideal vehicle when it comes to desert travel."

"No, sir. It is not."

Dan and I cleared our plates and rinsed what we could with what water we had left. We cracked fresh beers and settled into chairs for what remained of our evening. It was only about 7:00, but bedtime comes early in the desert. Eliminate televisions and radios and computers, and there isn't much to keep you up at night. I reached into my pocket for the last cigarette of the trip.

"You got another one of those, Harlin?"

"Last one, buddy. You wanna share it?"

"Nope. That's all you. I don't need it anyway."

The omega cigarette left this plane, along with a couple of melatonin tablets and most of a beer, in a thin wisp of smoke. Before the clock struck 8:00, Dan and I were hunkered down in the *hacienda*—me on a cot and my friend in a perch fit more for a mountain climber than an old bar owner. The temperature dropped rapidly, so we lit the little gas heater to warm the space around us. We were both asleep before the coyotes started their show.

FAREWELL TO A DESERT

We packed up and left without saying shit. There's not much you can say when you're giving up on an adventure and dragging your ass back to a world you have very little interest in being a part of anymore. Sure you got friends and lovers and family and pets, but all the shit you gotta put up with to stay close to those things can damn sure spoil them if you aren't careful. You could try to spark a mass relocation, but it's real, real hard to convince everyone you love to simultaneously give up everything and move to the desert.

The voices on the radio were all still talking about the dead Supreme Court Justice. I wondered what the hell he was doing out there on the edge of Texas. Then I started wondering if maybe that desert rat Richard was the Unabomber's brother and he had something to do with knocking off the judge. I tried to do some Google Fu to confirm my rampant speculation, but there weren't enough bars to get pictures.

We rolled through the Border Patrol checkpoint without raising an eyebrow. No one wanted to look in the back of the U-Haul or ask us any questions about Project Habakuk. I think maybe the guard was hungover because he looked like he was tired as fuck of standing out there in the sun, and it wasn't even 9:00 in the morning yet. The gantry raised up and then fell again after we drove past it. There was no going back. At least not today. Terlingua was in the rearview mirror before we ever got to say goodbye.

OFFICER CORNFED AND THE SWEETWATER PONCH

We were in the slow lane when I saw them. State Troopers. Two cars with the lights flashing. Had some old boy pulled over on the side of the road just outside Sweetwater. The lessons I learned as a Driver's Ed teacher, the single worst job I have ever had, came flooding back, so I slid into the fast lane to give our esteemed public servants some much-needed breathing room. Driving a ten-foot box truck through the middle of a windfarm can be downright hazardous. All it takes is one bitch of a gust, and things get dicey with a quickness. Clipping a couple of Troopers on our way out of the desert wouldn't have exactly been the cherry on top of our adventure. But my maneuvers had been flawless. We cruised past without a second thought. It was just an almost story, fading away in the passenger-side mirror.

Or so I thought. The sudden appearance of flashing lights suggested otherwise.

"What the fuck, Dan?"

"Are we getting pulled over?"

"Yeah. I'm pretty sure that's for us."

"You can't be speeding."

"Not in this thing."

"What the fuck do they want?'

"I guess we better find out. Goddamn U-Hauls."

I pulled off to the shoulder and reached for my wallet. In the driver's-side mirror, I saw two Troopers doing the big man walk up to our truck. They split at the back bumper and flanked us.

The young one, Sweetwater Ponch, stared me down through his Ray Bans. Dan's guy was playing good cop. Big shit-eating grin. Red-faced. Spinning his best bumpkin and calling us "buddy." Officer Cornfed and Sweetwater Ponch. I had a bad feeling about this, and it wasn't just the McDonalds I'd eaten at the last truck stop.

"Afternoon, sir. Do you know why I pulled you over today?"

"No, sir."

"Sir, I stopped you today for following too closely behind another vehicle."

You could have knocked me over with a feather. Following too closely. This was bullshit, and we could all smell it.

"You'll be getting a warning today, sir. I'll just need to see your license and insurance, and we'll get you on your way."

I handed him my license, and Dan started ruffling through his papers to find the insurance for the truck.

"Where y'all coming from," asked Cornfed.

"The desert. Down in Terlingua."

"The desert? What's out there?"

"I've got a friend with some land out there."

"Y'all do any hunting?"

"It's not in season."

"You need a license to hunt on private property?"

"Oh yeah. There's a game warden and everything."

Officer Cornfed either didn't know a damn thing about the rules and regulations of wild game hunting, which would make him a shit Texan, or he was playing a hunch that we were smuggling a U-Haul full of illegally slaughtered beasts, which would make us the world's worst poachers. Nothing about this was adding up quite right.

While Cornfed was setting us up with small talk, Sweetwater Ponch was examining our papers. There wasn't much to look at, two driver's licenses and a rental agreement, but Ponch was making a big fucking deal about being thorough.

"Where did you rent this van?"

"We picked it up in Weatherford. My buddy rented it."

"But you live in Denton?"

"Yes, sir."

"So why did you rent the U-Haul in Weatherford."

"His van blew up."

"Where is the van now?"

"At the Firestone in Weatherford."

"You left it?"

"We had to be somewhere, and the van was dead. We didn't have much of a choice."

"Why were you in such a hurry to get to the desert?"

"Actually, we had to get to Marathon first. Then we went to Terlingua."

"What's in Marathon?"

"Dan was putting on a show."

"A show?"

"A music show. A concert."

"A show, huh?" Officer Cornfed was feigning interest. "Anyone I know"

"I don't know," said Dan. "Maybe. Do you know Joe Pat Hennan? Cornel Hurd? Butch Hancock?"

"Don't sound too familiar. Maybe Butch Hancock, but I could be thinking of another Butch."

"It's a popular name," said Dan.

"It sure is. I'm a country music guy myself. That's probably why I don't know those fellas."

Officer Cornfed was most assuredly a shit Texan. Husky fucker probably has an iPhone chock full of red dirt schlock, and as long as I'm casting aspersions, there's bound to be a confederate flag hanging above his fireplace."

"All right, sir," said Sweetwater Ponch. "I'm gonna need to you come back to the car with me while I scan your license. It should only take a minute."

He was trying like hell to make everything seem routine, but this shit definitely wasn't on the up and up. I had no idea if they were dirty cops or bored assholes or both. I wasn't eager to arrive at a verdict, and I sure as shit didn't want to go sit in Sweetwater Ponch's cruiser.

It struck me that I might be looking somewhat derelict as I trudged along the highway from the truck to the squad car. Five straight days of drinking beer and showering infrequently will do that to you. My clothes were dirty, and I felt greasy from a couple of gruesome gas-station burritos I'd scarfed down in Alpine early that morning. I was innocent of any and all possible charges, but I couldn't help but think of how criminal I'd look in my mugshot if these fuckers decided to trump something up.

Quarters were cramped in the trooper's vehicle. Computers and radios and various gadgets made it feel like the cockpit of an airplane.

"They don't leave you a lot of room in here, do they?"

"Tell me about it. They keep adding new equipment all the time."

It was the only genuinely human, non-scripted, un-asshole thing Sweetwater Ponch ever said to me. He dialed up someone on the radio and started feeding in my license number. As if on cue, Officer Cornfed stuck his big fat head in the passenger window and started jabbering.

"So what'd y'all do down in the desert?"

"Not a whole lot. Played some washers. Checked out a couple local spots. Watched the sunset."

"Y'all meet anybody down there?"

"Couple of friends that have land down there."

"What did you do with them?"

"Cooked some dinner and drank a few beers. That's about it."

"What you got in the back of the truck?"

"PA system. Couple of giant speakers. A cooler. Our gear."

Officer Cornfed looked off in the distance, and Sweetwater Ponch finished up on the radio. He didn't look happy.

"All right, sir. Your license came back all clear. You'll be getting a warning today for following too closely. I just need to ask you a few more questions."

"Okay."

"What was the purpose of your trip?"

"Like I said, Dan was throwing a show down in Marathon, and I was going along for the ride."

"How do you know your friend?"

"He owns a club in Denton. I go to a lot of shows there."

"So you work for him?"

"No, we're friends."

"What's his business?"

"He owns a bar and music venue. Dan's Silverleaf in Denton, Texas."

"And how did you come to be associated with him?"

"I'm a regular at his bar. I throw shows there sometimes. We got to be friends over the years."

"But you don't work for him?"

"No. We're friends. Buddies."

They were trying to trip me up, but their interrogation techniques came straight from a TV cop show. That and they were too dumb to realize I wasn't hiding anything.

"Are you carrying any weapons with you today sir?"

"I've got a pocket knife, and Dan has a shotgun in the truck."

"Where is the shotgun?"

"It's in the back of the truck."

"Why do you have the shotgun?"

"For protection."

"From what?"

"There are wild animals and crazy people in the desert. The shotgun is just in case you run into something bad."

"What kind of shotgun does your friend have?" asked Cornfed.

"Not sure of the gauge, but just a regular shotgun."

"Sawed off?"

"No, sir. Normal barrel. Regular old shotgun."

I was getting tired of this shit, and Ponch knew it.

"Are you all right, sir," he asked. "You seem awfully nervous even though I already told you that you'll only be getting a warning."

"I'm in a police car, and you guys are hitting me with questions from both sides. This isn't exactly something I'm used to."

"This is just standard procedure," chimed in Cornfed. "Anytime someone gets stopped out here, this is how we play it. If I see my buddy pull someone over, I stop to check on him because we never know what we're gonna find."

"I can respect that. It's definitely a messed-up world."

"Plus, I'm just nosey, and I like to see what's going on."

Officer Cornfed wheezed a fake-ass chuckle. If I hadn't been sitting in the car, I'm fairly damn sure he would have slapped me on the back like we was old drinking buddies.

"Sir, I'd like to get the timeline of your trip straight," said Ponch. "When did you leave Denton?"

"Dan picked me up in Denton on Thursday morning."

"What time?"

"About 4:30 in the morning."

"And then you went to Marathon."

"No. Then we made it to Weatherford where the van broke down. That's when we rented the U-Haul, and then we went to Marathon."

"Why did you rent a U-Haul?"

"Because we had all the PA gear in the van. A big truck was the only thing we could fit it all in."

"Why didn't you rent a PA in Marathon?"

"It's not that big of a town. I don't think there is anywhere you can rent a PA down there."

"Where did Dan get the equipment?"

"He owns a music venue."

"So it's all his gear?"

"Some of it belongs to him. I think the big speakers belong to Joe Pat Hennan."

"Who is Joe Pat Hennan?"

"He was Dan's partner in throwing the show. He was also one of the acts that played."

"Do you have any drugs in the van?"

"No."

"No methamphetamines, cocaine, heroin, ecstasy, or marijuana?"

"No, sir."

"Do you have any large bales of money? Like on a pallet, wrapped in stretch film or tape?"

"No."

"Do you have any ingredients for making a bomb?"

"No."

"Is there any child pornography in the truck, sir?"

"No, and I'd like that noted as emphatic 'no.'"

"You'd be surprised what people we stop will admit to."

"I don't doubt that, but it's still an emphatic no."

"An emphatic 'no.'"

"Yes. Emphatic."

"Sir, did you meet anyone in the desert who asked you to bring something back with you?"

"No."

"Were you away from the truck at any point where someone could have put something inside it without your knowing?"

"No, sir. We packed up this morning before leaving, and there was nothing that shouldn't have been there."

"You're sure?"

"Yes. We had to go through Border Patrol, so we made sure to check our vehicle."

"What happened at the Border Patrol checkpoint?"

"Not much. The guy looked at our licenses, but that was it. I saw another guy with a dog in the rearview mirror coming up to the back of the truck. I figure it was sniffing for drugs."

Sweetwater Ponch nodded real seriously at that part of the story, as if he was an expert on Border Patrol search tactics. He paused for a second, adjusted his Ray Bans and went back to the grilling.

"Sir, do you have any people in the back of your truck?"

"People?"

"Yes, sir."

"No. There are no people in the back of the truck."

"Sir, would you be surprised if we searched the truck and found something suspicious?"

"No. Not surprised. Because there is nothing in that truck that I haven't already told you about."

"So you wouldn't be surprised."

"Surprise doesn't factor into it. There is nothing in that truck. There is no possibility of surprise."

"Would you give us your permission to search the truck?"

"Well, Dan rented it."

"You're the driver sir, and he's already given us permission. Do we have your permission to perform a search?"

"Absolutely."

"All right, sir. I'm going to need you to listen to me very carefully. Can you do that?"

Fucker.

"Yes. I can do that."

"I want you to get out of the car and walk to the edge of the grass median. Stop before you get to the frontage road. And then I want you to walk about a hundred feet straight forward and stand there until I call you. Do not look at, or attempt to communicate anything with, your friend as you pass the truck. Do you understand?"

"Yes, sir."

I got out of the car and did exactly like he told me. It was windy. I felt cold and embarrassed, standing on the side of the highway, next to a U-Haul, while state troopers got all up in our shit. Out of the corner of my eye, I watched Sweetwater Ponch and Officer Cornfed do Dan just like they'd done me. Grilled him up like flank steak to see if our stories matched.

After a while, I saw Dan climb down from the truck and start walking in my direction, but still keeping his distance. Apparently, Ponch didn't want us conspiring while they performed their questionable, and completely unwarranted, search. I gotta admit, I was hesitant to talk to Dan as we stood there in that field. I didn't want to piss the troopers off, but Mojica was having a little more fun with it than I was.

"Hey, Harlin. What are the odds Joe Pat drives by right now and sees us pulled over and standing in the middle of the fucking road?"

"That'd definitely be something, Dan."

"They give you the third degree?"

"And then some, buddy."

"Fucking U-Hauls."

"You can say that again."

Cornfed was tossing the cab, and I figured Ponch must be in the back because I could see the truck bouncing around. The search didn't take long, which is to be expected because there was jack fucking shit for them to find. Ponch jumped down from the back and slammed the door shut. He looked up, pointed at me, and then motioned severely for me to return to his car. I shrugged at Dan as I passed him.

I climbed back into Ponch's vehicle. He was already printing out my warning.

"In the future, you need to maintain greater distance between you and the other vehicles on the road. If you'd had to stop suddenly, there wouldn't have been enough time."

He proceeded to rattle off some speed-to-distance ratios that I'm pretty sure weren't even accurate, if I recall correctly. I wanted to tell him that the only damn reason I was following closely is because I'd changed lanes so as not to endanger him and Cornfed, but I didn't because I'm a coward when it comes to picking fights with law enforcement. He handed me a tablet and asked for my signature.

"This is a warning, Mr. Anderson. It will not go on your record, and you do not need to appear in court. Have a nice day."

I got out of the car, and Sweetwater Ponch gassed it, nearly clipping me on the ass as he zoomed down the highway. Dan and I climbed back in the truck and just looked at each other.

"What the fuck?"

"Those dudes were bad news, brother. They were out to find some dirt on someone."

"They sure as shit weren't happy to come up empty."

We got back on the road and drove for a while in relative silence. Static-choked, Tea Party pundits buzzed in the background. The passenger side AC vent began to rattle. Dan watched closely as it fell from its housing and landed at his feet. He picked up the vent and turned it over in his hands a few times before popping it back into place. Almost immediately after, he changed his mind and jimmied the vent free again and stared into the cool emptiness behind it.

"Figured I'd better check and make sure those guys didn't jam a bag of coke in there while they were searching the truck. Let us go just to pull us over a couple miles down the road. They seemed like the type. Crooked bastards."

It sounded funny at the time, but two overpasses down the road, we spotted them. Watching. Waiting. Maybe for us. Sweetwater Ponch and Officer Cornfed were having a hard time saying goodbye.

"Dan."

"Yeah, brother."

"Maybe you should check that vent again."

DOUBLE ASS BROKE

Fort Worth kicked our ass. Traffic slowed to a one-legged crawl and then stopped altogether. We were mostly broke and totally wiped out. We listened to The Ticket sports radio to try to distract ourselves, but all we really wanted was to be out of the damn truck. Instead we were suspended in midair, trapped on the wing of a cloverleaf waiting to get spit out into the shitstorm that is I-35 from the stockyard city to Denton town.

Every mile felt like ten. My legs and lower back dog cussed me for not having slept in a real bed for about five days. I missed my family, and I needed a shower just about as bad I could remember ever needing a shower. If you hit the Metroplex at the wrong time, getting home from a long trip is a lot like having a king hell itch on your back that you just can't reach. Door jams, pencils, rulers, or hunting knives. None of them seem to do the trick. It's a transit blue-balling of the highest order, and the only things that can ease your suffering are the landmarks.

Alliance Airport on your left. Starting to get there. Cabela's on your right. Making progress. Texas Motor Speedway. Left again. Getting closer. There's that liquor store you used to get a discount at because you worked at the Prairie House. Yet another left side of the highway milestone. Now we're cooking with Crisco. And finally, the majestic windmills of beautiful Apogee Stadium. Right-hand side of the road, and you're so close to home you wanna kick out the windshield and run the rest of the way every time you hit another snag or a red light.

I tried to give Dan directions for the quickest route to my house, but he was too tired to process, and sometimes, I'm not so good with words. We made it, eventually, but there was no fanfare. Just a couple of tired dudes dragging their asses out of a U-Haul, so they could unload, unpack, and begin the agonizing process of re-acclimating to a life with timeframes and deadlines and responsibilities. It wasn't going to be much fun.

Dan and I staggered to the back of the truck and pushed open the door only to discover the true depths of the havoc wreaked upon us by Sweetwater Ponch and Officer Cornfed.

"Oh shit, Dan."

"What the fuck?"

"Those assholes straight up tossed our shit."

Everything was in shambles. Both our duffels had been unzipped and dumped out. There was a box of Big Bender t-shirts Joe Pat and Susie had made, and those were tossed all over the place, too. Basically, anything those bastards could ransack, they did. I was almost surprised Sweetwater Ponch didn't take a piss in our cooler.

"Brother, it's your name on the citation," said Dan. "But if it were mine, I would be on the phone officially raising hell. This is bullshit."

"I hear you, but I fear retribution. They fucked our day when were completely innocent. Maybe next time they'd make sure to paint us in a guilty light."

"The more I think about this, the more it burns my ass. I'm fucking pissed, Harlin."

"So am I, Dan. But I don't guess there's much we can do besides put our shit back together and never drive another U-Haul down to the desert."

It took me four trips to get my scattered belongings from the back of the truck to my front door. I could hear my dogs barking inside. It would have been nice to think they knew it was me, but they bark like hell when anything cat-sized or bigger breaches the perimeter. I turned to Dan not knowing what to expect in terms of a farewell.

"Thanks for riding with me, Harlin. I hope you had fun."

"It was one of the best times ever, Dan. I can see why you love it out there. I can't wait to go back."

"Right on, brother. I'm sure I'll see you at the bar."

"I wouldn't bet against it."

And so our great adventure ended without so much as a bro hug. We were both too tired and grimy. Maybe there was a handshake or a half-assed salute, but mainly we just wanted to be inside our homes, showered and clean. I felt bad for Dan. He still had to drive that rig home and then get up in the morning to unload the PA and settle up on any overages with the U-Haul folks. I had taken the next day off. I didn't know it at the moment, but instead of doing any writing, I would spend the entire day watching *Friday Night Lights* on Netflix. Something about passing through that part of Texas had awakened a hunger in me. I wanted to get as close to that experience as I possibly could, even if it meant wasting an entire day with my ass planted on a couch cushion. At least I'd have that little beagle lying next to me and snoring like the most wonderful creature God ever created.

So yeah, no hug. At least not then. The hugs would come later. At unexpected times. I'd be ordering a drink at the Silverleaf and Dan would sneak up on me, throw an arm around my shoulders, and say, "How you doing, Desert Buddy?" Then we'd laugh and re-tell some Big Bender story we'd already told each other twenty times before. I love those moments almost as much as the journey itself. It's good to share stories with people who really mean something to you. To feel connected to them. That's the most important thing the desert taught me.

JEFF GLOVER AND THE TWENTY-DOLLAR BILL

There's treasure under the patio at Dan's Silverleaf. Twenty dollars' worth. I know because I saw how it got there. It was a Friday. The weather was damn pleasant, and the happy hour crowd wore their very happiest faces as they ditched the trials and tribulations of the working week. I had on my green bandana and my favorite red shirt. My hair was freshly cut, and I was feeling good. Jeff Glover was next to me at the bar. I could tell he was feeling good, too.

"Miss Kate," he said with a big grin. "I'm already closed out, but I'd like to buy Harlin a beer and get a double Hornitos for myself, and then I'm done."

Kate dialed up a Coors draft for me and started doling out the Hornitos. Old Glover reached into his pocket for his money while at the same time sorta winding up like he was fixin to say something.

"Harlin, I figure it's gotta be over a year since I bought you a beer. Now seems like a good time to rectify that."

"I appreciate that, buddy. You doing good?"

"Doing great. Yourself?"

"Damn glad it's Friday."

"Don't I know it. This whole week I've been just dragging myself along by the scruff of the neck. Trying like hell to get to today."

"Same here," I laughed. "I think I got the desert hangover."
"Oh yeah? You been out that way for a while?"
"I did the Big Bender with Dan and Joe Pat and the gang."
"Was it a good time?"
"The best."
"We couldn't make it this year, but I'm putting it on the schedule for next."
"You won't regret it. Marathon is beautiful, and you can run over to Alpine if you want to walk around the city or check out a cool bar. If you got the time, it's worth making the trip down to the desert, too. There ain't nothing like Terlingua."
"Well, I can see where it might take you some time to get used to the real world again. Sounds like a helluva trip."

Kate had our drinks ready right about then, so we did the whole toasting and clinking and drinking thing and all was good in the world.

"That'll be $8.50, Jeff."

I took another pull off my Coors, and old Glover started to count out his money. I saw the twenty fall from the bar through the bottom of my pint glass. My first instinct was to bend over and pick it up, but that was another man's money. Best to keep my hands off it. Besides, Glover was already reaching down to pick up what was his. At least until he handed it over to Kate. I drifted back to my beer and thoughts of the desert.

"No way!"

I snapped back to the sound of stupefied laughter.

"I cannot believe that just happened."

Jeff was standing there sorta dumbstruck and shaking his head. I looked down and it hit me.

"Did it fall through the deck?"
"Right between the fucking boards."
"What are the chances of that?"
"What happened?" asked Kate.
"I dropped a twenty dollar bill and it fell perfectly between the planks of the deck and is now somewhere beneath the patio."
"That will probably never happen in this bar ever again," said Kate.
"Well, I'm glad I could do my part to ensure the safety of all future barflies."

"I'm so sorry. Do you want me to ask Dan if there is a way to get under there?"

"No, no. It's okay. Really, it's okay. Someday they'll rip this up to repair it or make it bigger, and that twenty will be there waiting."

"You just made someone's lucky day," I said.

"Exactly, Harlin. And you were here to witness it. Years from now when someone does find that twenty, you and Kate and I will be the only ones that know the true story of how it got there. The only ones that saw it happen."

The three of us now a carried a secret truth. We'd joined the ranks of Richard the desert rat, who had faced God and solved his riddle. And all the other desert dwellers, alive or dead, that knew the truth behind all the things that disappear.

WHEN YOU GOT THE ITCH

Once you been to the desert, you never really leave it. You might think you kicked the habit, shook the longing, got your steady hands back, but you haven't. All it takes is a photograph, and you're fucked. You might have work to do. Back up against a wall. Double nostril full of deadline staring you in the eye. But you see that picture of a bit of cactus or the outline of a mountain against the horizon and you get straight cloudstruck. All you wanna do after that is go to a bar and drink cold beer with other folks who been out there. Marathon, Marfa, Alpine. It don't matter. You got a deep need for a hint of the feel of the land, or a little lubricated kinship with folks who ache from the same empty place at their core. The Texas high desert is something more severe than a landscape or an ecosystem. It's a fucking infection, and the only goddamned cure is leaving wherever the fuck you are and proceeding directly to the greater Big Bend area. Do not pass fucking go. Do not even fucking think about collecting 200 dollars. Just get your ass out there under the stars where the coyotes sing and the mountains stand tall. It's the only the very best thing about being stuck on this fucking rock.

PART FIVE
THE SECOND GREAT TEXAS COASTAL EXPEDITION

SAND RUNNERS

Birds glide sideways at the Padre Island National Seashore. Little gulls floating midair, only occasionally flapping their wings against the wind coming off the ocean. The beagle would lose her tiny mind out here. She'd get to hopping and howling like mad at the mysterious flying things just out of reach. I would like to bring her to this place, but the cautionary brochures given to us by the park ranger seem to think she'd be a coyote snack before she got to chase her first sand crab.

   Out there on the edge of Texas, time is a triviality that hardly warrants consideration. At least, that is, until you find yourself racing the sundown to Mile 60. Sixty miles on a highway is less than an hour of zoned-out, cruise control. Sixty miles on the beach is three hours of churning through sand, dodging washed up buoys and other mangled sea debris. It's a trip better made by daylight. Once the sun sinks into the ocean, the going gets even slower. Obstacles become harder to predict.

   There were three trucks in our caravan. Sinclair's Nissan, Morgan's Toyota, and Steven's big fuck-off Ford F-250. Every one of them had four wheel drive because it's an absolute necessity if you're gonna make the run to Mile 60. Sinclair used to have a Nissan with two wheel drive, but he traded the fucker in after Steven took him on his first beach ramble. Sinclair and Steven are coworkers who bonded over a mutual appreciation for Renaissance Faires. Sinclair taught Steven to play Kubb, and Steven introduced my brother to the Padre Island National seashore. Steven and his buddy Josh had been coming to beaches like this for most of their lives. They were our seaside gurus, the anchor team of our expedition.

   We made a quick stop around Mile 2 to fetch beers from the coolers in the backs of our trucks. Some of us smoked cigarettes. We were careful to hold on to the butts. Jam them in empty beer cans, so they didn't end up in the water or a turtle nest. There was already enough trash on the beach.

   "We need to be quick about this, Sinclair," said Steven. "That sun is going down fast. I'd like to be at least halfway before it's gone."

   "Well, all right. Let's move out, gentlemen!"

   Sinclair hopped in his truck and straight up gunned it. It was hard to judge just how far ahead he'd gotten on account of being stuck behind Steven's ark of a pickup. Every now and then, the big truck would swerve to avoid some flotsam or jetsam, and I could see Sinclair frontrunning a good fifty or so yards ahead of us. Obstacle avoided, Steven would fall back into place, and Sinclair would disappear again. Before we even made it to mile ten, Sinclair's lead foot got him pulled over by a park ranger. Morgan slowed way down so we could assess the situation as we passed, but Steven and

Josh were already on top of it. They were pulled over and had the binoculars out. Steven drank beer. Josh manned the glasses.

"Sinclair was hauling ass, man. I told him to keep it cool until we got to Mile 15."

"What happens at Mile 15?" I asked.

"That's where it changes from being a state park to a national park," said Steven. "After that you don't see any park rangers. Only thing they got out there is turtle patrol. And they don't give a shit about anything but turtles.

"What you think is gonna happen to Sinclair?"

Steven shrugged and took a sip of beer.

"Probably get a ticket. Might have been going too fast for a warning. Lots of kids around. We'll know everything's cool if the ranger gets out of the truck with his little clipboard. If he just keeps sitting there, we might have a problem."

I got out to have a smoke and grab some fresh beers, all the while keeping an eye on my brother. Getting hit for speeding was one thing, but an open container citation would be a shit way to start his bachelor party weekend. When I thought back to the confluence of undesirable circumstances that derailed our previous attempt at this journey, it seemed only fitting that we'd run into some manner of trouble before we ever reached the campsite.

"The ranger's getting out of his car," announced Josh. "We've got visual confirmation on the clipboard. Looks like it's a ticket or a warning."

Sinclair caught up with us a few minutes later.

"He get you for speeding?" I asked.

"Yeah."

"Ticket?"

"Warning."

"Let's move boys" yelled Steven over the noise of the ocean. "We're running the fuck out of daylight."

We fell back into formation—Sinclair and Ben in the front; Steven, Josh, and Bruns in the middle; and Morgan, Greg, and me bringing up the rear. In the thickening dusk, I noticed flashes of reflected light in the sand. Swarms of tiny crabs zig zagging eight-bit patterns in and out of the surf, their jagged dance interrupted only by the occasional crunch of the tires smashing them.

Up ahead, Bruns and Josh climbed halfway out their windows and rode down the beach Duke Boys-style. They threw their arms up over their heads to catch the wind as it blew their shirts back, turning them into tails that would trail them all the way to Mile 60. I was jealous. But nothing was stopping me from climbing out of my own window except me. Maybe on the way back, I thought. But I didn't really believe it.

The further down the beach we got, the more interesting the campsites, and the people inhabiting them, became. Some folks had only a tent, chairs, and fishing poles, but other adventurers had trailers with makeshift patios set up in front of them. There were surf casters with rows of PVC pipe driven into the beach, each one holding a fishing pole connected to bait by hundreds of feet of invisible line. Flags were popular among the beach dwellers. American, Texas, and even one that was army green with a white silhouette of a machine gun on it. Federal land or not, this felt like unincorporated territory. The one and only law was "Harm no turtle."

Somewhere between miles twenty and thirty, Steven hit the brakes and Josh bolted out the passenger door and went running past our truck. I hopped out to investigate, but he was already jogging back with the lid to a cooler in his hand.

"What the hell?"

"Dude. Sinclair hit a big bump and everything went airborne in the back of his truck. This lid didn't come back down. It went fucking flying."

"We lose anything else?"

"I don't think so. Beer might be shook the fuck up, but it'll still drink."

Sinclair noticed that we'd stopped, and he was backing up his truck to see what the delay was all about it. Josh and I waited for the taillights to turn into break lights before walking over to the bed of the pickup. Our cargo was certainly jostled, but nothing else seemed to be missing. Steven popped the lid back into place while I reconfigured our gear.

"What's going on back here?"

"You lost the lid to your cooler," said Josh. "You got some serious air."

Everyone was out of the trucks now. Smoking cigarettes, passing liquor bottles, and getting fresh beers for the next leg of the journey. The crabs were running everywhere.

"Holy shit," said Greg. "Look at all these little guys! I'm gonna catch one."

I watched as a group of thirty-something men changed into children right before my eyes. Greg and Josh scampered in the headlights, lurching on soggy legs in pursuit of the tiny pinching creatures.

"Shit! One of them got me," shouted Greg, proudly displaying a hand adorned with a plucky little sand crab clinging to his finger.

"Can we eat these?"

"I don't think so. You'd need too damn many of them even if you could."

"Anyone else hear the crunch when you run one over?"

"Fuck yeah, man. Gnarly."

It was all the way dark now, but no one cared. The tide was rolling out and the road ahead was smooth. Drivers and navigators need only keep an eye out for any random shit left in their path by the ocean's recession. Instead of watching the sun set from Mile 60, we'd streaked through it, spraying color all across the horizon. The salty sting of the wind off the ocean promised us everything.

MILE 60

Brunsie was fucking green by the time we got to camp. Everyone else was pulling coolers and tables and chairs out of the beds of trucks, but he was just sitting in the sand with his head between his legs looking like he was about to toss his guts.

"What's wrong with Bruns?" I asked. "He have one too many?"

"Nah, man," replied Steven. "He's dip sick."

"Y'all gave him some Skoal?"

"He said he wanted to try it."

"Something tells me that dude ain't gonna last too long."

It was true. Bruns had a few ambulatory moments over the course of the evening, but for the most part, he slept and moaned and regretted. The rest of us had a camp to set up.

We built our base of operations on a little rise overlooking the beach on one side and the intercostal channel on the other. It was Josh and Steven's favorite spot. A handful of sand dunes blocked the wind and gave us a little privacy from the other campers and fishing enthusiasts scattered about Mile 60.

Josh and Steven had known each other basically forever. They were teammates on their high school baseball team, and they'd been roaming the beaches of Texas since a long time before that. They work together now, and work has a funny way of not seeming like such a horrible thing when your oldest, best friend is right there with you every day. Sinclair has that with Morgan and Bruns. And I had it, too, for a while at the cartoon factory. But those days are long gone. I miss them more than I care to think about.

The cooler lid wasn't the only casualty of the ride to Mile 60. As I went to unload my awning from the back of Sinclair's truck, I noticed that some of the contents of the cooler were dislodged by the same bump that sent the lid flying.

"Shit, Sinclair. There goes breakfast."

"What?"

"We lost the eggs, brother."

"Where did they go?"

"All over our shit and the back of your truck."

Sinclair and I surveyed the wreckage. Some of the eggs had died in the cooler, but most of them made their way into the truck. There was yolk on the case to my awning, yolk on the outside of the cooler, and a substantial amount of yolk all over his bed liner.

"That shit's nasty," said Sinclair.

"It's gonna be even worse once the sun hits it."

"Fuck."

We had four awnings in the beginning, but one of them busted when we tried to set it up, so we broke it down as best we could and tossed it aside. We strung the other three into an "L" and weighed them down. Morgan and I started setting up tables so we'd have a place to eat and mix drinks, and Sinclair started playing music like he always does. My brother doesn't do shit without music.

Bottles of tequila and whiskey circulated like clockwork. We were full of beer and anticipation of good times. The night was electric in those first few hours. The possibilities endless. Laughter came easy in the beginning, and we never wanted to go to bed. Some of us didn't.

GLOVES

My first Denton date was at Rubber Gloves Rehearsal Studios. It was hip hop night. BYOB. Back in the late '90s before they built a bar and got a liquor license. She was a steakhouse waitress with those big-ass, high-beam Disney eyes that can shrink a man on the spot. It wasn't even fair. We went on one or two more dates before she decided she wasn't quite ready to give up on the high school boyfriend that was off playing minor league baseball somewhere. Well, fuck him. And fuck her, too. She didn't return my copy of *Ethan Frome*, and I got ten bucks says she never even cracked the cover.

I saw a lot of cool shit at Gloves. Johnathan Richman. Little Grizzly. Supagroup. Corn Mo. Lift to Experience. Tons of young local bands busting their asses to make a name for themselves in a town like Denton. Small-time touring acts with big-time talent just hoping to sell enough CDs to make it to the next gig. I also missed a lot of badass shit. That Modest Mouse show before they got huge still stings. And I probably should have seen Boris at least once. Never get the chance now. Not at Rubber Gloves.

We did our best to send Gloves out in style. Tailgated in the parking lot for three nights straight. Practice rooms became party spots that lived and breathed between sets. Tony Donate, the Puerto Rican bass player, grilled meats. Folks passed around magic brownies and contraband vape pins and even old school hog-legs. Clouds of smoke gathered in corners or between cars. High up above them, dark clouds marched in like stormtroopers ready to fuck shit up. Rain came and went. When the sun returned, the boys from Armazilla waded into the muck water next to some old railroad tracks out back to have their band photo taken while they lounged in pool floaties. We crowded around them to watch the scene go down.

The party vibe came easy on Friday, when there were still two days left and we didn't have to think about the end. Saturday we were on a mission. Kick it up to eleven and fucking throw down because this was the last ever Saturday at Gloves. Sunday we carried heavy hearts and swollen livers. One by one, bands took the stage, played their songs, and then gave way to the next act. Rumors of a liquor shortage began to circulate. Folks without safety beers started thinking of making a run, but no one wanted to miss any of what was left. In the end, they ran out of booze before they ran out of music.

We lost a hell of a lot more than just a venue when they shut the doors for the last time. The Rehearsal Studios had always been the heart of Gloves. It gave all those misfits hoping to become a band someplace they could suck in private for a while, so when they went on stage for the first time, they sucked a little less. And then it was back to the practice spot where they would continue to suck until the day they had sucked together long enough to get fucking decent. After that, the sky was the limit. Adoring fans. Platinum records. Shows that charged a cover.

That's how you build a fucking music scene. You start out with more ambition than talent. Then you go to work. And there was always someone working at Gloves. They might be in the practice rooms writing songs and recording demos. Or they could be higher up the food chain. Established musicians tending bar to pick up extra cash before their next tour. Rubber Gloves was a home to them all. A nurturing biosphere in the rapidly shifting Denton scene.

We got a bunch of festivals and shit now, and some bigger names are starting to swim through our waters. Some dude slapped an "ing" on Denton and turned it into a verb. Then they turned that into a hashtag and then the visitor's bureau started selling t-shirts with that bullshit. I think it might even be an Instagram filter, whatever the fuck that is. Folks that get off on marketing and promoting took our wonderfully strange scene with all its freaks and beardos and dirty bathrooms and spun it into something shiny to attract the masses. We got bars on rooftops with real live music these days. But you can't keep building up if you destroy the roots and implode all the basements and forget to leave room for all the people that created the thing in the first place. You can try, but that shit will ring hollow.

INVERTED TOTALITARIANISM

Out in the dunes next to the jetty, if you step beyond the illumination of the Coleman camping lanterns, you're instantly in impossible darkness. There are no rules at Mile 60. Especially not at night. What feels right is the law. So you stand on the jetty and do the mannequin piss for what seems like hours because you've suddenly realized that you've desperately needed to for a very long time, which, in reality, has only been a very short time, but it's the time of night where nuance slips away in the receding surf. You hear voices coming from camp. Drunken alarmists.

"What the fuck is that?"

Still pissing, you crane your neck to see a group of hunched-over folks walking single file with head lamps and weird sticks. They are off to your left, creeping you the fuck out. The craning throws you off balance and the sand shifts beneath your feet. Vertical is a challenge, so you lean into the wind.

"Do I need to get my fucking gun?"

"No, dude. These guys are either nerds or scientists. We have nothing to fear."

The scientist nerds turn out to be crabbers. You discover this when they pass by a little too close for comfort considering the business you're doing. You know they are crabbers because their sticks have little claws on the end to protect them from pincers. The crabbers pay you no attention as they crab their way down the beach, one after another, eyes and headlamps fixed on the ground. There could be rattlers anywhere, you think. The brochures the Lady Ranger gave you said so. Crabbing ain't for cowards.

You return to camp where Stephen and Sinclair are listening to the new Sturgil Simpson album. Stephen hands you a Bulleit and Red Bull, and you don't hesitate. Bruns is still asleep. Most everyone else is up, drifting in and out of the conversation in various stages of drunkenness. June bugs congregate around the lantern as if they can't get enough of that Sturgil. Sinclair's tongue gets looser the tighter he gets on the brown.

"Inverted totalitarianism, man. That's the United States right there."

"What are you talking about?"

"The Nazi government, man. It controlled—it fucking dominated—the German economy. But the U.S. is all fucked up. We're run by big business. Corporations control everything."

"So?"

"So it's gonna be our downfall. It will fucking destroy the fuck out of us."

Normally, you'd be right there with Sinclair, but it's late and you're drunk and the waves are crashing and now the new Weezer is blasting and you're feeling good and calling it the best record since *Pinkerton* and you're pretty much not worried about a goddamned thing. That's Mile 60.

JETTY WALK

Over the course of writing this book, I've told you about sleeping in some pretty wretched places. The back of a U-Haul box truck; on the cold, hard ground in the middle of a Texas wind farm in December; and even the back of a Nissan Xterra with a large man named Jackson. But none of those spots did a number on my back like a night spent tossing and turning on the Padre Island National Seashore.

There's a chance I could have made it work, but Sinclair wouldn't let me bring my sleeping bag on account of us being short on stowage space.

"We don't need sleeping bags or a tent," he's said. "I've got a couple of camping chairs we can crash in. Same as we did on Mustang Island. We'll be fine."

I'd had my doubts. For starters, I gave the fuck up on sleeping in that chair when Sinclair and I visited Port Aransas. After he passed out, I snuck into his truck and spent a mostly miserable night leaned back in the passenger seat. No pillows. No blankets. No dreams or snoring.

Ben was as skeptical as I was, but he didn't say a word. Mainly because he's a quiet, thoughtful dude by nature. A wandering philosopher of sorts. But also because he'd slipped his bag and tent in the back of Sinclair's truck without anyone noticing. The perks of living a somewhat nomadic existence is that you get real damn good at cramming everything you need into a burlap duffel. Ben had his gear set up in a sweet spot overlooking the surf about five minutes after we arrived. His efficiency as a camper was hard-earned and impressive.

While Ben had slumbered peacefully in the comfort of his tent that first night, I attempted to master the art of sleeping curled up on a discarded tarp in the damp sand. It didn't go well. Sand seems all soft and warm while you're walking through it on your way into the ocean, but once it gets a little wet and compacted that shit is concrete.

Greg was already fishing when I crawled out of my tarp cocoon. Dude's a well-coined tech success who's actually lived all the shit you see on shows like *Silicon Valley*, but all he really wants to do is go fishing. I don't blame him. If some asshole tried to steal my million-dollar company and turn it into a billion-dollar juggernaut, I'd need a way to relax, too. Besides, Greg didn't get into that shit for the money. Ever since he and Sinclair were little dudes, computers were all that ever made sense.

I went looking for a sandwich in one of the coolers in the back of Sinclair's truck. There was a rank, half-scrambled egg buffet between the ridges of his bed liner that the flies were way into. A quick dig through the icy depths of the cooler produced a cold beer and half a ham and cheese sandwich. It wasn't even nine in the morning.

I stuffed a hunk of sandwich in my mouth and walked over to where Greg was fishing.

"Catch anything?"

"Just a little fish. Nothing worth eating, but we can use it for bait."

"Anyone else up?"

"Josh and Stephen are out on the jetty. Maybe Bruns, too. I think Morgan is about to head that way."

"Maybe I'll go with him. I bet the view is badass."

There was a big dune near where Greg was fishing. I scrambled up it to get the lay of the land. It was the first time I'd seen everything in the daylight. Our camp was right above a quiet fishing spot on the back side of Mile 60 next to where the jetty juts into the ocean. Morgan was fishing knee-deep in the intercostal waters. I wondered if I could swim from our shore to the beach across the channel. It didn't seem that far, but I was hungover and old, and I hadn't done any serious swimming in a hell of a long time. Maybe once upon a time it wouldn't have been such a terrible idea.

Morgan saw me, waved, and started heading back toward camp. I met him at awning city and lit a smoke.

"Any luck?"

"Not a damn thing. Fixin' to head out on the jetty."

"Mind if I join you?"

"Not at all."

"How long those guys been out there?"

"Maybe an hour or two."

"Think we ought to bring them something cold to drink? Probably hot out on the rocks."

"Golly gee, mister. That'd be real swell of you!"

"Dick."

I tossed some beers and a couple bottles of water in a plastic sack, and Morgan and I hit the jetty. Our friends were only halfway out, but that was plenty far. If you've ever spent any time on a proper jetty, you know exactly what I'm talking about. Some hardworking bastards a long time ago found a way to pile up hundreds, maybe thousands, of big-ass stones until it became a treacherous obstacle course for folks that want to fish as far out to sea as you can get without being in a boat. To get from the shore to the end of the jetty requires a lot of jumping from rock to rock. You got to keep you wits about you. Learn to read the stones. Simultaneously watch where you're stepping now, where you're about to step, and where you'll be stepping three moves from now. It's not that you can't traverse the jetty with a quickness, but you got to build up to it slowly.

It took Morgan and me about twenty or thirty minutes to reach our friends. Some of it was being cautious, and some of it was being tired and not used to physical exertion in that kind of sun and heat. Along the way, I noticed all kinds of interesting things between the jetty rocks. Abandoned beer cans, lost clothes, hats, love graffiti, and general trash. It pisses me off that people are so willing to shit all over something so beautiful, but that ain't a problem unique to the beach.

Josh and Steven were watching a sea turtle cruise by when we finally got to them. It's shell was at least a foot long. Maybe sixteen inches. It banked to its right as it approached a submerged jetty rock, rolling onto its back like an amphibious jet fighter traveling in slow motion. The shell looked like leather. It was a beautiful, peaceful creature in a serene environment. I began to understand the passion of those brave men and women of the Turtle Patrol.

"If you hook a turtle, you're not supposed to try and remove it," said Josh. "You just cut your line and start over. They don't fuck around when it comes to the turtles."

"Can't say as I blame them. Y'all need a beer or something? Got some water, too."

"Beer sounds good," said Steven.

"Same here."

I tossed them beers and then scanned the jetty. There were little clusters of fishers all over the place. Some old dudes that looked like they wanted to be left the hell alone—but also a fair share of younger kids. Teenagers who were probably using fishing as a cover for making out or smoking dope. Or maybe teenagers don't need a cover for that kind of shit anymore.

I slipped into a little daydream of what it must be like to grow up that close to the ocean. Instead of going to bullshit malls or waiting for someone's parents to go out of town so you can have a party, you just pack up and go sleep on the beach for the weekend. It sounded a hell of a lot better than growing up in Waxahachie, Texas. That town was so little back then that they didn't even sell beer.

"How you like it out here?" asked Steven.

"It's fucking gorgeous, man. The hike's a bitch, but the view is worth the sweat."

"Be careful on the jetty. I seen a girl running on it once. She fell and her leg got caught between the rocks. Snapped her fucking shin like a chicken bone. Had to get the coast guard to haul her out of here. Made me wanna puke."

"I don't even want to think about that shit."

But I did think about that shit. Just as soon as the sun got too hot for me to ignore the fact that I wasn't even fishing and all the beer and shade and sunscreen was back at camp. Steven and Josh, as fishermen do, were keeping mostly quiet, so I decided to head back. His warning still echoing in my head.

But all I gave a shit about was being fast. I wanted to best the jetty. To master it. I started slow, trying to find the pattern in the stones that led all the way to the sand. Hop here. Sidestep to the left and then two quick jumps forward. Aim for the middle of the rocks. Never trust an edge because you might slip off or miss it altogether. After the first fifty yards, I was in the zone. I had this fucked-up, shin-snapping, game of jetty Frogger absolutely figured out. There was no slowing down. Just a compulsion to go faster and faster and faster. Morgan was heading back to camp with me. At first, I tried to set a pace he was comfortable with, but that shit didn't last long. I was hell-fucking-bent. How fast can I make it back to the beach? The sweat was pouring down my face and burning my eyes, blurring the stones and the spaces between them. Still I refused to slow down. When I made that epic final leap from stone to sand, I was gassed. Morgan was still a hundred, hundred and fifty yards out. I looked back for half a second and then headed to camp. The sun was angry, and I wanted the coldest beer I could find.

INVASION

I was standing next to Sinclair as he fished the little channel from the beach by our camp. It was peaceful, and the water was warm. We were up to our waists, and I was thinking of going deeper.

"Fuck!"

"What's wrong, brother?"

"Fucking jellyfish."

I backed out of the water to watch from the safety of the sand. A half dozen or so baby jellies were floating in on the current. Ghost white bordering on translucent. Thin tendrils like bad dreadlocks on a balding albino. It seemed wrong that something so delicate and pretty could inflict pain. Or maybe it was the most natural thing in the world. I wanted to swim with them, but I figured that would be a stupid thing to do.

Sinclair was stubborn and kept right on fishing. He got stung about five or six times. No one tried to pee on him.

INTERLOPERS

The rains came after sundown on Saturday. We were in the middle of a Kubb match, a Swedish lawn game often referred to as Viking Chess. It plays a little like a hybrid of horseshoes and croquet only with wooden pegs and batons instead of bent metal and ceramic balls. Steven and Sinclair had recently started handcrafting Kubb sets to sell at Renaissance Faires. It gave them something to do on weekends. Work with their hands. Dream of lawn game empires. Sales had yet to explode, but the Lone Star Kings of Kubb remained steadfast.

We played on through the steady drizzle. Soggy, not soaked. It was nothing new. We'd been some degree of damp since the moment we arrived. Sinclair stripped down to his boxers. The man of the hour strutted around drinking beer and whiskey and instructing the newbies on the rules of the game.

"Why the fuck are you mostly naked, Sinclair?"

"Why the fuck do you care?"

"There's fucking people all around, and you're hanging out in your underwear."

"I'm wearing boxers. How is that any different from swimming trunks?"

"You're wearing boxer briefs, bro. Big difference in the crotchal region."

"I think you're fucking repressed, Harlin. No one else has a problem with it."

I want to say that's when Morgan sidled over and nonchalantly mentioned that he had a problem with it because that's a totally Morgan thing to do, but the beers and lack of sleep or decent food were adding up at that point, so I won't put words in an old friend's mouth. I'll just suggest that you imagine them there.

"Don't you have some actual trunks you could put on?"

"I'm fucking chaffing like a motherfucker, man. These are moisture wicking. They breathe better than nylon shorts or whatever the hell they make swimming suits out of. I don't get why this is such an issue."

These were the types of exchanges that drove my poor mom crazy when Sinclair and I were younger. Bickering for no other reason than to do it. Getting older hasn't done much to abate the endless verbal sparring over shit that doesn't mean shit to anyone but us.

"Dude. Stop worrying about what I'm wearing, and play the game."

"Be a hell of a lot easier to do without an eyeful of your fucking dingus."

"So stop fucking looking."

I didn't actually give a shit, but I do love bitching at my little brother. Even now that he lives so close, I don't get to see him enough. Same goes for my mom and my dad. They split when I was fourteen, so making the rounds takes some time. And life doesn't get any less busy the older we get.

We took a quick break to grill some hotdogs and SPAM on Morgan's Coleman camping stove. A small gang of scrawny wanderers walked up to our makeshift compound and interrupted our meal. I didn't want shit to do with them, so I drifted to the back of our crowd and watched. Sinclair was quick to greet them.

"What's up, fellas? Y'all keeping dry?"

"Um, what was that game y'all were playing just now?" asked Scrawny Dude No.1. "It looked cool."

"It's called Kubb."

"What's that?"

"It comes from Sweden. It's one of the most popular games in the entire country. My friend Steven and I made this set."

"Cool."

"We were just about to start another game. You guys wanna play?"

Scrawny Dude No. 1 looked hesitantly at his Scrawny Brethren and shrugged. Kids today are virtually incapable of making any fucking decisions on their own. They're too used to having Mom or Dad or the entire social media world weigh in on everything from what glasses they should buy to what they should jam in their mouths at lunch. Why in the hell was Sinclair inviting the Scrawny Bunch to Kubb with us?

"We don't know the rules or anything."

"It's cool," said Sinclair. "I'll teach you."

Sinclair divided the teams up and started handing scrawny fuckers beers like we had an endless supply of them. This went against the very core of my being. I don't give shit to strangers. Haven't ever since some motherfucker claiming to be a broke-down army man swindled me out of ten bucks on the San Antonio Riverwalk during a class trip back in high school. But whatever. I didn't want the Scrawnies to get too comfortable digging through our coolers. We had liquor out the ass, but beer was beginning to be in short supply, and a trip to the corner store for a fresh six pack wasn't an option that far from civilization.

I took my spot for the next Kubb match. Most of the Scrawnies somehow ended up on the team with me and Morgan. I was even less pleased about that than the giving away of beers. If Sinclair was gonna invite some empty-handed strangers to join in our game, he should have had the decency to give me a chance to kick their asses. Instead, my hopes of victory were dashed by scrawny fucks with virtually no wood baton chucking skills. Morgan and I fought valiantly, but it was not enough to overcome our flaccid arsenal of scrawny arms.

Sinclair's Kubb warriors emerged victorious, and the interlopers shuffled back into the night after I made a slightly ostentatious display of sitting on one of the coolers and not offering to refresh their beers. Sinclair, still in his briefs, walked up and slapped me on the back.

"Good game, brother. You've got some skill. A little practice and you'll be a tough opponent. We'll send you home with one of our sets."

"Funny how all those scrawny little bastards ended up on me and Morg's team."

"Huh," said Sinclair. "I didn't even notice."

I'll never be able to prove it, but I swear there was a mischievous Loki twinkle in his eye as he went looking for more whiskey.

SLOBBERDERBY

"Change never stops, Harlin. Old things disappear and new things take their place. It's the way it's always been. But that doesn't mean change is always bad."

Joe Pat Hennen told me that while we sat next to the fireplace on the patio of the Marathon Motel and RV Park. I'm probably paraphrasing a bit because he said it very late at night, but the meaning remains pure. He'd meant to comfort me. I know that. But all I could think of were the things I didn't want to disappear.

My thoughts drifted back to that moment as I drove toward the Denton North Branch public library. It was Saturday, and I needed to be writing. Deadlines were looming. But fuck it. Slobberbone was playing a matinee at the Silverleaf directly following the Kentucky Derby. Post time was 5:26 pm. Slobberbone would take the stage at 5:30 on the dot, blow the doors off the joint for exactly ninety minutes, and it would all be a memory before the sun went down.

I expected a bigger crowd outside the library. It was Election Day, but I guess voting on local issues doesn't draw like the presidential primaries. A couple months back, I'd waited for hours in a line that spilled out the door and ran the length of the front of the library to vote for a candidate I knew had no chance of winning the nomination. It was a waste of my fucking time, but I felt obligated to play my part in the charade of regular people still having a say in who leads their country.

There were a handful of folks in the parking lot holding signs advertising their choice for city council, but other than that, it was fucking crickets. Took me about a minute and a half to get through the line and cast my votes. I've got friends a lot smarter than me that didn't even bother to do their civic duty. Don't guess I can blame them. Ever since that reprehensible fuck Greg Abbott and his cronies down in Austin took exception to our decision to ban fraking in the city limits and decided, in their infinite fucking wisdom, to make it illegal for cities to do such a thing, there just doesn't seem to be much point.

But I was worried for my city. Leah and I were homeowners. The permanent kind. Not the type who can reasonably expect to trade up at some point in the future—or buy land outside of town where we might have more freedom. We'd cast our lot with the 940. It was our present, past, and future, and we wanted to do whatever we could to protect it.

I checked the little electronic boxes in support of local professor Deb Armintor and attorney Sara Bagheri because I believed they care more about our town's air quality and transparency on the part of our local government than luring new businesses to town with tax breaks or publically funded incentives. Armintor was running against Dalton Gregory, a longtime council member who was only even eligible to run again because of a loophole that desperately needs amending. Fat fucking chance of that ever happening when the people charged with doing the amending are the same ones doing the exploiting. Bagheri was up against Greg Johnson, a real estate mini-mogul with a silly race car, a horrendous goatee, and a questionable history of brokering deals the city council has to vote on while he's on the damn council.

A lot of talk and rabble-rousing surrounded the city council elections this year, but judging by the turnout on voting day, that's all it was. The gap between the folks with money who make all the decisions and the artists and musicians who make Denton special has been steadily widening. It's hard not to sense a certain inevitability to the fact that this town so many of us love so much will eventually become the next Frisco as we try our very best to morph into the Austin of the north. But we could never be Austin. We'll stall out long before that, probably just after it's gotten so expensive that all the things that made us Denton can no longer survive.

This all weighed heavily on my mind, and it's probably why I took no comfort in Joe Pat's reassuring words. Armintor and Bagheri had their work cut out for them. They were up against incumbents, and the chips were all stacked on the other side of the table. The only thing left to do was vote and hold your breath. By the time

Brent Best belted out his last note of the night, the people, at least some of them, would have spoken.

Things were much happier in close proximity to tap handles. Dan's wife Pam Chittendon stole the show with a straw hat adorned with googly eyes, a robotic parakeet, and a potted plant sprouting out the top. The parakeet would move its head and chirp every so often.

Juan Verde was there with his little Green Bean. She was rocking festival beads and eating Cheerios. When the music started, he put her head phones on, and she took off teetering and tottering into the crowd. A lot more people bring their kids out to shows now that you can't smoke inside. There was widespread resistance to that ordinance in the beginning, but we can see the benefits now. Live music is the soul of Denton. No reason someone should have to miss out on a Slobberbone show just because they're a baby.

I was standing in the back of the room shouting along to a song called "Man of Note."

> *I am a man of note. I am. A footnote. A footnote.*
> *Take these words for rote. I am. A footnote. A footnote.*

The rest of the crowd was shouting right along with me. And I do mean shouting. There was no fucking singing coming from the audience. Brent was up on stage growling lyrics we could never forget and looking like a rock-n-roll yeti. At a twelve-dollar cover charge, it was the cheapest form of therapy you could get after a week of bad news. We shouted along to get all the angst and anxiety over the future of Denton out of our systems. That and because it felt fucking good as hell.

As the show wore on and the beers started to lean into us, the vibe intensified, and I started getting emotional. Verde's little girl was dancing just as hard as she could on wobbly toddler legs. Juan gave her space to explore, but he was watching with daddy eyes. A Slobberbone show at Dan's is the perfect place for a little one to cut their scene teeth. The crowd is always friendly and in a good mood. There's no drama. Just folks having fun.

In a moment of sublime beauty, I looked up and saw Andy Knapik standing near the front of the stage with his daughter

Isabella on his shoulders. Brent was ripping through a guitar solo, and Izzy stretched her arms toward the rafters and flashed double peace signs. I took me a mental photograph and retreated to the patio for a smoke. Mojica was at a table by himself.

"Godammit, Dan. This is our band. Can't nobody else in the world lay claim to them. They belong to Denton."

"Hell, brother. This band is Denton."

My friend and I just looked at each other and nodded silently. Days like this spent watching bands like Slobberbone made me never want to leave Denton even after two degrees and never having much luck finding a cool job within the city limits. And these are the days I fear for when speculation runs rampant that more garish pseudo luxury condominiums would rise from the ashes of what was once Rubber Gloves.

It was nearing 7:00 pm, now. I checked my phone. Sara Bagheri was well on her way to defeating that carpet-bagging real estate dude-bro, but the best Deb Armintor could hope for was a run-off election, and that was only if the provisional votes came out in her favor. It was a little victory, to be sure, but between that and Slobberbone, it was just enough hope for a Saturday night in Denton.

GOODBYE TO MILE 60

The trip home almost always feels shorter than the journey to get somewhere. Maybe it's the anticipation that agonizes as you count down the miles to arrival. Whatever the reason, there are only two trips I've ever taken where the road back seemed to last longer than the ride out. One was mine and Dan's long run back from the desert—and the other was the return from Mile 60.

We woke up to storm clouds, so we struck camp and packed the trucks in a hurry. Sinclair finally put on pants, some Texas flag swimming trunks, and he herded us into position for a group photo while Morgan set the timer on his phone. We were a haggard and motley crew, but the picture makes you feel like you were there for it all. Leah had a print made at a local superstore for me and put it in a four-dollar frame. I look at it all the time.

The business of commemorating our weekend on the edge of Texas complete, we climbed back into our vehicles and fell into formation. Sinclair led the way back. I brought up the rear with Morgan. He punched some buttons on his dashboard video screen and Daft Punk began to mix with the sound of thunder rumbling behind us. We'd raced the sunset on the way out to Mile 60. Now we would race the storm back to civilization.

A mile marker slipped into the rearview mirror and just like that it was over, a handful of memories waiting to fade.

There were no stops for beers or cigarettes or to retrieve cooler lids on the drive back to where the sand ends and the paved roads begin. No skittering herds of sand crabs to get crushed under our tires. The tide was coming in, making our road far narrower than it had been two days earlier. We passed retired fishermen with trailer rigs who looked like they may never leave the beach. High school and college kids with tan skin and lean torsos in bikinis and board shorts, radiating explicit youth. We saw everything and left all it behind.

Our tires kicked up the last of the sand then made contact with asphalt a few hours later. We stopped to unload our trash in the dumpsters provided by the park service. Empty beer cans, eggshells, half-eaten bags of chips, an empty can of spam, and the broken awning.

"You guys want to head into town and get some lunch before we head back?" asked Sinclair.

"I could definitely eat."

"We can check out this Mexican place I tried while I was waiting for y'all on Friday," said Greg. "I thought it was pretty badass."

"Everyone good with that?"

Morgan and I responded in the affirmative, but Steven and Josh just sort of nodded silently and got back into their truck. By the time we hit the main road outside the park, it was pouring rain. Corpus Christi was flooding. Visibility was shit. It was a motherfucking apocalyptic deluge. Siri, struggling to be heard over the downpour, announced that Morgan had received a text message.

Great weekend guys. We're gonna skip lunch and head straight home. Had a blast.

Josh, Steven, and Bruns were out. It was no surprise. Steven woke up that morning missing his wife and kids. Sunday was rapidly evaporating, and Monday would be kicking us all in the teeth soon enough. If I could have blinked my eyes or clicked my heels together and been transported home at that very moment, I would have done it without a second thought. But I don't have that kind of magic, so I just sat there and wished until we got to Greg's Mexican joint.

The food was decent, but according to our waitress, the water was all tainted or toxic or poisoned. I forget the exact word she used. We ate quickly and then scampered back through the rain to our vehicles. Sinclair was fading, so Ben took a turn at the wheel. Fifteen or twenty miles down the road, it was still raining. We stopped at a gas station for running water and snacks. When I walked by Sinclair's truck, I saw my brother passed out in the passenger seat, head bent awkwardly, chin resting on his collar bone. My lungs seized. I've seen him like this before, only he was younger—a little kid with soft blonde hair and little boy cheeks. He is so much older now with his thick dark beard and thinning hair. I wonder what my mom and dad think when they look at me.

Everything changes or gets old and dies. There is no avoiding it. But that's okay because it means that Padre Island National Seashore will always have a perfect balance of old fishermen, beautiful youths, and travelers like me and Sinclair and our friends, wandering with wide eyes somewhere in the middle for as many days as we can.

The drive back was long and boring and painful, but I'd make the trip any day of the week if it meant even just one more night on the beach with my brother.

WEDDING WALK

The thing about not having a rehearsal dinner, or in Sinclair's case, turning your rehearsal dinner into a party at the oldest bowling alley in Texas the day after the ceremony, is that no one in the wedding party knows what the hell they are supposed to be doing when it finally comes time to get the bride and groom hitched.

Especially when you're trying to get the groomsmen lined up in the right order.

"Bruns is tall, so he should be at one end of the line."

"Harlin is the next tallest after that. He needs to be next to Bruns."

"But Eddie is the co-best man and keeper of the ring, so he needs to be next to Harlin. Bruns can be at the other end.

"How do y'all not know where you're supposed to be standing?" asked some sage observer. "Didn't you pay attention at the rehearsal dinner?"

"We don't know yet," I shot back. "It's tomorrow."

When we finally thought we had it all figured out, someone noticed that we were all sorts of backward. Had we proceeded in our current configuration, Eddie and I would have ended up furthest away from Sinclair, which would have made passing the ring a hand-over-hand-over-hand-over-hand type of maneuver, not unlike a double-quick bucket brigade trying to put out some blaze threatening an entire town.

We flipped the script easy enough, and I took my new place at the back of the line to watch Sinclair's closest friends join arms with Dawn's leading ladies and head down that aisle with the beautiful view of all of Austin town. You could just make out the little boats down on the river below us. A breeze made it a little less unbearable for all us dudes dressed in black. One by one, the boys and girls in front of me walked the walk and took their proper places at the front of the audience.

I turned to my left to greet my temporary lady friend only to find the biggest, scariest, hairiest looking Maid of Honor I've ever seen in my life. It was Dawn's brother Scotty.

Time was of the essence. Wait too long to figure it all out, and people would start to notice the delay. We had to act fast.

"We heading down together?" I asked.

"Looks that way."

I held out my arm. "We mine as well own it."

"Damn straight."

We rolled down the aisle heads high with shit-eating grins on our faces. Two big-ass, burly dudes with thick beards. Mine a fading red and his the sort of jet black you find on a younger man. Me in my pearl snap shirt and classic Wrangler old-man rancher pants, and

Scotty blacked out in a more rockabilly style. Folks were cheering and clapping. It was a special moment on the most special of days, and just to show I'm a forward-thinking, liberated, fair-minded guy, I let Scotty lead when it was time to walk back the way we came and straight over to the bar for a cold Shiner Bock.

REDIAL

Fall creeps slowly into Denton. Cool weather visits for a day or two before being chased away by the return of triple-digit temperatures. The time between sun up and sundown dwindles. Very soon there will be days where dawn has not yet broken on my way to work and the walk to my car after doing my time will be lit only by the tall, electric lamps in a parking lot with nothing but a solitary letter for a name.

I didn't notice the stretching and shrinking of days so very much when I was younger. But now I wake up in the night. Panicked. Anxious. Crying over dreams I can't fully remember. Clawing in the darkness. Searching for a trail back through the ether to wherever I was before I woke up.

Sometimes I reach for my phone to record lines from unwritten songs or bits of stories that have thus far eluded me. But mostly I close my eyes and extend my arm hoping to make contact with the wiry scruff of my dog Jake—and not some lurking thing even darker than the darkness. Leah sleeps even less than me. Takes longer to nod off. Wakes up easier. Barely manages to reclaim her slumber before the Beagle fills our house with pitter-patter steps and chirping pleas for freedom.

"What the fuck is wrong with you assholes?" I ask them as I stumble toward the back door. "The sun's not even up yet."

But they never answer. Beagle pogos on her hind legs and scratches at the door while Jake trembles and unleashes sharp little yelps that pierce the heart of silence. Earl watches from a distance, old and tired and unwilling to stray too far from his humans. I open the door and Jakey and the Beagle race into the darkness. They have nowhere to go, but they are free, so they will run.

"You can all go to hell. Maybe not you, Earl, but your brother and sister can fuck right off."

Almost as if on key, the Beagle and her mighty snout pick up the scent of something that may be in the trees—or may have been here hours, or even days, ago. The racket is infernal. A hellish juxtaposition of bloodcurdling howls and short, ear-murdering barks.

"Motherfucking assholes."

The leaves have already started to fall. Another thing that must be dealt with. Do I pay someone or do the work myself? We finally got paint on the walls in the most frequented half of the house, but that was only the beginning. Pictures litter the hallways, leaning against walls and waiting to be hung. There is a sunroom that needs tile to cover up the bare concrete that is harsh and ugly. The queen-size mattress in the guestroom needs to be fashioned into a murphy bed in the record den, and then the guestroom will require a transformation of its own. I am worried the light will run out before I can cross off everything on a list that grows longer as the days get shorter.

Leah and I have an appointment next week. Neither of us talk about it much. Only when absolutely necessary. There are two possible outcomes, and I'm scared to death of them both. Everything is either about to change—or we'll soon be reunited with a familiar tragedy.

Next week Leah and I go looking for a heartbeat.

MY MORNING RAMBLE

I was hungover and the day was already getting hot even though Fuzzy's on Industrial Street was still serving breakfast. I stopped in on the way back from my mechanic for some chorizo and egg tacos and an ice-cold cup of Powerade. I've got no real love for Powerade, but I talked myself into gulping down the artificial red liquid on account of the electrolytes.

The walk from Fuzzy's to the shitty rental house Leah and I were living in at the time was probably only a couple miles, but I'd stayed out too late at the Silverleaf the night before. One of my favorite things to do is take a Friday off, so I can spend Thursday night acting like I'm still younger than I am. Thursdays are magic. You can stumble into a good show or an even better conversation. Order a beer, hit the patio, and walk up on Scotty Danbom and Brent Best swapping stories of life on the road.

I finished my breakfast and cruised by Recycled Books and the Mini Malls, but I didn't go in. No sense in carrying vinyl around in the hot sun or lugging a dusty old receiver all the way home. It's cool, though, because I had a double handful of memories to keep me company. I passed the ghosts of two first dates somewhere near Locust Street. One at a hippie grocery store full of bullshit homeopathic remedies—and the other at the Greenhouse, a longstanding Denton restaurant with a beautiful bar that used to have great jazz on Thursday nights. They might still, but I wouldn't know. I spend my Thursdays exclusively at the Silverleaf. It's the place that's the closest to what it used to be. You don't have to worry about getting the Lone Star Attitude treatment and having some corporatized version of Texas blown up your ass while you pay too much for a burger and listen to some out-of-town hack. But that's just my opinion.

The heat was draining the bounce from my step as I approached the big white house across the street from TWU. Place looks like a smaller version of the President's digs. They've been remodeling the outside for what seems like years. Should be something special when it's all done. It makes me a little sad, though, to see such a place crammed in between dentists' and doctors' offices, insurance agencies, and accounting firms. Some of the best houses in Denton have been turned into businesses as the square spreads and developers attack from the outskirts. I would have liked to seen the place when it was first built. I bet it had a kick-ass yard instead of parking lots.

The big boxer that lives in the white house barked at me as I hung a left to cut over to our place on Bolivar. I smiled and reminded him that he'd seen me walking my boys, Jake and Earl, many times before. He cocked his head and got silent for a moment, then went on barking.

"Yeah, yeah. Save it for the squirrels, buddy. You and I go way back."

I was feeling out of sorts about how fast my little town was changing when something up ahead caught my eye. There was a big boarding house on the corner, and from where I was standing, I could see a guy and girl, college-age, laying under a blanket on the roof of a patio that jutted out from beneath the second-story windows. They'd drug out a little futon mattress so they could lounge in relative luxury. I could hear music. I didn't recognize the band, but it was good music. The stuff college kids spend all their spare time making sure they hear before any of their friends do.

They were wearing pajamas. Or rather, she was wearing pajamas, and he was in the casual state of undress that constitutes pajamas when you didn't expect to be sleeping in a strange place. The girl was pretty, and she was sorta sitting up. The boy was lying on his side. She had a slim paperback in her hands, and she was reading to him over the music. They were the only two people in the world.

I stopped near a large shrub, so I could watch them. Not like a pervert or anything. But I wanted to see if I could feel a little of that moment. One minute I was waxing nostalgic about first dates, and I now I was privy to the intimate morning after some manner of first. The boy must have said something clever because the girl laughed, then leaned in and kissed him. It was a reset kiss. A kiss that said last night was a little more exciting than either of us expected. Now let's go back to sweet and innocent. When the night returns, we'll can be bold again. But let's be bashful in the daylight.

So many memories came rushing back to me. The night before my first date at the hippy health food store, the awkward aftermath of my Greenhouse first date, and the shitty Cajun joint, just a few blocks away, that Leah took me to on our first official night out. The onslaught of feelings wrecked me there in the shadow of that shrub. For all the changes in our town, boys and girls and girls and girls and boy and boys were still falling in love over words and music. It hurt that I would never again meet and fall in love with somebody in the time between nightfall and daybreak. But it was a wonderful hurt. There was still adventure in the night. There were streets to wander and roofs to climb on and days custom-made for playing hooky.

CLINICAL

A nurse opened the door and called Leah's name. She was a big lady. Not in an overweight way, but more matter-of-factly. Tall. Strong shoulders. Somebody who looked like she didn't take shit from anyone. Her bedside manner was a bit on the gruff side, which didn't exactly do wonders for our wrecked nerves.

Leah laid down on the little table, so the nurse could use machines to look inside her. The room was nothing like I'd expected. The lights were down low and there was a big screen television on the wall. I doubt it had ever shown a football game or had someone fall asleep watching Netflix on it. Womb-o-Vision was its only channel.

I kept my eyes fixed on the big screen because there were things I was afraid of seeing. Leah pursing her lips or clenching her jaw. Leah breathing like she does when she's anxious. Leah crying. And even if the news was good, I didn't want to see Leah's body as something to be examined scientifically instead of something that I could hold and love.

Nothing on the screen looked like anything to me. Shades of white against a black background. An X-ray of an ambrosia salad from the inside out.

"Okay," said the nurse. "I'm going to need to take a closer look. Have you ever had an intravaginal ultrasound?"

"The first time," said Leah. "You can't find the heartbeat?"

"I can see one..."

"Did you say can or can't?" asked Leah. Pleading.

We spent time in two different rooms after we left the one with the television on the wall and the ultrasound machine. Three different medical professionals spoke with us. I think one was a doctor. We walked through a hallway where I desperately searched for a water fountain, but all I saw was the big nurse again. She said something to me that I couldn't quite make out over the reverb in my ears. When it finally cleared up and the world stopped tumbling all around me, I found myself on the very same campus where I met Leah so many years ago. It was 5:00 pm, and the clock tower was warbling out this distorted-as-hell version of a song I knew I recognized.

"Is this fucking 'Bridge over Troubled Water?'"

The only creature within earshot was this little gray squirrel who was foraging for slightly trampled french fries or potato chips abandoned by college kids. It was just one of the hundreds, maybe thousands, of squirrels that lived on campus. It looked right at me for a second, and then we both looked back in the direction of the clock tower.

"That is most definitely 'Bridge over Troubled Water.'

I could finally make out the words the big nurse had said to me in that hallway when I was looking for a fountain.

"Somebody came back. And this time they brought a friend. Better get ready for those twins, Dad."

The little squirrel chirped out something that was either "good luck" or "you're so fucked" and then took off in search of more forgotten morsels.

"Sail on silver girl," I said as it dissapeard into the bushes. "Sail the fuck on by."

THE INDUSTRIAL STREET POP FESTIVAL

The Beatles were playing on the roof of Hoochies oyster house when I spotted Lucinda the Patron Saint of Desert Wanderers and Honky Tonkers. Not the real Beatles, obviously, but a fair approximation of them. Saint Lucinda was puffing on this vape pin she'd picked up on a recent trip to Colorado and enjoying a musical walk down memory lane in the form of cover bands doing their best to recreate the magic of the Lewisville Pop Festival from back in the once upon a time days. I was a few beers in and feeling good, so I wrapped her right up in a big bear hug.

"How you doing, friend?"

"Doing damn good, Saint."

"Where's your better half?"

"Leah's at the office right now, but she'll be here soon."

"It'll be good to see here. Feels like a long time since the last time."

"Well, there's a reason for that."

"Oh yeah? She busy at work?"

"That and we're having twins."

"Twins? Really?"

"Would I lie to you, Lucinda?"

I never saw the smile I expected when I told the Saint about our twins. She talked to me about it for a little bit, asked some questions and tried to seem excited. But there was a sadness to the exchange that would have troubled me more if I'd been drinking less. Leah showed up not too long after that and she and Lucinda got to talking, and I wandered off to see some more music. I don't remember if I made it back around for one more hug, but I damn sure hope so because it was the last time I would ever the Saint.

A week or two later, I was back at the Silverleaf drinking beers with Dan and Pam and Chris Hawley, one of the founding fathers of Denton's Little Guys Movers. Talk turned to Lucinda because the hurt was too fresh for us to ignore. All the stories I knew about her were right on the tip of my tongue because writing this book was keeping her alive in a way. At least for me. I told my drinking buddies about her hauling my ass in from the cold and making me a sandwich. They all laughed, but not too hard.

"I wish I'd had that experience," said Hawley. "I only ever got to see her at shows, and I'm grateful for that, but I'm envious that you got to spend time with her in the desert."

"She loved it out there," said Dan. "I'm just happy she got to see her place in Terlingua one last time."

Pam wasn't saying much of anything. Just nodding and sipping. Sipping and nodding.

"You know, she wouldn't let me use her real name in my book. Said she didn't want any extra attention. So I had to call her Lucinda. Lucinda the Patron Saint of Desert Wanders and Honkey Tonkers."

Pam chuckled.

"Well, I guess you can use her real name now," she said.

"Nope. I promised I wouldn't, and I'm gonna keep that promise.

Dan was on empty, so he wandered off to the bar for a refill. Pam and Chris and I sat there for a minute staring anywhere but at each other.

"Leah hasn't been out much lately, but I talked her into coming to the pop festival. Thank fucking God she got to see her one last time. She would have been inconsolable."

"We were all lucky to have that day with her," said Pam.

"I got to tell her about our twins."

I had more to say than just that. I was gonna keep moving my mouth and spitting words out into the air. I was going to tell my friends that the Saint seemed sad when I told her about our babies. Sad like she knew what was coming. Like she knew she'd never get to meet them. But Pam started shaking and then crying a little and then sobbing, so I swallowed all the shit words I was about to spew. Better to leave them right here for people to look at when they finally feel ready. If they ever do.

"I miss my friend," said Pam.

I tried to give her a hug, but it was awkward because her shoulders were still heaving a little, and I wasn't sure if she actually wanted to be hugged. She'd known the Saint so much better than I had. Her hurt went deeper. It would never fade.

We gave Pam some time to navigate the sadness. When it seemed to have passed for the moment, Chris Hawley proposed a toast to the Saint using her real name. The one her parents gave her when she was born. Pam wasn't having that shit.

"No," she said. "To Lucinda."

We clinked our glasses in the air, knocked their bottoms on the bar top, and drank deep enough to forget everything we'd lost.

AFTERTHOUGHT

It all comes to an end in the City of Fountains. At the Red Front Bar. Some shotgun brick dive that popped up on my phone when I googled "best dive bars in Kansas City." I was sick and fucking tired of the hotel-shopping mall combo work had put me up at for the international conference on some shit I don't feel like telling you about. Once upon a time, I would have ordered room service and dialed up some pay-per-view. But not anymore. I needed to stretch my legs. Get the fuck away from that twenty-bucks-a-peep aquarium prison down the street and the eight-dollar lobby beers. I needed to find something real.

The Uber dumped me off out front just as it started to rain. I hustled through the door, and it was like the record skipped. All eyes swung toward me. A handful of greybeards took one look and decided they didn't give a shit, and this forty-something bartender who was spilling out of her top shot me a look like what the fuck was I doing there.

"Could I get a beer and a shot of tequila, please?"

"Sure, hon. You wanna keep it open?"

"Yes, ma'am."

I hit the patio for a smoke and watched the storm clouds assemble. The app on my phone told me it was raining back in Denton same as it was here. I wondered if my friends were on the Silverleaf deck and wished that at least one of them were along for the ride. After a couple beers, keeping to yourself can get lonely.

I drank the first beer real quick and headed back inside. The Royals game must have been rained out because there was a crowd of ladies raising hell and passing around this replica of the World Series trophy. All the old dudes in the bar were loving it. They took turns getting their pictures made with the imposter and buying rounds of shots for total strangers. Myself included.

"Where you from, son?"

"Texas."

"No shit."

"Yessir. Live just north of Dallas."

"I shoulda guessed you were from Texas. You talk polite like a cowboy would. Sir. Ma'am. Thank you. Please."

"My mom taught me right."

The old guy laughed and bought me another shot. We tossed 'em back and slammed our glasses on the bar. I heard the front door swing open, and my new drinking buddy shouted "Gray!" right over my shoulder. An old black dude and his son walked up to us, and they all started talking like they went way back. Next thing I know, the room was getting wobbly, and all the white folks were gone, and it was just me and Gray and his son Torrence and this Mexican dude who was a manager forced into duty behind the bar because some girl was late for her shift. Gray and I were watching the NBA playoffs and talking ribs. Torrence was on the phone getting real serious about something I couldn't quite make out.

"You had any BBQ on your trip, Harlin?"

"I made it over to Arthur Bryan."

"Good spot."

"Damn straight. Last time I was here, I ended up at that Jack Stack place."

"That ain't bad."

"I thought it was bullshit. I don't want table service at a BBQ joint. I wanna go through the line. I want old school."

"You tried Gates?"

"Got a buddy from KC who told me Gates was the way to go, but I ain't made it over there yet."

Gray yelled at Torrence and told him to get off the damn phone and go get us some ribs from Gates BBQ. I told him they didn't need to go to any trouble, but he said he was hungry anyway. Torrence disappeared out the front door, and I hit the bar to get another round. A beer for me and a vodka and soda for Gray. Tito's. Because that's the only shit he drinks. I threw a couple bucks in the juke box and played some R. Kelly for Gray and some Swamp Dogg for me. We were jamming and watching hoops and drinking with abandon by the time Torrence got back. He laid out a couple racks and a big pile of fries on the table. We dug in and nobody said shit for about three or four ribs. Torrence broke the silence first.

"Motherfuckers robbed me today."

"What?"

"I was getting a fucking haircut and some punk put an AK in my face. Took my fucking wallet."

"Holy shit, man. That's fucking insane."

"I ain't worried. Got my people on it. Folks always run they mouth. Sooner or later, I'm gonna hear something and then somebody gonna be sorry. I'ma find them motherfuckers. You can believe that."

Gray and Torrence and I kept drinking for about three more quarters of basketball. When it was time for them to leave, we traded cell numbers. They had family down in Texas, and I was adamant that they join me in the Barage for some Texas BBQ. Give me a chance to repay the hospitality. And just like that, they were gone, and I was alone again. So I wandered up to the bar and took a seat across from Johanna. This German immigrant Uber-driving, bartending, school teacher. A messy beauty with virtually no bartending skills. There was an investigative journalist sitting next to me who couldn't stop talking about this story he was about to break on a bunch of cops fucking people up with Tasers. I was a stranger when I'd walked through the door, but everyone knew my name before I left.

On the way back to the hotel, I made small talk with the driver.

"Nice city you got here. Had a lot of fun tonight."

"Where you from?"

"Texas."

"Where at in Texas?"

"Denton."

"Never heard of it."

ACKNOWLEDGEMENTS

I've got a lot of these, but I'll try to make it quick.

    This book never would have existed without the Goliad Family. They believed and championed and listened every step of the way. I did my best to make you all proud. And to anyone who read this, these are the guys to see if you want your money back. I'd suggest you start with Welch. Can we put a picture of Welch here? Just so people know what they're up against?

I want to thank my Mom for all the trips to the library and my Dad for challenging me to explore as much of the world as I could get to. (Even though I didn't always listen.) And I want to thank them both for giving me a brother.

Eternal gratitude to Kody Jackson for my first hunting trip, cold beers and windmills, and all the backroads history lessons.

Dan Mojica, my desert brother. I love the fucking shit out of you.

Big thanks to MSP for getting me hired at the cartoon factory, where I probably learned more about writing than I'd like to admit. I miss the days of roadies and mix CDs, buddy.

Thanks to Earl for his loyal company during all those early mornings by the smoker. And thanks to Jake and the Beagle for being noisy assholes every time I sat down to write.

Darin Bradley gave me all the right books at all the right times to keep me writing. He believed I could do this before I ever did. He knows about a hundred ways to start a fire, and he's the only person who's ever had to spend as much time in my head as I have. (Maybe that's more of an apology than an acknowledgement, but what the hell.) Thank you, Darin. The world would be a better place if we all lived according to your code.

Thanks to that pretty girl who wouldn't come to my Super Bowl party all those years ago for finally realizing that she kind of liked me and eventually agreeing to put up with me forever. I love it, darlin.

And to Sinclair. I'll see you at Mile 60, brother.

As for the rest of you fuckers, I'll be at the bar. (Sorry, Tex. Couldn't help it.)

www.ingramcontent.com/pod-product-compliance
Lightning Source LLC
Chambersburg PA
CBHW050532300426
44113CB00012B/2053